CISTERCIAN STUDIES SERIES NUMBER TWO HUNDRED TWENTY-EIGHT

David N. Bell

Orthodoxy

Evolving Tradition

CISTERCIAN STUDIES SERIES NUMBER TWO HUNDRED TWENTY-EIGHT

Orthodoxy
Evolving Tradition

by

David N. Bell

Cistercian Publications

LITURGICAL PRESS
Collegeville, Minnesota
www.litpress.org

A Cistercian Publications title published by Liturgical Press

Cistercian Publications
Editorial Offices
Abbey of Gethsemani
3642 Monks Road
Trappist, Kentucky 40051
www.cistercianpublications.org

Publication of this book was made possible by support from
Western Michigan University to
The Institute of Cistercian Studies.

© 2008, David N. Bell. All rights reserved.

Published by Liturgical Press, Collegeville, Minnesota 56321. No part of this book may be reproduced in any form, by print, microfilm, microfiche, mechanical recording, photocopying, translation, or by any other means, known or yet unknown, for any purpose except brief quotations in reviews, without the previous written permission of the publisher. Printed in the United States of America.

1   2   3   4   5   6   7   8   9

Library of Congress Cataloging-in-Publication Data

Bell, David N., 1943–
 Orthodoxy : evolving tradition / by David N. Bell.
  p. cm. — (Cistercian studies series ; no. 228)
 Includes bibliographical references and index.
 ISBN 978-0-87907-228-5 (pbk.)
  1. Orthodox Eastern Church—Doctrines. 2. Oriental Orthodox churches—Doctrines. I. Title. II. Series.

BX320.3.B45 2008
281.9—dc22   2008017492

*To John and Nancy Condon
who first suggested this book*

TABLE OF CONTENTS

Introduction   1

1   Taking a Look Around   11

2   Two Orthodox Families   19

3   Organization and Administration   35

4   Holy Icons and Holy Spirit   47

5   More About Icons   59

6   Tradition and Traditions   73

7   Becoming Like God   85

8   Going to Church   99

9   Becoming Orthodox   111

10   Sex, Marriage, and Celibacy   125

11   The Way of the Angels   139

12   Doing Your Own Thing   157

13   The Body and Blood of Christ   171

14	Orthodoxy and the West	183
15	Orthodoxy in the West	197
16	Orthodoxy: Principles and Problems	211
Index		223

INTRODUCTION

LET ME STATE at the outset that this is neither a history of the Orthodox Church nor a history of Orthodox belief. True, it is impossible to discuss the Orthodox Church or Orthodox belief without bringing in a certain amount of history, but there is a great difference between discussing, say, the schism of the Old Believers in seventeenth-century Russia in order to explain the importance of ritual gestures, and presenting a detailed history of Russian Orthodoxy from the conversion of the Slavs to President Putin.

Similarly, in the long history of Orthodox belief there have been many deviations from official teaching which, either at the time or later, were condemned as heretical and wrong. Some of these, such as the Arian controversy in the fourth century, must certainly be mentioned if we are to understand why the vast majority of modern Christians believe in a coequal and coeternal Trinity. Others, such as the beliefs of the dualistic Bogomils in the Middle Ages, are of great interest historically, but play no part in modern Orthodox, or indeed Christian, belief. If this were a history of Byzantine or Bulgarian thought, the Bogomils would have to be included. As it is not, we can safely leave them aside. In any case, those interested can easily find the information elsewhere.[1]

My approach therefore differs from that taken (for example) by Bishop Kallistos Ware in his excellent handbook *The Orthodox Church*.[2] More than half of that book is taken up with a history of

---

1. See David N. Bell, *Many Mansions. An Introduction to the Development and Diversity of Medieval Theology West and East* (Kalamazoo-Spencer, 1996) 125–134.

2. Timothy Ware (Bishop Kallistos of Diokleia), *The Orthodox Church* (London-New York, 1993 [new edition]).

Orthodoxy, but if one is interested in, for instance, the Orthodox understanding of the sacraments, one is limited to a couple of dozen pages. That they are very sound pages is not in question, but they did not and do not answer the down-to-earth questions of some of my friends and many of my students. Other popular studies are even more historically oriented, but it is questionable whether someone interested in the possibility of Orthodoxy as a practical, spiritual path needs to know the details of the precise legal status of Greek Orthodox Christians under the Ottoman Empire.

So what is this book? Or, more precisely, what have I tried to make it? I have tried to make it a reasonably wide-ranging account of modern Orthodox beliefs primarily for non-Orthodox readers, but it is certainly not comprehensive. You will not find in these pages (for example) a discussion of the fourteen *anaphoras* used in the Ethiopian Liturgy, nor an account of the differences between Greeks and Slavs in the singing of the *megalynaria*. Indeed, I have tried to reduce technical terminology to a minimum, not least because Orthodoxy is not monolingual and what is called a *sticharion* in Greece is called a *qamis* in Ethiopia and a *patmucan* in Armenia.[3] They are all equivalent to what, in the west, is called an alb: a simple, ankle-length, white, sleeved tunic.

What I have also tried to do is suggest how Orthodoxy might be adapted to modern western ideas. This has nothing to do with creating a 'Western Orthodoxy', but with looking realistically at certain beliefs and attitudes common in the West and discussing whether they can or cannot be accommodated to traditional Orthodox teachings. Some western Christians, for example, are sympathetic to the idea of reincarnation, though reincarnation is, emphatically, neither an Orthodox nor, indeed, a Christian belief. But is it possible for an Orthodox Christian to subscribe to the idea while still remaining an Orthodox Christian? The answer given by most Orthodox will be an impassioned No, but the question deserves to be put and examined fairly. Similarly, our modern western scepticism may produce some hesitancy in accepting the doc-

---

3. Those interested in such details will find a wealth of information in *The Blackwell Dictionary of Eastern Christianity*, edited by Ken Parry *et al.* (Oxford, 1999, 2001), but this dictionary cannot be called an unqualified success.

trine of the corporeal assumption of the Virgin Mary or in believing in the efficacy of prayers to saints whose lives are chiefly legendary. But does a scholarly scepticism with regard to the events in the life of, say, Saint Mary of Egypt[4] necessarily prohibit one from being an honest Orthodox Christian? Personally, I do not think so, but, again, the question must be honestly discussed. That this is dangerous ground is not in doubt, but courage, surely, is no more than being afraid and going on.

One of the problems with Bishop Kallistos's admirable survey is that it is not really an account of the Orthodox Church as a whole, but (as he himself says) an account of the history and beliefs of those Christians 'who are in communion with the Ecumenical Patriarchate of Constantinople',[5] in other words, the Greek-Russian-Slav tradition. When his book was first published in 1963 that was a reasonable standpoint; it is much less reasonable now, especially when we examine recent developments in North America, where the Antiochian and Coptic Orthodox Churches are extremely active. In this present book, therefore, I have tried to include at least a glance at these other traditions, though it is only right and proper that the huge Greek-Russian-Slav majority—the Byzantine tradition—should be given greater space. But since (for example) Greek and Coptic Orthodox Christians do not receive communion in quite the same way, and since a curious visitor is as likely to wander into a Coptic as into a Greek Orthodox church, it is interesting to point out the differences.

Not all Orthodox Churches, however, will make an appearance in these pages: not because they are not important—far from it—but simply because of space. To take but one example, I will not discuss the teachings of the Apostolic Catholic Assyrian Church of the East, sometimes simply referred to as the Assyrian Church, and sometimes, incorrectly and in the past, the Nestorian Church. It came into existence in the fifth century as a result of disagreements over the relationship of divinity and humanity in the incarnate

---

4. Saint Mary of Egypt is discussed briefly in Chapter Five. All that we can say with any confidence is that there were certainly women living as hermits in Palestine in the fifth century, and that one of them was undoubtedly called Mary, a very common name. The rest of Mary's legend must be read as a pious novel.

5. Ware, *Orthodox Church*, 4.

Christ, and despite a troubled and isolated history, it has survived until the present day. Its membership is estimated at about 350,000, and the Patriarchate is located in the United States where many Assyrian Christians have immigrated, especially as a consequence of the turmoil in Iraq. In 1968 there was a schism in the Church and a minority broke away to form the Ancient Church of the East, which is almost entirely confined to Iraq and India.[6] But despite its present involvement in the ecumenical movement, the Assyrian Church is a minority tradition (though a very interesting one), and in a book of this nature we simply cannot include everyone and everything.

Speaking generally, the Orthodox world is divided into two main groups: Eastern Orthodox and Oriental Orthodox. Neither name is particularly satisfactory, since Orthodoxy is now a world-wide phenomenon and one of the fastest growing Christian traditions in the United States.

The Eastern Orthodox Church is sometimes referred to as the Graeco-Russian Church, and, as we shall see in due course, it is not so much one Church as a family of self-governing Churches, all of which acknowledge the honorary primacy of the Ecumenical Patriarch of Constantinople. This, too, is a matter we shall discuss a little later. The vast majority of Eastern Orthodox comprise Greek Orthodox, Russian Orthodox, the various Slav Orthodox Churches, and the Orthodox Church in America (OCA).

The Oriental Orthodox Churches are those Churches which refused to accept the decisions of a church council held in 451, primarily to try to resolve controversies pertaining to the person of Christ. This was the Council of Chalcedon, and we will discuss its importance in Chapter Two. Until recently there were four Oriental Orthodox Churches: Armenian, Coptic (Egyptian), Ethiopic, and Syrian. Since the independence of Eritrea in 1991, there are now five. They used to be called 'Monophysite' by those who did not belong to this branch of Orthodoxy, but the term is misleading and best avoided. It is still used in books and papers dealing with ecclesiastical and theological history, but nowadays the Ori-

---

6. On Christianity in Iraq, see Suha Rassam, *Christianity in Iraq* (Leominster, 2005).

ental Orthodox Churches find it, understandably, offensive, since it misrepresents their teaching. The Eritrean Orthodox Church used to be part of the Ethiopian Orthodox Church, just as Eritrea used to be part of Ethiopia. The Church, like the country, became independent in 1991 when the Coptic Patriarch Shenouda III consecrated two bishops for Eritrean émigrés in England and the United States, but these and subsequent consecrations have led to very strained relations between the Coptic, Ethiopian, and Eritrean Orthodox Churches.

As we said above, both 'Eastern' Orthodox and 'Oriental' Orthodox are misleading terms. They may be historically correct, but they are no longer geographically correct. Some eastern eastern Christians—those who live or who were born east of Italy—may see in the terms the traditional basis of their identity; but many western eastern Christians—children of immigrants to Europe or North America, for example, or western converts to Orthodoxy—may hear in them only unfortunate overtones of ethnicity, or a romantic and anachronistic yearning for the 'old country' alien to the universality of the Orthodox tradition. In this book, therefore, I have tried to avoid easternizing Orthodoxy and, where possible, have used different expressions.

The Orthodox Church, as we have said, is really a family of Churches, but as we shall see in the first chapters of this book, it tries to be a united family. That it does not always succeed in this is evident, but the fact remains that there are a number of essential ideas, themes, and practices which are shared by all, or virtually all, the Orthodox Churches, and which are referred to as Holy Tradition. The content of this Tradition will be a matter for later discussion, but it is Tradition that enables us to speak of 'Orthodoxy' in general. There are certainly plenty of local and national variations in custom among the various Churches, but custom is not Tradition, and from the point of view of Tradition, there is an impressive degree of unanimity. There is not, however, always an impressive degree of harmony.

We have already mentioned the tension between the Coptic, Ethiopian, and Eritrean Churches, and they are not alone. In December 2000, fifteen patriarchs and leaders of the Eastern Orthodox Churches met at the Ecumenical Patriarchate in Istanbul to discuss the present state and needs of the Orthodox Church. They called for regular meetings to deal with Orthodox issues, particularly moral and ethical matters (especially bioethics[7]), they expressed a desire for the unity of Christendom (especially Orthodox Christendom), and they vowed to cooperate more actively in Orthodox matters than had hitherto been the case. Their meeting, however, was marred by the absence of the Patriarch of Moscow and All Russia, the leader of the largest Orthodox Church, who had boycotted the meeting. Why? Because of a dispute over whether the Moscow Patriarchate or the Ecumenical Patriarchate in Istanbul should have jurisdiction over the Orthodox Church in Estonia (though Ukraine is also a problem), a situation not helped by the fact that the Russian patriarch himself, Alexy II, is of Estonian birth, and served as a bishop there before his election to the Patriarchate in 1990.

At the same historic meeting the patriarchs expressed their concern over a lingering schism in the Bulgarian Orthodox Church, but when they attempted to draft a special document addressing the question, their attempt came to nothing since certain of their members complained that its tone was too mild.

Again, at the moment of writing (2008), the Greek Orthodox Archdiocese of America is in a state of some disquiet, if not disarray, and there is now another serious rift between the Patriarchs of Constantinople and Moscow over yet other jurisdictional questions in Europe. The divisions are so serious that there have been calls, especially from the Orthodox laity in the New World, for an international Pan-Orthodox Synod; but despite the fact that the Ecumenical Patriarchate realized, as early as 1993, the need for such a Synod, divided Orthodox Christians are still waiting, not always hopefully, for some official indication of its possibility.

Similar tales could be told from other areas, and the problems are certainly not confined to Orthodoxy, but enough is enough. The Orthodox family is not wholly united, there is no doubt about it, but if we were to judge Christianity as a whole from the divisive behaviour of some Christians—the sectarian warfare in Northern

---

7. See further John and Lyn Breck, *Stages on Life's Way. Orthodox Thinking on Bioethics* (Crestwood, 2005).

Ireland, for example—there would be few left in the Christian fold.

On a happier note, the old schism between Eastern Orthodoxy and Oriental Orthodoxy—those who recognize the authority of the Council of Chalcedon and those who do not—is well on its way to being healed. Unofficial consultations between the two groups began in 1964, and they were followed by the establishment of a Joint Commission of the Theological Dialogue between the Orthodox Church and the Oriental Orthodox Churches which began holding meetings in 1985. The members of the Joint Commission included representatives of all the Oriental Orthodox Churches and all the independent Eastern Orthodox Churches (and some semi-independent ones as well), and in 1989 the Commission published its First Agreed Statement, which effectively cleared up the misunderstandings which had occurred after the Council of Chalcedon and established a clear path to ultimate reunification. The Fourth Meeting of the Heads of the Oriental Orthodox Churches in the Middle East, held in Cairo in March 2001, confirmed the ideals and aims of the Joint Commission, and suggested ways in which the process might be accelerated. At subsequent meetings of the Heads of the Oriental Orthodox Churches, the goals have been reiterated and the process of reconciliation continued. But we must note, sadly, that the Apostolic Catholic Assyrian Church of the East, which we mentioned above, has taken no part in these deliberations, and remains somewhat isolated within the Orthodox tradition.

But while it is undeniable that there are serious rifts in certain areas of Orthodoxy, it is also undeniable that there is sufficient doctrinal agreement within the Tradition to allow us to speak of 'Orthodoxy' as a whole in a meaningful way. Precisely how we can do this will be the subject of our first chapters. The major rifts nowadays are administrative and jurisdictional rather than doctrinal (especially since the First Agreed Statement of the Joint Commission mentioned above), but administrative and jurisdictional problems date back to the very beginnings of the Christian Church. The book of Acts testifies to serious disagreements between Peter and Paul, and the First Letter of Pope Clement I, written in about 96, offers us our first glimpse—a cloud no bigger than a man's hand—of what, in time, would become the problem of the papal claims and the contrast between primacy of honour and primacy of jurisdiction.

There are also, of course, other problems, some integral to the Orthodox Tradition, some peripheral to it. Orthodoxy's opposition to the ordination of women to the priesthood, for example, is integral to the Tradition; its ethnicity, however deeply rooted, is peripheral. But both alike may serve to dissuade some people from looking at Orthodoxy more closely. In this book, therefore, I have tried to indicate both the good and the bad points of the Orthodox Tradition, though not all Orthodox will be happy with the attempt. Indeed, there are those who will object to the title itself, maintaining that there is no evolution in Orthodoxy, and that the Tradition of the Church has remained unchanged, immaculate, and inviolate since the time of the Ecumenical Councils. In many fundamental matters this is true, but the nature and vision of today's Orthodox Church in America (for example) must obviously be different from the nature and vision of, say, the Moscow patriarchate under Communist rule. Orthodoxy is a living faith, not a dead legacy, and if Tradition is not open to inspired and creative development, then it becomes rather like a stuffed animal: pretty to look at, but not a great deal of use. Traditions, like animals, are better alive.

One last point before we get under way. Those interested in Orthodoxy today no longer have to rely on books. There is a huge amount of information now available on the Internet, ranging from anti-ecumenical, ultra-Orthodox hysteria to fuzzy and all-embracing offshoots of the Orthodox Tradition invented by followers of 'Wandering Bishops' unattached to any larger Church. All the major Orthodox Churches have their own websites, many of them excellent, accurate, and informative, and all of them provide huge amounts of material in English. Other sites—just type 'Orthodox Links' into the search engine—provide easy access to all these homepages, together with equally easy access to articles, documents, literature, icons (with an abundance of illustrations), church buildings, liturgy, monasteries, magazines, news, organizations, saints, seminaries, and, in case anything has been overlooked, 'miscellaneous'. On the other hand, like much else on the Internet, the wealth of information is not always wholly reliable, but if (for example) you want an English version of the minutes of the Seventh Meeting of the Heads of the Oriental Orthodox Churches in the Middle East, 20–21 October 2004, you can find it and download it in a minute or two. This sort of access is invaluable, and offers an up-to-date view of the entire Orthodox world at the click of a mouse.

We may add that the Apostolic Catholic Assyrian Church of the East also maintains an admirably informative website with a large amount of material in both English and Syriac.

So with these preliminary comments safely behind us, let us begin at the beginning with Chapter One, and visit an Orthodox church on a Sunday morning at the time of the Divine Liturgy.

1
TAKING A LOOK AROUND

LET US SUPPOSE for a moment that a non-Orthodox Christian decides to visit an Orthodox church. I say non-Orthodox Christian not because Christians are any better than Hindus, Buddhists, Jews, or others, but because a Christian may have more idea than a Hindu or Buddhist as to the basic principles and essential symbols of the Christian religion. In today's secular society, this is not always the case, but there is a reasonable chance that if someone brought up in, say, the Roman Catholic tradition sees a crucifix, he or she will recognize it as something having Christian significance, and not see it simply as a prop for some weird cult specializing in sadism and bondage.

Furthermore, if our visiting non-Orthodox chooses to visit an Orthodox church, it is probable that he or she will also have visited non-Orthodox churches and have some familiarity with what happens there. An Anglican, for example, may have some acquaintance with the Bible, a vernacular liturgy, bishops with mitres, priests or ministers male or female (and, if male, bearded or clean-shaven), clerical vestments (ranging from the very elaborate to the very simple), a congregation of men and women, male or female servers, hymns, an organ, a sermon, pews, stained glass windows, religious imagery (paintings more than statues), and—if they are lucky enough to find a church with a really good choir—a great deal of extraordinarily good music, classical, gospel, or contemporary.

What, then, may they see if they attend a service in an Orthodox church, and how would what they see differ from what they are used to?

First of all, the actual form of the church may be different. A Russian Orthodox church, for example—if it is not second-hand (i.e., bought from, say, Episcopalians who had no further need of it or no congregation to fill it)—may have a ground-plan in the form of an equal-armed cross rather than the usual western crucifix. An inscription near the door may say to whom the church is dedicated in Cyrillic script rather than English, and the dedications may not be familiar. We do not find Protestant churches dedicated to the Protection of the Mother of God, for example, and a Roman Catholic church dedicated to Saint Silouan the Athonite or Saint Herman of Alaska would be rare indeed. The church may be capped not by a spire or tower, but by one or more onion-shaped domes, and on top of each dome will be a Russian Orthodox cross with three cross-bars: a short one at the top, a longer one beneath it, and a short one at the bottom, but this last cross-bar will be on an angle, slanting down from right to left. Why? To answer such questions is the purpose of this book.

Once in the church, visitors may be startled by the lack of seats. In the majority of Orthodox churches there are no pews (though accommodation is made for the elderly or those with physical difficulties) and the congregation stands for the duration of the liturgy. But if our visitors stay for the liturgy, they may be surprised to find people coming in and going out at all sorts of times, and when people come in, they will always complete a brief but very important ritual. They will buy a candle (or candles) from a stock of candles near the entrance to the church, and take it (or them) to one or more of the icons with which the church will be decorated. What is an icon? Essentially a two-dimensional stylized representation of a religious theme or person—Christ, Mary, angels, saints, scenes from the Old or New Testament, for example—painted in colour on a gold background. They will then make the sign of the cross, kiss the icon, and place the lighted candle in front of it. They may then kiss the icon again, make another sign of the cross, and bow to the icon. They may, in fact, do almost any combination of these things in any number, but one salient fact remains: an Orthodox entering an Orthodox church will always venerate the icons, and for a non-Orthodox, the icons are surely the most characteristic feature of the Orthodox tradition.

On entering an Orthodox church, you will see in front of you the iconostasis—the icon screen. You can't miss it. It's right there in the front of the church, and it separates that part of the church where the congregation stands and worships from that part of the church where the ordained clergy celebrate the liturgy. In modern non-Orthodox churches, all that remains of this structure is the altar rail, though in medieval churches one can sometimes see a chancel-screen, choir-screen, or rood-screen—they all amount to the same thing—which separates the choir of the church from the nave. An Orthodox iconostasis is normally of solid wood, and is pierced by three doors—a double door in the centre and a single door to either side—and decorated with icons. The number of icons will vary depending on the age and wealth of the church, but immediately to the left of the central door there will always be an icon of the Virgin Mary, and immediately to the right there will always be an icon of Christ. The screen will also be decorated with other icons—anything from one to seven rows of them—and the rest of the church may be decorated with them as well. Icons, in fact, are everywhere in an Orthodox church, and since most of them will have candles burning in front of them, the gleam of the flames on the gold backgrounds produces a dramatic and, indeed, exotic effect.

Lighting a candle or lamp is, of course, a universal symbol, and the light it sheds may symbolize anything you like. It may represent the light of life, the light of love, the light of learning, the light of grace, the light of knowledge, the light of intuition, and so on. For Christians it symbolizes, above all, the light of Christ, who is called in John's gospel 'the light of the world'. Those who follow him, the evangelist continues, 'will not walk in darkness, but will have the light of life' (Jn 8:12). Other religions say much the same thing about their own inspired teachers, but that is another matter for another time.

When the liturgy begins, non-Orthodox visitors may then be surprised to find that everything is chanted or sung, and nothing (save the sermon) said or spoken. This has been the Orthodox tradition for many centuries, and what used to be called, in Roman Catholicism, a Low Mass, has never existed within Orthodoxy. The type, language, nature, and quality of the singing and chanting naturally varies from country to country, and some of it—to western ears—may sound odd. Russian Orthodox music is, on the whole, easily accessible; Greek Orthodox music somewhat less so. But non-Orthodox westerners attending a Coptic or Ethiopian Orthodox liturgy in Arabic, Coptic, or Ge'ez may well be astonished at the sort of music they will hear. The intervals and rhythms sound strange to those accustomed to the straightforward diatonic scale, and, for those not brought up in oriental traditions, it can take a while to get used to the music. Some people never get used to it, but that is their loss. We should also add that the chanting and singing will be unaccompanied. Orthodoxy does not use organs, guitars, pianos, or other instruments. Why not? Because the liturgy is regarded as prayer, and an organ or guitar cannot pray.

Non-Orthodox visitors who enjoy singing may now be disappointed. The congregational hymns which play so important a role in the Roman Catholic, Anglican/Episcopalian, and (especially) Protestant families, play virtually no role in Orthodoxy. There are hymns, certainly, very many of them, but not many are sung at a regular Sunday morning service, and those that are sung are sung by the choir on behalf of the congregation. Nor do they change much from week to week. In other words, if a non-Orthodox enjoys a good sing-along, he or she will not find it in an Orthodox church. What visitors will hear is the continual repetition of 'Lord, have mercy' or 'Grant it, O Lord', for what are technically known as litanies play a very important role in any Orthodox service. The term 'litany' comes from the Greek word *litaneia* or 'supplication', and a litany consists of a series of petitions or prayers to which the choir and congregation make fixed responses. The idea of the litany seems to have originated in Antioch in the fourth century. From Antioch it spread to Constantinople, and from Constantinople to Rome. In Orthodoxy the litany is the main way in which the members of the congregation, separated from the ordained clergy by the iconostasis, express their devotion.

The Great Litany, with which the ordinary Sunday service begins, opens with prayers for peace, then moves on to prayers for the welfare of the ecclesiastical and civil authorities, then for the city and country, then for seasonable weather and the fruits of the earth, then for all travellers, the sick and suffering, and those in captivity, then for deliverance from affliction, and so on. And to each of these petitions the choir and congregation sing 'Lord, have mercy' in whatever language is being used. The most common languages are Greek (*Kyrie eleison*), Old Slavonic (*Gospodi pomilui*), and (especially in the Orthodox Church in America) English. One will also hear two shorter litanies, a litany of fervent supplication, a litany for the departed, a litany for catechumens, another litany of supplication, and a litany before the Lord's Prayer. This all takes a long time, but a full Orthodox service generally takes quite a lot longer than most non-Orthodox services. It is rare to finish in less than about an hour and a half, though not all Orthodox will stay for the whole service.

After the first three litanies (the Great Litany and two Little Litanies) comes what is known as the Little Entrance, when the priest carries the Gospel Book in procession around the church. He will be accompanied by others, carrying candles and icons, and, after the procession, non-Orthodox visitors may feel rather more at home and somewhat less bewildered when they hear a reading from the letters by or attributed to Saint Paul and a reading from one of the four canonical gospels. Then, as in non-Orthodox churches, the gospel reading may be followed by a sermon, though this is sometimes added at the very end of the service. It is not usually very long, and biblically-based Protestants might be surprised and disappointed at its brevity.

What visitors will not see or hear is a female priest or female reader. They do not exist in Orthodoxy. We shall explain the reason why they do not exist in due course, but Orthodoxy, rightly or wrongly, does not ordain women to any of the holy orders, major or minor. There are certainly Orthodox nuns, but nuns are not ordained. Nor do we find altar girls serving in Orthodox churches, and women are not generally permitted behind the iconostasis. Non-Orthodox reaction to this will doubtless vary from outrage to delight, depending on a variety of circumstances, but that is the way it is.

The priest will normally have a beard. That has been the tradition from the earliest times. Western priests were also usually bearded until about the fifth century, but after that, largely because of the influence of monasticism, clean-shaven priests became the rule. Nowadays, of course, one sees a variety of facial ornamentation among western clergy, but Orthodoxy has retained the old tradition.

Visitors may also be impressed (or startled) by the priest's vestments, which are rather more elaborate than they are used to seeing in non-Orthodox churches. Bishops, who wear not mitres but splendid crowns, are even more gloriously apparelled. Once again, vesture is a matter of tradition, and the Orthodox tradition has changed less than that of any of the non-Orthodox churches. This, as we shall see, can be both good and bad. It can provide a wonderful sense of continuity with the past; it can also lead to stagnant ossification. But visitors to an Orthodox church, seeing the icons and gold and candles and vestments, smelling the scent of the rising incense (an integral part of Orthodoxy), hearing the chant of the litanies and liturgy, watching the processions and entrances, are being transported back to medieval Byzantium, to the imperial church of Constantinople in the Middle Ages. There the liturgy was intended to represent heaven on earth, a momentary experience of resurrected life in a transfigured cosmos. Again, reactions to this will vary. Anglo-Catholics, if we may still use the term, may find themselves comfortably at home. A staunch Calvinistic Protestant may simply be amused or, if devoid of a sense of humour, horrified.

We have just mentioned entrances in the plural, but have so far identified only one of them, the Little Entrance. There is also another entrance, the Great Entrance, in which our splendidly vested priest carries the eucharistic bread and wine out of the left-hand door in the iconostasis to the altar (or Holy Table, as it is called in Orthodoxy). While this is going on, the choir sings the Cherubic Hymn, which begins 'Let us, who mystically represent the cherubim, and who sing the thrice-holy hymn to the life-creating Trinity, now lay aside all earthly cares'. Musically, this can be the most impressive part of the liturgy, especially in Russian Orthodoxy, and some of the greatest Russian composers have produced exquisite settings of this all-important hymn. If you want a recommendation, try the Cherubim Hymn (*Kheruvimskaya*) No. 7 by Dmitry Bortnyansky (1751–1825). But non-Orthodox music-lovers should beware: the magnificent settings of the liturgy are not, of themselves, sufficient reason to convert to Orthodoxy.

After the Great Entrance, the priest will disappear behind the iconostasis, and visitors to the church will find themselves singing 'Lord, have mercy' and 'Grant it, O Lord' in yet another litany, the

Litany of Supplication. Then comes the Creed, Sanctus ('Holy! Holy! Holy!'), and Benedictus ('Blessed is he that comes in the name of the Lord')—Anglicans, Episcopalians, and Roman Catholics will find themselves more or less at home here—and that is followed by a hymn to the Mother of God which begins: 'It is truly meet to bless you, O Theotokos, ever-blessed and most pure, and the Mother of our God.' The meaning of the title 'Theotokos' is something we shall discuss in due course. Roman Catholics will be happy with this hymn, though Protestants may find it idolatrous. Anglicans and Episcopalians, being a law unto themselves, will find it as they find it.

Then comes the actual communion, and at this point non-Orthodox visitors may indeed be surprised. The priest does not offer the faithful the bread and wine separately, but bread and wine are mixed together in the chalice, and communion is given by means of a long-handled communion spoon. The communicant approaches the priest, opens his or her mouth, the priest takes a morsel of bread-and-wine from the chalice, and delivers it from the spoon right into the open mouth of the communicant. This was certainly not the practice in the early church, when bread and wine were each given separately, and when it became the custom in the eastern Church is unclear. It *may* have begun in the sixth century, though the evidence, both archaeological and documentary, is ambiguous, but it was certainly regular practice by the early Middle Ages. In theological jargon it is referred to as intinction, though Anglicans and Roman Catholics may not recognize it by this name. For them, intinction usually refers to taking communion by dipping a piece of consecrated unleavened bread into the wine in the chalice. This is not Orthodox intinction, which remains—as some would say—primitively unhygienic.

After the liturgy has ended, non-Orthodox visitors may have questions, not only about the liturgy itself, but about what Orthodox believe and how what they believe differs from what members of other Christian Churches believe—Roman Catholics, for example. Some of the answers will be familiar. Visitors will hear of the Trinity, the Incarnation, the Atonement, the veneration of Mary and the saints, angels and guardian angels, a Church guided by the Holy Spirit, Ecumenical Councils, apostolic succession, holy tradition, seven sacraments, the communication of grace, judgement and forgiveness, and heaven and hell. But some of the answers may contain terms and ideas less familiar: autocephalous and autonomous churches, for example, or the ecumenical patriarch and other patriarchs, metropolitans, archimandrites and archpriests, the schism of the Old Believers, the importance of Mount Athos, hesychasm and the Jesus Prayer, synergy, and, above all, the goal of deification, which does not mean that one becomes God. It means that one becomes God-like. It is my intention in this book to try to explain all these—and many more—Orthodox terms and ideas, but it is necessary, indeed essential, to begin with a little history.

2
TWO ORTHODOX FAMILIES

ORTHODOXY MEANS correct belief or correct doctrine. It can also mean correct worship. This means that we need to answer two questions: what do Orthodox Christians believe, and why do they think that what they believe is correct? The first question is not too difficult to answer; the second is more delicate. But do all Orthodox believe the same things? Not entirely, though all Orthodox share a belief in certain basic principles, even though, in the past, they sometimes did not think they did. But to explain that, we need to say something of the history of Orthodoxy. We do not need to say a great deal—as we said in the Introduction, this is not a history of the Orthodox Church—but we do need to say something. Without some idea of Orthodox history it is impossible to understand the separation between the great majority of Eastern Orthodox who belong to the Greek, Russian, and Slav family, and the minority who belong to the Oriental Orthodox Churches: the Copts, Ethiopians, Syrians, and Armenians. Furthermore, without some knowledge of history it is also impossible to understand the bane of Orthodoxy, namely, its ethnicity, its tendency to identify religion with nationality and culture.

So where do we begin? We can begin with the death and resurrection of Jesus of Nazareth and the gradual growth of the Christian Church in a non-Christian environment. For almost three centuries Christians were a persecuted minority, but early in 313, essentially for political reasons, the Roman emperors Constantine and Licinius met at Milan and passed an edict or semi-edict (its exact legal status is unclear) which recognized the legitimacy of the Christian religion and required that all religions be tolerated equally. This, in theory, ended the persecution of Christians, and Constantine's support for the faith gave it a tremendous boost. On the other hand, the removal of external threat meant that Christians could now do openly what they had hitherto done discreetly: argue about their beliefs. And the belief which engaged their attention in the years immediately after 313 was the doctrine of the Trinity.

The doctrine of the Trinity is one of the two great pillars on which the Christian tradition stands or falls. The other is the doctrine of the Incarnation, i.e., the belief that Jesus of Nazareth was not merely an inspired man or great prophet, but the infinite deity appearing in the finite bounds of mortal flesh. No other religion maintains these two principles (the 'trinity' of Brahma, Vishnu, and Shiva in Hinduism is quite different, and an *avatar* is not an 'incarnation' in the Christian sense) and it may be debated whether a 'Christian' denomination which does not accept both of them (the Unitarians, for example, or the Jehovah's Witnesses) may accurately be called Christian. Orthodox—all Orthodox—accept both, and both are essential and necessary beliefs for any Orthodox Christian.

But in the years following 313 the doctrine of the Trinity was still being hotly debated, and one point in particular occupied the attention of theologians and laity alike: what was the position of the Son with respect to the Father? Was the Second Person of the Trinity equal to the Father in rank, status, and power, or was he in some way inferior or subordinate? Some thought one thing; some thought the other. Since the main protagonist of the subordinationist position was an Alexandrian priest called Arius who died in 336, the controversy is referred to as the Arian Controversy.

It cannot be denied that Arius had a point—several points in fact. First of all, according to the Gospel of John, Christ himself said 'the Father is greater than I' (Jn 14: 28), and according to John and the other Evangelists, Christ did a number of things which, if he were truly and completely God, were impossible to explain. He was tempted, he 'advanced in wisdom' (Lk 2: 52), he wept, he did not know the hour when the world would end, and he cried out in desperation when he was on the cross. But how can an omniscient Deity grow in wisdom? How can an all-knowing God be ignorant? How can the perfect Creator be tempted? Surely the only way to explain these things is to say that Christ was not, in fact, God in the same sense that God the Father is God, that he was not quite perfect and not quite all-knowing.

Furthermore, if Christ is the mediator between God and the human race (and Scripture leaves us in no doubt on the matter), then how can he be a mediator, a 'middle-man', without being in the middle, i.e., without being something more than human but less than divine? And if the way to salvation involves the imitation of Christ (and the Church was and is convinced that this is so), how can we hope to imitate a being who is infinite in all things? If someone suggests to us that we imitate an Olympic runner and try to run a hundred meters in so many seconds, we might give it a try. We may not succeed, but success is at least a theoretical possibility. But if someone tells us that we have to run at the speed of light and cover a hundred meters in no time at all, we would be perfectly justified in shrugging our shoulders and walking out of the changing-room. Such a thing is manifestly impossible. If, then, Christ is God—totally God—how can we hope to imitate him? But if, on the other hand, he is something less than God, then we may at least have a chance, we may at least make the attempt. Subordinationism, in other words, provided sound and convincing answers to the questions of how Christ could exhibit human emotions, how he could mediate between God and us, and how we could aspire to imitate him with some hope of success. It brought him within our reach.

About half a century later these questions would be answered in a different way: by insisting that in Christ there was not only the fullness of divinity, but also the fullness of humanity; and that the fullness of humanity involved true human flesh and—more importantly—a true human soul which felt human emotions and which had human limitations. But that was in the future and, for the moment, Arius had both logic and tradition to support his case.

Both sides, Arian and anti-Arian, bolstered their arguments with appropriate biblical quotations, but it was not long before the controversy—originally theological—became enmeshed in politics and turned violent. The emperor Constantine, to say the least, was not pleased. Ecclesiastical civil war was not conducive to the smooth running of an empire, and the emperor therefore did what, in future years, emperors would generally do in cases of difficulty and major divergences of opinion: he called a council. This was the First Ecumenical Council. It was attended by representatives of what, at the time, was the whole Christian world (in essence, the world around the shores of the Mediterranean), and it was held in the small town of Nicaea (now Iznik in modern Turkey) in the year 325.

The most important decision of the council was that Arius was wrong, subordinationism was wrong, and that Father and Son were truly coequal in divinity, rank, and power. There was never a time when the Father alone existed (which was what Arius had maintained, though he maintained it with great subtlety[1]), and from the very beginning of eternity there was a Father and a Son who were both alike fully God and fully divine. Arius's most effective adversary was Athanasius, bishop of Alexandria, who was appointed to the position in 328, and Athanasius had no doubt that Arius was utterly, totally, and blasphemously wrong. Why? For three main reasons.

First of all, Christianity has always maintained that God is, in some way, One *and Three*. This is one of the essential features that distinguishes Christianity from Judaism and, later, Islam. The Trinity, in other words, did not develop; it always was. To maintain that there was a time when God was one and not three (said Athanasius) may be a form of Judaism, but it is not Christianity.

Secondly, Christianity has always maintained that worship may be offered to God alone. To worship anything less than God is idolatry, the worship of idols, and idolatry, as Saint Paul makes clear, is a very grave sin indeed. But if, as Arius maintained, God the Son was subordinate to God the Father and was not truly God, then to worship Christ was to worship a being less than God, and that (said Athanasius again) is not Christianity, but idolatry.

Thirdly, Christianity maintains that salvation involves two essential principles: first, that the iniquities of the human race have been forgiven and its many sins paid for by the death of Christ on Calvary; and second, that this same human race is, by God's grace,

---

1. For a more detailed account, see David N. Bell, *A Cloud of Witnesses. An Introductory History of the Development of Christian Doctrine* (Kalamazoo, 2007 [2nd ed.]), 64–68.

permitted to share in the divine nature of Christ and become, in a sense, divine. Scripture is clear on the point: through the promises made to us by Christ, we 'may escape worldly corruption and become partakers of the divine nature' (2 Peter 1:4). The technical term for this—and it is arguably the most important single term in the whole Orthodox tradition—is deification, and we shall have much more to say about it in due course. But to redeem the whole of the human race, past, present, and future, from all its infinite wickedness requires an infinite being who is not himself part of that race, and the only infinite being is God. This had been clearly stated by an earlier Greek theologian, Irenaeus, who had died in about 200. The world cannot be redeemed, he said, by someone who is part of that world, and we cannot be saved by a Saviour who is himself in need of salvation.

As for the second point, we may summarize the principle in Athanasius's own words: 'God became human that in him humans might become god'.[2] He did not mean by this that 'God became 70% human that in him 70% of humans might become 70% god'. In other words, if Christ was not *fully* God, not 100% God, then redemption may not be complete, and the New Testament is wrong. But since the Christ of Arius is not 100% God by nature, we cannot hope to share fully in his divinity since he has no full divinity in which we can share. And that, said Athanasius yet again, is not what the New Testament teaches, and it is not Christianity.

The principle that Father and Son were coequal and coeternal was enshrined at the Council of Nicaea in a document which has come to be known as the Nicene Creed, and all the bishops but two signed it. The two who did not sign were immediately deposed and sent home in disgrace. The Creed also stated that Father and Son were *consubstantial*, which meant that they were both of the same substance. The substance, in this case, was 'Godness' or divinity, and to say that Father and Son were consubstantial meant that both were completely, wholly, and perfectly God.

But what about the Holy Spirit? Father and Son may have been coequal, coeternal, and consubstantial, but could the same be said of the Spirit? That was quite another problem. Virtually nothing,

2. Athanasius, *Ad Adelphium*, 4.

in fact, was said on this subject at Nicaea, and it would take about another sixty years before another council called by another emperor—the Second Ecumenical Council held at Constantinople in 381—made any official statement on the matter. At that council, the bishops stated, logically and correctly, that if the Trinity was also a unity, then whatever was said of Father and Son must also be said of the Holy Spirit, and that the entire Trinity, not just Father and Son, is at one and the same time consubstantial, coequal, and coeternal. Nor was this merely dotting an I or crossing a T. The idea that the Holy Spirit is 100% divine is an essential feature of the Orthodox tradition, and (as we shall see in a later chapter) any apparent threat to this principle was to be adamantly resisted. If the Church is to be inspired and guided by the Holy Spirit, then the Church must be inspired and guided by a Holy Spirit who is fully divine. Or, putting it crudely, if the Holy Spirit is only 70% divine, then there is a 30% chance that the Church is wrong. It may be wrong in some areas, and certainly has been in the past, but that is the fault of human beings, not the Holy Spirit.

Let us note, however, that the doctrine of the Trinity was a doctrine that evolved over a number of centuries. In the pages of the New Testament we certainly find mention of a Father, a Son, and a Comforter, but we will look in vain to find details of their nature and relationship. Working out these details was a matter for theologians and Ecumenical Councils, and what they decided did not come easily. What they decided, however, has remained part of the Tradition of the Church, and it is the business of Tradition to elaborate truth with truth. But truth (says Orthodoxy) is to be found in the inspiration of the Holy Spirit, and a Church Council inspired by the Holy Spirit is a Church Council inspired by God.

No sooner had the Trinitarian controversy been settled (or, more accurately, had begun to be settled) than another great conflict arose to divide the Christian world. The question this time concerned the second fundamental pillar on which the Christian tradition stands: the Incarnation. By the time of the Council of Constantinople in 381, Christians generally agreed that Christ was both fully human (with human flesh and a human soul) and fully divine, but there was no agreement as to how these two natures were related, nor was there any agreement on what terms should be used to describe the relationship. Was the divinity in Christ *mixed* with the humanity? *Conjoined* with the humanity? *Mingled* with the humanity? *United* with the humanity? Or what? The question may not seem of much significance today, but it was certainly significant fifteen hundred years ago; and the point at issue, hidden behind the subtleties of the Greek language, personal rivalries, and (just as at Nicaea) secular and ecclesiastical politics, was as vital then as it is now. Any description of Christ must state, or at least imply, that he was 100% divine and 100% human, and that when the divinity was conjoined or united with the humanity, both divinity and humanity were unaffected by the relationship. In other words, the divinity of Christ was not in any way diminished by its association with his humanity, and the humanity of Christ was not transformed into some sort of super-humanity by its association with his divinity. Christ was neither half a God nor half a man, but fully both. He was neither a superprophet nor an arch-archangel, but God incarnate. In him, the divinity and the humanity were never separated, but they *were* distinct.

It cannot be denied that these are important points and they have major theological consequences, and the importance of the issues was matched by the violence of the controversy. This time the two major antagonists were Nestorius, bishop of Constantinople, and Cyril, bishop of Alexandria, and the issue at stake was whether it was right to refer to the Virgin Mary as 'Mother of God' or 'God-bearer'. Nestorius advocated caution. To call Mary 'God-bearer' (*Theotokos* in Greek) might imply that Christ was only God—i.e., that he was not also human—or, if he were human, that his humanity had in some way been swallowed up by his divinity and lost. The title 'God-bearer' was not *wrong* exactly, but it was dangerous; and if one were going to use it at all, then it would be best to be on the safe side and balance it with the title 'Man-bearer'; and if 'God-bearer and Man-bearer' is too cumbersome, then the safest title to use is 'Christ-bearer', a term which nobody can dispute. Nor did Nestorius like to speak of the divinity and humanity being *united* in Christ. The term 'union', he thought, might imply that in Jesus of Nazareth, the humanity and divinity had merged into a sort of amorphous oneness, and he much preferred to use the term 'conjunction'. No one can mistake a conjunction for a blurred union, and we must at all costs make it clear that Christ was truly God and truly human, and not either God alone or some sort of confused 'Hugomand'.

It is not difficult to appreciate Nestorius's concerns, but Cyril pounced upon his comments, misrepresented them, and accused Nestorius of *denying* the title 'God-bearer' to the Virgin. If that had been true, it would indeed have been grave heresy, for if Mary did not bear God, then what she bore was no more than an ordinary human child, and Nestorius has denied the divinity of Christ! The charge was not true. Nestorius never denied the Virgin the title of 'God-bearer', nor did he ever deny that Christ was truly God, but some of his language was misleading and his theology was not always as clear as it might have been. There is no doubt, however, that he left himself wide open to attack by Cyril, and Cyril was more than happy to avail himself of the opportunity. He loathed Nestorius, and resented his being appointed to the great see of Constantinople, a position to which Cyril himself aspired and which he thought (with some justice) he well deserved. Although he was a very good theologian, Cyril was not always scrupulous when it came to ecclesiastical politics, and his campaign against Nestorius proved extremely effective. In due course, Nestorius would be condemned for holding views he did not hold. But, as may be expected, not everyone agreed with Cyril, and his attack on Nestorius soon came to involve the whole Church.

Once again, the reigning emperor, now Theodosius II, saw his empire ravaged by theological war, and, like Constantine before him, he called a council. The council—the Third Ecumenical Council—met at Ephesus in 431, but it was hardly a success. True, it led to a compromise in 433 which resulted in fifteen years of uneasy peace, and it gave formal approval to the title *Theotokos*/'God-bearer' for the Virgin Mary, but it did not settle the issue. On the contrary, the council actually gave rise to further factions, and when the unsatisfactory truce of 433 began to collapse in 448, the situation rapidly worsened and became much more difficult to deal with. The details can be read elsewhere,[3] but three years later, in 451, a new emperor called a new council in the hope of resolving what, by now, was a complicated and heavily politicized controversy.

3. See Bell, *Cloud of Witnesses*, 122–133.

The great Council of Chalcedon (now Kadiköy, a district of Istanbul), the Fourth Ecumenical Council, was attended by more than five hundred bishops and was the largest ecclesiastical council yet convened. As usual, political lobbying played an important role, but political lobbying does not necessarily preclude the inspiration of the Holy Spirit. The Holy Spirit, after all, has to use whatever resources it has to hand, and human resources are sometimes far from ideal. At this important council Nestorius was condemned and Cyril (who was now dead) was regarded as a spokesman for the Orthodox tradition. The final resolutions of the council were then summarized in a document known as the *Chalcedonian Definition of the Faith*, and the essential part of this document stated that the holy fathers taught unanimously that

> our Lord Jesus Christ is one and the same Son, perfect in his divinity and perfect in his humanity, truly God and truly human, like us in all things except for sin. In his divinity he was begotten from the Father before all ages; in his humanity, for us and for our salvation, he was begotten in these last days from the Virgin Mary the God-bearer (*Theotokos*): one and the same Christ, Son, Lord, only-begotten, made known in two natures without confusion, without change, without division, and without separation.[4]

The *Chalcedonian Definition* is not merely an historical document. It is actually a statement of what the vast majority of contemporary Christians of all denominations believe about their Lord and Redeemer. But is it a *clear* statement? In English it is. In Greek, especially in the Greek of the fifth century, it is not. The problem lay in the meaning of the word 'nature'—*physis* in Greek (the root of the word 'physics')—which, at that time, was unfortunately ambiguous. It could mean 'nature', which is what the bishops at Chalcedon intended it to mean, but it could also mean 'person'. If we take *physis* to mean 'nature', then there were indeed two 'natures'—one divine and one human—in the one person of Jesus of Nazareth. But if we take *physis* to mean 'person', then to say that Jesus of

---

4. Translated from the Greek text in *The Oecumenical Documents of the Faith,* ed. T. Herbert Bindley, rev. F. W. Green (London, 1950 [4th ed.]), 193.

Nazareth was two 'persons' or two people is to imply some sort of schizophrenic split personality. As we have seen above, in the Christian tradition, the divinity and humanity of Christ are distinct, *but not separate*. Nestorius was accused, unjustly, of separating them.

The complex ramifications of the problem need not concern us,[5] but since the Council was talking about one of the two unique features of the Christian faith, it is understandable that many theologians were deeply concerned. The tragedy of the matter is that both sides, on the whole, believed the same thing: that in Christ there was an unconfused union of perfect divinity and perfect humanity. Unfortunately, they found it impossible to express their belief in the same words. For those who took *physis* to mean nature, Christ was two *physeis* (*physeis* is the plural of *physis*). For those who took *physis* to mean person, Christ was one *physis*. The first group came to be called Chalcedonians (i.e., those who agreed with the ideas and the terminology set out in the *Chalcedonian Definition of the Faith*) or Dyophysites/Diophysites ('Two-*physeis*-ites'). The second group came to be known as Monophysites or 'One-*physis*-ites'. Each group was wholly convinced that it was right, and the two groups hated each other with a holy hatred.

From the second half of the fifth century to the second half of the seventh there were a number of attempts at reconciling the two parties, but by this time the theological terms 'one *physis*' or 'two *physeis*' had become nationalist slogans. To ask a sixth-century Monophysite Egyptian to admit that in Christ there were two *physeis* would be like asking a Second World War Nazi general to sing 'God Save the King' and admit that he meant it. So it is hardly surprising that none of these efforts was successful, and the final break occurred in the course of the sixth century, when the Monophysite movement consolidated itself into three major Churches, one in Egypt and Ethiopia, one in Syria, and one in Armenia.

Today, the terms Dyophysite and Monophysite are rarely used (save by ecclesiastical historians), and all Orthodox Christians are at one with Roman Catholics, Anglicans, and the great majority of Protestants in maintaining that in the one being of the incarnate

---

5. See Bell, *Cloud of Witnesses*, 143–152 (chap. XI).

Christ there coexisted, in some mysterious way, the fullness of divinity and the fullness of humanity.

Nevertheless, the national Churches which did not agree with the Chalcedonian Definition still exist. The Coptic Orthodox Church traces its lineage to Saint Mark who, according to the third/fourth-century ecclesiastical historian Eusebius, established and organized Christianity in Alexandria. But the bitter rivalry—theological, ecclesiastical, and political—between Alexandria and Constantinople in the fifth century led the Egyptian Church to separate itself from the 'Chalcedonians' and to become increasingly isolated. Coptic Orthodoxy is now centred in Egypt and the Sudan, though other dioceses are to be found outside Egypt in areas of large Egyptian immigration, especially the United States. The Ethiopian Orthodox Church (which has a number of unique traditions and some curious links with Judaism) was for many centuries a daughter-church of the Coptic Church, but became fully independent and self-governing, with its own Patriarch, in 1959. The head of the Coptic Church is the Patriarch of Alexandria, who now resides in Cairo. But the Egyptian situation is further complicated by the fact that there are two Orthodox patriarchs of Alexandria: the Greek Orthodox patriarch, who represents those Christians (the small minority) loyal to the Council of Chalcedon, and the Coptic Orthodox patriarch who represents those Christians (the great majority) who disagreed with the Council's decisions. There are also two other Alexandrian patriarchs representing very small groups of Egyptian Christians in communion with Rome.

Of this plethora of patriarchs, the Coptic Orthodox patriarch is certainly the most important, and he is normally referred to as the Pope of Alexandria. The Greek Orthodox patriarch is also referred to in this way. The title is an old one—it dates back to the third century—and the use of the term 'pope' to designate the patriarch of Alexandria (both Coptic and Greek) actually predates its use as a title for the bishop of Rome. Technically, therefore, if someone asks you the name of the pope, you should reply 'Which pope?' There are three.

Of the other Oriental Orthodox Churches, the Syrians have the most convoluted history: there are Syrian Orthodox, Syrian Catholics in communion with Rome, Syro-Malankara and Syro-Malabar

Churches in India, Maronites, and a number of others, including the Apostolic Catholic Assyrian Church of the East. But we cannot present the details here, and those interested must seek the information elsewhere.[6] The Syrian Orthodox Church is also known as the Jacobite Church, though nowadays only the Syrian Christians in India use the term. The name derives from Jacob Baradaeus, a sixth-century monk who was primarily responsible for establishing the Church in Syria. The Syrian Orthodox have had an unhappy history. Great numbers of them were slaughtered by the Mongols in the fourteenth century; at the end of the eighteenth century a considerable number entered into communion with Rome and became Syrian Catholics; and at the turn of the twentieth century there were appalling massacres at the hands of the Muslim Turks. Among Syrian Orthodox, 1915 is called 'the year of the sword'. The largest group of Syrian Orthodox is actually to be found in south India (where they have their own complicated history), but Syrian immigrants took the tradition to North America where the Antiochian Orthodox Christian Archdiocese of North America is today doing booming business.

As to the Armenians, they were converted in the third century, and were the first nation to embrace Christianity officially. For political rather than theological reasons, they rejected the decisions of the Council of Chalcedon, but never completely identified themselves with the other non-Chalcedonian Churches. For much of its history, the Armenian Church has been a persecuted Church, and the persecution culminated in the Turkish massacres of the late nineteenth and early twentieth centuries, when a large portion of the nation was slaughtered. The vast majority of Armenian Orthodox are centred in present-day Armenia, but, as may be expected, there are Armenian churches wherever there are sufficiently large numbers of immigrants. We shall meet some of them in Chapter Fifteen. The Armenian Church is unusual in having not one head, but two: it is organized as two Catholicates, each administered by a Catholicos. Congregations can choose their own jurisdiction, but most Armenian Orthodox owe allegiance to the Catholicos of Etchmiadzin. The

---

6. There is a sound account in *The Blackwell Dictionary of Eastern Christianity*, 46–76.

title 'Catholicos' is also used by the heads of the Georgian Orthodox Church and the Apostolic Catholic Assyrian Church of the East, but in the combined form Catholicos Patriarch.

Nowadays the differences between these Oriental Churches and the great mass of Greek, Russian, and Slav Orthodox are national, cultural, and linguistic rather than theological, though Ethiopian Orthodoxy exhibits a number of distinctive features not shared by any other major Christian Church, Orthodox or otherwise. But all are agreed on the doctrine of a coequal, coeternal, and consubstantial Trinity, and all are agreed that Christ was indeed the God-man, God incarnate, truly divine and truly human. He was not just God (with no real humanity), and he was not just a man inspired by God, a sort of megaprophet.

We must note, however, that all the Oriental Churches were, at one time or another, persecuted Churches, and none more than the Armenians. This is important, for persecution always strengthens societal bonds, and a persecuted people often finds its unity in its religion. It's like a snowball: if you squeeze it, it certainly gets smaller, but it also gets harder. 'The blood of the martyrs is the seed of the Church', said Tertullian (more or less),[7] and what was true of the early Church amid persecuting Romans was equally true of the national Churches amid persecuting Persians, Mongols, Arabs, Turks, or Bolsheviks. And even if we speak of pressure rather than out-and-out persecution, the result is much the same. There were long periods when the Egyptian Church was not actively persecuted, but when, nonetheless, it was under the enormous cultural pressure of Arab/Muslim domination. The same was true of the Russian Church under the Mongols or the Communists, and the Greek Church under the Turks. In all cases, the Church, together with monasticism (which will be the subject of a later chapter), played a vital, indeed essential, role in preserving much of the cultural treasury of the ruled rather than the rulers, and one can understand why some Orthodox look with a wary eye on non-Orthodox seeking entry into their national traditions. Even for an English-speaking North American seeking to convert to Greek

---

7. Tertullian, *Apologeticum*, 50.13. What Tertullian actually said was simply 'the seed is the blood of Christians'.

Orthodoxy the situation can sometimes be difficult (though much depends on the local priest). Think what it could be like for a Turk seeking entry into Armenian Orthodoxy. This nationalistic exclusivism is certainly not Christian, but given the vicissitudes of history, it is certainly understandable.

But before we go further in this matter, let us return to the Council of Chalcedon. As we have seen, the *Chalcedonian Definition of the Faith* was rejected by the Oriental Churches, not so much for what it said as for the words it used to say it. The Chalcedonians, however, had no problem in accepting the entire document, and nor did the western half of Christendom, which had its centre in Rome. Furthermore, when Orthodox missionaries moved into Moravia, Bulgaria, Serbia, Russia, and other Slav areas from the ninth century onwards, they took with them the Chalcedonian principles of Greek Orthodoxy, and the result was inevitable: the Chalcedonian branch of the Orthodox Church came to outnumber by millions the much smaller group of the old and venerable Oriental Churches. Which Churches constitute the Chalcedonian family? The patriarchates of Constantinople, Alexandria, Antioch, Jerusalem, Moscow, Serbia, Romania, Bulgaria, and Georgia; the Orthodox Churches of Cyprus, Greece, Poland, Albania, and the Czech Lands and Slovakia; and the Orthodox Church in America (OCA). All these Patriarchates and Churches are wholly independent and self-governing, and are referred to as *autocephalous* Churches.[8] Orthodox Churches which enjoy a limited independence, but which are ultimately under the jurisdiction of one or other of the autocephalous Churches are referred to as *autonomous*.[9]

---

8. The Orthodox Church in America is recognized as autocephalous by Moscow, Bulgaria, Georgia, Poland, and the Czech Lands and Slovakia, but not by the other Patriarchates or Churches.

9. There are seven autonomous Churches: (1) Sinai, (2) Finland, (3) Estonia, (4) Japan, (5) China (which is almost non-existent), (6) Ukraine, and (7) the Archdiocese of Ohrid. Only Sinai and Finland are recognized as autonomous by all the Patriarchates and Churches. Estonia is recognized as autonomous by Constantinople but not by Moscow. Japan, China, and Ukraine are recognized as autonomous by Moscow but not by Constantinople. And the Archdiocese of Ohrid is recognized as autonomous only by the Church of Serbia.

The Chalcedonian/non-Chalcedonian distinction is actually quite useful. It avoids the limitations of using 'Eastern' and 'Oriental' for Churches which are no longer exclusively eastern or oriental, and it is not anachronistic. In the Second Agreed Statement of the Joint Commission of the Theological Dialogue between the Eastern Orthodox Church and the Oriental Orthodox Churches issued in 1990, the Commission stated that both families of Orthodox Christians 'accept the first three Ecumenical Councils, which form our common heritage.'[10] The decisions of the Council of Chalcedon and three later councils, considered by Eastern Orthodox to be dogmatic teaching, are regarded by the Oriental Orthodox as 'interpretations', but given this distinction, the Oriental Orthodox Churches were happy to respond 'positively'.[11] In other words, the terms Chalcedonian and non-Chalcedonian are still legitimate—unlike Dyophysite and Monophysite—though the disagreements and misunderstandings which originally caused the rift have now been overcome. We should add here, perhaps, that the Apostolic Catholic Assyrian Church of the East does not agree with the rest of the Orthodox world that the first three Ecumenical Councils form part of a 'common heritage'. The Church of the East does not accept the decisions of the Council of Ephesus (431), the Third Ecumenical Council, and that is no small stumbling-block in the quest for reunion.

But this is to go too far too fast. It is all very well to speak of patriarchates and patriarchs, but what exactly are they and how did they come into being? We have seen that the Orthodox Church is actually a family of Churches, but what is the precise relationship between the heads of the various Churches, and is there an Orthodox equivalent of the Roman pontiff? And if there is not, to whom does the Orthodox Church look for authoritative guidance? These are important questions, and we shall try to answer them in our next chapter.

10. The document can be found on the Internet at http://www.uk-christian.net/boc/2church.htm. The three councils are Nicaea (325), Constantinople (381), and Ephesus (431).
11. *Ibid.*

3

ORGANIZATION AND ADMINISTRATION

THE PROBLEM OF AUTHORITY is one that faces every Church. Roman Catholicism is the most centralized of the major Christian Churches and has (in theory) the fewest problems. Some of the Protestant Churches—those that take the doctrine of 'the priesthood of all believers' to its logical conclusion—have the most. Orthodoxy, like Anglicanism, stands somewhere between the two. In technical terms, the Orthodox Church is an episcopal Church, a collegial Church, a conciliar Church, and a spiritual Church. But is it *a* Church at all? That is to say, is it one Church or many? And if it is not one Church, can we ever speak of Orthodoxy as a whole and mean what we say? Once again, in order to understand what is going on, we need to go back in history and return for a moment to the First Ecumenical Council, the Council of Nicaea, called by the emperor Constantine in 325.

As we saw in the last chapter, the main theological concern of this council was the mutual relationship of God the Father and God the Son, but it was not its only concern. The establishment of some system of administration and government was also of major importance, for the Church of 325 no longer consisted of small, scattered communities of persecuted Christians. On the contrary, it was now a rapidly growing organization with a clearly defined hierarchy of bishops, priests, deacons, and deaconesses; and although it was still to be found for the most part around the shores of the Mediterranean, the shores of the Mediterranean covered no small territory.

For organizational purposes, therefore, the bishops at Nicaea decided to divide the Christian world into four administrative districts, each centred on a major Christian centre, and to rank them in order of precedence. No one had any doubt that Rome should come first. Not only was it the old capital of the Roman Empire, but it was to Rome that the message of the Gospel had been taken by Peter and Paul, and it was in Rome that both Peter and Paul had met their deaths. Next, in the east, came the great city of Alexandria, the second city of the Roman Empire and the intellectual capital of the ancient world. Then, following Alexandria, came Antioch in Syria (the third city of the Empire), and, finally, Jerusalem.

Nearly sixty years later, however, at the Second Ecumenical Council in 381, a change had to be made in this structure to take account of Constantinople. In 330, five years after Nicaea, the city had been inaugurated as Constantine's capital, and by 381 it was the chief city of the eastern Roman Empire. It was also where the Second Ecumenical Council was taking place. But where was Constantinople to be placed in the list? As the eastern imperial capital it could certainly not just be tacked on at the end, but it was equally certain that western imperial Rome took precedence over all. Constantinople was therefore inserted in the list between Rome and Alexandria, to the great displeasure of both. Rome looked askance at what it saw (not without reason) as a dangerous and threatening newcomer; Alexandria objected to losing its preeminence in the eastern Christian world. But the die was cast. Constantinople would not and could not be dislodged from its position as 'Second Rome', and, from the fifth to about the tenth century, the Christian world was administered through what came to be known as the Pentarchy: the five ancient patriarchates of Rome, Constantinople, Alexandria, Antioch, and Jerusalem. Each was governed by a patriarch and each was autocephalous, or independent and self-governing.

With the conversion of the Slavs, which began in the 860s, and the rapid development of Slavic Orthodoxy, this old administrative system required expansion; and over a period of time (and not without opposition) five new patriarchates were added to the five old ones: Russia, Serbia, Romania, Bulgaria, and Georgia. As with the Pentarchy, each of these new administrative districts was (and is) governed by a patriarch, and once again, each is autocephalous. The same is true of the Coptic, Ethiopian, Syrian, and Armenian Churches, whose lineage, as we have seen, is non-Chalcedonian and whose patriarchs are sometimes called by different names.

But what is a patriarch? No more and no less than a bishop. As we said at the beginning of this chapter, the Orthodox Church is an episcopal Church, a structure it shares with Roman Catholicism and Anglicanism. It is the view of all three traditions that authority to govern the Church, administer the sacraments, and preach the Gospel was given by Christ to his apostles, and from the apostles to the successors of the apostles; and all three agree that the successors of the apostles are the bishops of the Church. The germ of this idea can be seen as far back as the end of the first century, though it reached its full development only with the full development of the idea of the episcopacy in the third century. In technical terms, what we are talking about here is the doctrine of Apostolic Succession, but we must take careful note that Apostolic Succession is collegiate, not individual. What do we mean by this? What we mean is that Christ did not hand on the power to govern the Church, administer the sacraments, and preach the Gospel to any one individual: he handed on these powers to the *group* of the apostles as a whole. Then, from the group of the apostles the same powers were handed down to the group of their successors, the bishops, who are sometimes referred to as the 'post-apostolic college'. Bishops may delegate certain of these powers to the priests in their dioceses, but priests (and, below them, deacons and subdeacons) do not possess them by right, but only by delegation.

This is a very important point. As far as Orthodoxy is concerned, this principle of collegial authority means that all the bishops share this authority *equally*. No one bishop has any more authority than any other, and if a matter concerning the government of the Church were to come to a vote (as, for example, at a council) then the principle of 'one bishop, one vote' necessarily applies, and any decision implemented will be the decision of the majority.

That all bishops share this authority is not to say that all bishops have the same rank or status. They do not. The great patriarchates are divided up into provinces (the name varies with the different Churches, but the principle remains the same), and the provinces subdivided into dioceses. Patriarchates, as we have seen, are administered by patriarchs, provinces generally by metropolitans or archbishops, and dioceses by bishops, though in the Greek Orthodox Church the titles of metropolitan and bishop are not always clearly distinguished. Even so, patriarchs and metropolitans, who are now generally elected (hair-raising stories of how they obtained their positions in the past are now happily a matter of history), cannot be any more episcopal than their episcopal colleagues. They may hold a superior position in the administrative hierarchy of the Church, but they do not receive an extra helping of grace. They occupy much the same position as the chairman of a board—they take more responsibility, they run the meetings, and they report the decisions—but they still have only one vote, and if the other members of the board out-vote them, so be it.

Just as a patriarch is a sort of chairman of the board of his own patriarchate, so the patriarch of Constantinople is a sort of chairman of the board of all the patriarchs who trace their lineage back to Chalcedon. Since the sixth century, the patriarch of Constantinople has borne the title of Ecumenical Patriarch, and the twentieth century witnessed the life and example of a truly great Ecumenical Patriarch, a true spokesman of Orthodoxy and a man of great spiritual authority: Athenagoras, who died in 1972. He was, as the Oxford historian Owen Chadwick has said, exceptional:

> His knowledge of French and English, his acquaintance with the western world, his openness to international ideas, his range of friendships in the world-wide church, his earlier experience with the seamier intrigues of Balkan politics, his deep learning in the Greek Fathers and some modern writers—it is safe to say that Constantinople had never seen an archbishop like him in the long line of ecumenical patriarchs.[1]

This is true. Athenagoras was indeed exceptional. But the present Ecumenical Patriarch, Bartholomew I, whose patriarchate falls in more difficult and dangerous times, looks to be a worthy successor.

---

1. Owen Chadwick, *Michael Ramsey. A Life* (Oxford, 1990) 290.

An Orthodox Ecumenical Patriarch is not, however, a Roman Catholic Pope, and he is certainly not the head of the Church. The Orthodox Churches recognize only one head, and that is Christ himself. An Ecumenical Patriarch may be a spokesman for Chalcedonian Orthodoxy (and sometimes, too, for the Oriental Churches), and he may even represent and symbolize Orthodoxy, but he cannot overrule his colleagues and he cannot speak on behalf of the Orthodox Churches without consulting them. The powers of a pope are quite different. Consider, for example, the question of contraception. The Orthodox view of the matter is something we shall discuss in Chapter Ten, but the official view of Roman Catholicism, as stated by Pope Paul VI in the papal encyclical *Humanae Vitae* in 1968 and confirmed by Pope John Paul II, is that artificial means of birth control are 'intrinsically evil' and forbidden to Roman Catholics. That most Roman Catholics simply ignore the encyclical is beside the point.

The principle had already been laid down by Pope Pius XI in 1930 in the encyclical *Casti Connubii*, but in the early 1960s a Pontifical Commission met five times to reconsider the question. At all the meetings, the majority view was that the old ban on artificial contraception should be lifted, and at the final session of the Commission, in answer to the question 'Is contraception intrinsically evil?', nine bishops voted No, three voted Yes, and three abstained. On the question as to whether contraception could be reconciled with the teaching and tradition of the Roman Catholic Church, nine bishops again voted Yes, five voted No, and one abstained. All the bishops then endorsed the majority report of the commission, *Responsible Parenthood*, which recommended to Pope Paul VI that the Church's teaching on the subject should be changed. It took two years for Paul VI to prepare his encyclical, but when it was published, on 25 July 1968, it simply over-ruled the majority report of the bishops and reiterated the prohibition of 1930: artificial contraception remained 'intrinsically evil' and wholly forbidden.

This could not happen in Orthodoxy. As we said above, the Orthodox Church is episcopal *and collegiate*—a bishop is a bishop is a bishop—and the Ecumenical Patriarch could no more over-rule the majority decision of his co-bishops than the chairman of a meeting could substitute his own personal views for the majority decision of his colleagues. In technical terms, the Ecumenical Patriarch has a primacy of *honour* with regard to his fellow bishops, but not a primacy of *jurisdiction*; and in the view of all the Orthodox Churches, the same is true of the pope. It is not, however, the view of the Church of Rome, and the question of the nature of Roman Primacy (which remains the chief obstacle to any real reconciliation between the Orthodox Churches and Roman Catholicism) is a matter which demands our attention.

The story begins at the end of the first century when Pope Clement I wrote a letter in the name of the Roman church to the church at Corinth, where a rancorous dispute had resulted in the deposition of certain presbyters. The point is not whether the letter was necessary or not (it was), but that the bishop of Rome—Clement—had no hesitation in intervening in the affairs of another diocese, telling them what to do, and expecting them to do it. Over the subsequent centuries the doctrine of the Roman Primacy was further elaborated by a number of popes, especially Damasus I (366–384), Innocent I (402–417), Leo I (440–461), and Gregory I (590–604), and by the Middle Ages, the bishops of Rome were wholly convinced that they were the pastors of *all* Christians, eastern and western, and that the see of Rome was not only first in honour among all the other patriarchates, but also first in authority. It is significant that when John the Faster, an austere and ascetic patriarch of Constantinople in the late sixth century, first used the title Ecumenical Patriarch, Gregory the Great refused to recognize it. It seemed to him that the patriarch of Constantinople was claiming some sort of universal jurisdiction, and this was wholly incompatible with the claims of the see of Rome. It is true, said Gregory, that the pope is no more than a Servant of the Servants of God (a title assumed by Gregory's successors), but Gregory himself was indefatigable in upholding the Roman Primacy, and, as pope, was wholly convinced that the Roman pontiff possessed unique authority throughout the entire Church.

Not one of the other patriarchates agreed with this, and although they were (on the whole) prepared to concede to Rome primacy of honour, they would not and could not concede primacy of jurisdiction. In other words, in a hypothetical board meeting of patriarchs, the patriarch of Rome—the pope—would naturally act as chair and spokesman, but each of the other patriarchs round the table would possess exactly the same juridical and legal authority. No one patriarch would be able to impose his will on the others. But the concept of Roman Primacy involves still more than this. According to Pope Leo I, who died in 461, when Christ transmitted to his apostles the authority to govern the Church, administer the sacraments, and preach the Gospel, he did not transmit this authority *directly* to the apostles. He transmitted it to the apostles *through Peter*, and Peter, according to tradition (and here we must ignore a number of major historical problems), was bishop of Rome. It follows from this that the successors of the apostles—the bishops of the Church—also receive their authority indirectly. It comes to them from Christ through the successors of Peter: through those, namely, who succeeded Peter as bishop of Rome—in other words, through the popes. This is emphatically not the view of Orthodoxy. Orthodoxy maintains that the authority to govern the Church was transmitted directly from Christ to his apostles, and equally directly from the apostles to the bishops of the Church.

Over the centuries, Leo's idea—it is referred to technically as the Leonine doctrine of the Roman Primacy—was further elaborated in the Roman Church, and the end result can be summarized by three statements: (i) decisions made by Roman Catholic bishops (even unanimous decisions) are authoritative only if they are approved by the pope; (ii) the pope may speak on behalf of his bishops without actually consulting them (their approval being tacitly assumed); and (iii) decisions of Ecumenical Councils are authoritative only if they, too, have been approved by the pope. No Orthodox patriarch possesses this power, and no Orthodox Church would agree with any one of the three statements.

It was the disputed matter of the Roman Primacy, and, as usual, ecclesiastical and secular politics, which really lay at the basis of the Great Schism of 1054, when strained relations between the Orthodox Church and the Roman Catholic Church reached breaking point. Relations had, in fact, been deteriorating for a very long time, and the root of the problem reaches back to the fourth century. By that time the Roman Empire had spread far and wide, but its very extent caused it to split apart under its own weight. If we draw a line through the Adriatic Sea between Italy and Greece and continue the line south, hitting the coast of North Africa about midway between modern Tripoli and Bengasi, most of the Roman world to the left of that line constituted the western half of the Empire, centred on Rome, with a Latin culture. Most of the Roman world to the right of that line constituted the eastern half of the Empire, centred on Constantinople, with a Greek culture. As the centuries progressed, the two halves became ever more isolated politically, culturally, and linguistically, and by the sixth century it was rare for a Greek to understand Latin or a Latin to understand Greek. The conversion of the Slavs, who spoke neither Greek nor Latin, merely made the problem worse.

Furthermore, over the centuries there had been a number of occasions when relations between the Ecumenical Patriarchate and the Papacy had been severely strained. There had been one schism in the fifth century (the Acacian Schism), another, more serious, in the ninth century (the Photian Schism), yet another in the tenth century (the affair of the Diptychs), and a number of other occasions of less dangerous tension.[2] Over the same centuries, the eastern and western Churches had naturally developed their own liturgies and ecclesiastical practices, and these sometimes differed radically. The eastern Churches worshipped God in their own languages; the western Church worshipped him in Latin. The eastern Churches held that the Holy Spirit proceeded from the Father alone; the western (for reasons we shall discuss in the next chapter) believed that the Holy Spirit proceeded from the Father and the Son. The east (except for the Armenians) used leavened bread in the Eucharist; the west used unleavened. In the east, married men could become priests; in the west they could not, though clerical concubinage—what we would now call common-law marriage—was rife. Priests in the east were bearded; priests in the west were clean shaven.

In the first half of the eleventh century the pope was Leo IX, a man of true personal humility, great reforming zeal, and an unshakeable belief in the absolute and universal primacy of Rome. The patriarch of Constantinople was Michael Cerularius (more accurately Keroularios), a politician *manqué*, and a man who was violently

---

2. See Bell, *Many Mansions*, 41–53.

anti-Latin. When Leo, as part of his policy of reform and centralization (and also for political reasons) demanded that Greek communities in southern Italy should follow western liturgical usage, symbolized by the use of unleavened bread in the Eucharist, Cerularius responded by demanding that the Latin Christians in Constantinople should follow Greek liturgical usage. When they refused, Michael closed their churches, and had one of his bishops write a ferocious letter to the pope condemning a number of western liturgical practices, of which the use of unleavened bread in the Eucharist was the most important. The pope then had his private secretary, Cardinal Humbert, write an equally ferocious rejoinder, which not only demanded that the eastern churches adopt the use of unleavened bread, but that they also accept the pope as pastor of *all* Christians, and acknowledge that Rome possessed not only primacy of honour, but also primacy of jurisdiction.

The results were predictable. Last-minute attempts at salvaging the situation came to nothing, and, on 16 July 1054, just before the afternoon liturgy, Cardinal Humbert entered the great church of the Holy Wisdom (Hagia Sophia) in Constantinople, strode up to the altar, and placed upon it a bull[3] excommunicating the patriarch of Constantinople and all who followed him. Just over a week later Michael replied with a similar bull which excommunicated the bishop of Rome and all who followed him. The Great Schism was complete.

That, at least, is the tradition, though it is not quite accurate. First of all, Leo had died before Cardinal Humbert delivered the excommunication in Leo's name, and, over the following years, the mutual excommunications of 1054 were quietly overlooked. Indeed, it is possible that the whole unfortunate affair might have been forgotten had it not been for the catastrophe of the Fourth Crusade (1202–1204). The Crusaders were on their way to Egypt when they were approached by the eastern emperor, who, having recently lost his throne, sought the help of the westerners to regain it. Regain it they did, but when it came time for payment, the emperor reneged on his agreement. The treasuries of Constantinople

---

3. Not an animal with horns, but a formal papal document sealed with the pope's seal (*bulla* in Latin).

were almost empty. So since they could not take their pay, the Crusaders took Constantinople instead, and on 6 April 1204 they stormed the city and captured it in less than a day. It was then given over to the soldiers, who indulged in a three-day orgy of rape, mutilation, torture, murder, arson, looting, pillage, and sacrilege. Whatever was valuable was stolen; whatever was holy was desecrated; whatever was neither valuable nor holy was, so far as possible, destroyed.

The east never forgave the west for this appalling event, and it took more than nine hundred years before the mutual excommunications were simultaneously lifted in 1965 by the Ecumenical Patriarch Athenagoras I and Pope Paul VI. Then, in May 2001, in a generous and courageous gesture, Pope John Paul II visited Athens, expressed his 'deep regret' for misdeeds committed by the Roman Catholic Church, and lamented the 'disastrous sack' of Constantinople. 'For the occasions past and present', he said 'when sons and daughters of the Catholic Church have sinned by action or omission against their Orthodox brothers and sisters, may the Lord grant us the forgiveness we beg of him.'[4] The pope's words were greeted with applause by Archbishop Christodoulos, the leader of the Greek Orthodox Church, and other Orthodox bishops, though there were protests from ultraconservative Orthodox, both priests and laity, for whom no apology from the west could ever heal the breach. What eventually will come of this gesture remains to be seen, for even after the apology it was still considered too risky for pope and archbishop to pray together. Some have seen it as the hopeful beginning of a long-awaited thaw in east-west relations, but we do not know, as yet, how things will develop under the present pope, Benedict XVI.

Earlier attempts at healing the breach had been made at the Council of Lyons in 1274 and the Council of Florence in 1438-1439, but the agreements they produced were of little worth. The so-called 'Union of Florence' which was, at heart, political (the Muslim Turks were almost at the walls of Constantinople, and the Greeks were looking for support from the Latin west) was formally repudi-

---

4. The essential parts of the pope's speech can be found in the *New York Times* for Saturday, May 5, 2001, and at a number of sites on the Internet.

ated in 1484, and from then to the twentieth century, the churches of the east and the churches of the west have gone their own separate ways. What happened in the twentieth century is something we shall consider in due course.

In this third chapter, then, we have seen how the Orthodox Church is episcopal and collegial, and how its understanding of collegiality differs from that of Roman Catholicism. But at the beginning of this chapter we also said that the Orthodox Church is conciliar *and spiritual*, and that is something we have not yet discussed. Nor have we yet answered the fundamental question as to whether the Orthodox Church is *a* Church at all? That is to say, is it one Church or many? And if it is not one Church, how can we ever speak of Orthodoxy as a whole and mean what we say? We need to pursue these questions in the next chapter, though it may seem, at first, that we have wandered off course. We shall begin, in fact, with a discussion of religious art, and those readers eager to find the answer to the questions we have just posed must follow the advice of Jesus of Nazareth, and possess their souls in patience.

4
HOLY ICONS AND HOLY SPIRIT

IN THE LAST TWO chapters we glanced at the first four Ecumenical Councils—Nicaea (325), Constantinople (381), Ephesus (431), and Chalcedon (451)—and saw how the majority of Orthodox Churches accept the decisions of all four. Theologically, Nicaea and Constantinople were concerned with the doctrine of the Trinity; Ephesus and Chalcedon with the doctrine of the Incarnation. Both doctrines are unique to the Christian tradition, and no two doctrines are more important. After Chalcedon, however, there were three other Ecumenical Councils and, once again, their decisions are regarded as authoritative by most, but not all, Orthodox Christians. The fifth and sixth councils need not much concern us; the seventh is a different matter.

The fifth and sixth councils were both held at Constantinople, one in 553 and the other in 680-681. Both were concerned with the Monophysite-Dyophysite schism, attempts to heal it, and the authority of the Council of Chalcedon. Their decisions are of great historical interest, but practically, nowadays, we can pass them by with no more than a glance. The Seventh Ecumenical Council, held in 787 at Nicaea (the same venue as the first council), dealt with an entirely different subject, and a subject as important to western Churches as to those in the east, namely, the question of religious art.

In Orthodox terms, we are talking here about icons, though a quick visit to any Catholic or Anglican bookstore (and a few Protestant ones as well) will reveal immediately how popular the eastern iconographic tradition has become in the west. Indeed, it is not only in western bookstores that we see the holy icons: in many non-Orthodox western churches they play an important liturgical role, and may often be seen on or near the altar. Just recently, while visiting the home of a young French Roman Catholic seminarian, I noticed that his own little oratory was decorated entirely with Orthodox icons.

The typical icon is painted on wood on a gold background and represents Christ, Mary, an angel or angels, one or more of the saints, or a biblical scene. The depictions follow traditional, formal patterns, and no icon-painter has anything like the freedom of expression enjoyed by other painters. In the case of the Virgin, for example, what we might call the 'genus' Mary is divided into a number of 'species', each of which is referred to by a technical term, usually in Greek. 'The All-Holy, Bringer of Victory' (*Panagia Nikopoia*), for example, depicts the Virgin seated on a throne holding the Christ child before her as if he were enthroned on her knees. In 'The God-bearer Showing the Way' (*Theotokos Hodegetria*), Mary usually supports Jesus on her left arm and points to him (as the Way to salvation) with her right hand. If the Christ child is shown embracing his mother or putting his arm around her neck, we have the tender *Theotokos Glycophilousa* or 'The Loving Godbearer'. And so on. Within these different species there are also sub-species, with variants of colour and posture. The Virgin's robe may sometimes be red or sometimes blue, and in some icons of the *Theotokos Hodegetria*, Jesus 'the Way' is not held in Mary's arm, but seated on her lap. But the formal pattern remains, and specialists in iconology (the study of icons) have little difficulty in classifying the traditional depictions. Older, rarer, or more venerable icons are sometimes protected by a metal cover on which is carved the form and clothing of the figure beneath, but which leave the face and hands visible. Icons, we might add, are all two-dimensional, and three-dimensional religious statuary, so common in the west, plays no role in the Orthodox east. We shall say more about icons in our next chapter: here we shall say something of their history.

Icons became popular and widespread in the east from about the fifth century, but there is no doubt that by the seventh century they were being abused. Saint Anastasius of Sinai, who died in about 700, complained that there were too many people who thought that they fulfilled all their obligations as Christians if they simply kissed all the icons in a church while ignoring the Divine Liturgy.[1] There was clearly a problem here, and something needed to be done. But in the course of the next century, a number of influences came together which, for a time, resulted in a wholesale ban on icons, and precipitated a long and violent controversy—the Iconoclastic Controversy—which, ultimately, would be settled only by an Ecumenical Council, the Seventh Ecumenical Council, held (as we have mentioned) at Nicaea in 787.

The Iconoclastic Controversy lasted for more than a century, from 726 to 843, but there is no need to trace the details of its history here. Suffice it to say that it began with an eighth-century emperor—Leo III the Isaurian—who saw icons as the chief obstacle to the conversion to Christianity of Jews and Muslims, neither of whom would countenance the representation of the human figure in religious art. Leo supported his case by quoting the second of the Ten Commandments: 'You shall not make for yourself an idol, whether in the form of anything that is in heaven above, or that is on the earth beneath, or that is in the water under the earth. You shall not bow down to them or worship them' (Ex 20:4-5). Nothing could be clearer to Leo. Orthodox Christians *were* bowing down to icons and worshipping them, and so were guilty of idolatry. And does not Saint Paul tell us to flee from idolatry (1 Cor 10:14)? And is not idolatry one of those works of the flesh which prevent entrance into the Kingdom of Heaven (Gal 5:19-20)? Certainly it is. Let us not, therefore, imperil our immortal souls by bowing down to wood and paint. Let us rather cleanse our churches from these objects of iniquity and do away with all idolatrous pictures.

There were, of course, a vast number of Orthodox Christians who did not agree with the emperor, and as time went on, the controversy became more theological, more political, and much more violent. The details can be read elsewhere.[2] But time and death played into the hands of the party which supported the use of icons, the anti-icon party (the Iconoclasts) gradually lost ground, and at the Second Council of Nicaea in 787 it was decided that

---

1. Anastasius of Sinai, *De sacra synaxi*.
2. Those interested will find a brief account in Bell, *Many Mansions*, 43–47, 267–282.

> the revered and holy icons, whether in paint, mosaic, or any other appropriate material, are to be displayed in God's holy churches, on sacred vessels and vestments, on walls and wooden panels, in houses and by the roadside: these are [icons] of our Lord, God, and Saviour Jesus Christ, of our immaculate Lady the holy God-bearer, of honoured angels, and of all holy and saintly people. For the more often we see them in pictorial representation, the more we are drawn to remember and desire their prototypes, and to accord to them due greeting and respectful veneration.[3]

In fact, this was not quite the end of the affair, for there was a resurgence of iconoclasm in 814 which lasted nearly another thirty years before the controversy was finally settled in 843. The final triumph of the icon-supporters was celebrated by a great feast on the first Sunday of Lent in that year, and ever since that time the Chalcedonian Churches have celebrated the 'Triumph of Orthodoxy' on that day.

One of the most important points to be made in the course of the long controversy was that 'worship' is not the same as 'veneration'. 'Worship' is something which can rightfully be offered only to God, and if we were to 'worship' an icon we would indeed be guilty of idolatry. But 'veneration' is different. When we venerate, say, the Mother of God, we revere her, we honour her, we exalt her, we admire her, we esteem her, and we see her as a model, an archetype, a pattern, a paradigm. The angels and saints are other such paradigms, but there is a world of difference between admiring and emulating the virtues of, say, Saint John of Damascus (who did much to bring about the downfall of the Iconoclasts) and worshipping the Trinitarian God. Given this important distinction, the prohibition of Exodus 20 becomes immaterial: we may bow down to an icon (for reasons which will become clear in a moment), but we certainly may not and do not worship it. The emperor Leo had the right text, but the wrong interpretation.

---

3. Translated from the Greek text in *Decrees of the Ecumenical Councils: Volume One, Nicaea I to Lateran V*, ed. Norman P. Tanner (London/Washington, 1990) 136.

Furthermore, when we venerate an icon, we are not venerating wood and paint. The essential principle was stated by Saint Basil the Great, bishop of Caesarea, as early as the fifth century: the honour or veneration we give to an image or icon passes on to the prototype (the exemplar or model) of the image or icon.[4] In other words, and in modern terms, an icon is like an interactive TV screen with a built-in phone line. On the one hand, whatever we do or say to the saints represented in the icons passes on to the saints themselves; on the other, it is through the medium of the icons that the saints are present to us. Orthodox churches, therefore, which are full of icons, are not just full of religious pictures. They are full of those beings represented in the icons, whether we are speaking of God, the Son of God, the Mother of God, the angels, or the saints. The 'communion of the saints', therefore, is not an abstract concept in Orthodoxy, but a living presence. A worshipper in an Orthodox church is partly on earth and partly in heaven, and he or she is never alone.

We should perhaps add here that the Seventh Ecumenical Council was concerned not only with icons, but also with relics, for relics and icons work in exactly the same way. Saints are present to us in their relics just as they are present to us in their icons, and the veneration of their relics is just the same as the veneration of their icons. There can be no doubt, of course, that many relics are not what they purport to be. In the east, the trade in relics never reached quite the same proportion as it did in the west, and the vast displays of relics which the western Reformers rightly ridiculed was not generally to be found in the Orthodox world. But the fact remains: we cannot be sure that a fragment of bone said to be from the right arm of one of the apostles is really from that apostle—all things considered, it probably is not—but if the believer truly believes it is, we can leave it to God to attend to the details. Grace is not dependent on osteal identity, and all religions sometimes require us to emulate the White Queen in *Alice Through the Looking-Glass*, and believe six impossible things before breakfast.[5]

4. Basil the Great, *De Spiritu sancto*, 18.45.
5. Lewis Carroll (Charles L. Dodgson), *Through the Looking-Glass and What Alice Found There* (first published 1872) Chapter V.

As far as Orthodoxy is concerned, the Seventh Ecumenical Council was the last Ecumenical Council. Most had been attended by representatives from the entire Christian world, east and west (though the western presence was usually minimal), and although the decisions of certain later councils were considered to be of major importance, no later council had the same authority. This is not the view of Roman Catholicism, which counts a further fourteen Ecumenical Councils, beginning in 869–70 (the Fourth Council of Constantinople) and ending (so far) with the Second Vatican Council held in 1962–65. Official delegates from the Orthodox Churches were indeed present at this last council, but only as observers, not as voting members. As a consequence, from an Orthodox point of view, the council cannot be considered truly ecumenical.

The Orthodox Church, therefore—or, more precisely, the Chalcedonian majority—is sometimes referred to as the 'Church of the Seven Councils', and it is in the teachings of these councils that Orthodoxy finds its unity. We said in Chapter Two that the Orthodox Churches are autocephalous or autonomous, and so they are. Each autocephalous Church is its own master, but they find their concord and coherence in the decisions of the Ecumenical Councils. The fundamental doctrines of Christianity (the Trinity and Incarnation, for example), the essential apostolic/episcopal structure of the Orthodox tradition, and many of its characteristic features and essential practices are to be found in conciliar decisions. Nowadays, even the Oriental Orthodox Churches accept most of these decisions, though they do not recognize the authority of all the councils. How is this possible? One way is by maintaining (justly) that ideas which appear in later Ecumenical Councils actually formed part of the earlier Tradition of the Church. In 1990, for example, in the Second Agreed Statement of the Joint Commission of the Theological Dialogue between the Orthodox Church and the Oriental Orthodox Churches, the members of the Commission stated that

> in relation to the teaching of the Seventh Ecumenical Council of the Orthodox Church, the Oriental Orthodox agree that the theology and practice of the veneration of icons taught by that Council are in basic agreement with

the teaching and practice of the Oriental Orthodox from ancient times, long before the convening of the Council, and that we have no disagreement in this regard.[6]

On the other hand, we will not find all Orthodox beliefs and practices set forth in the teachings of the seven Ecumenical Councils. We do not find any discussion of *in vitro* fertilization or contraceptive pills at Nicaea in 325, or any consideration of the morality of multi-national corporations at Ephesus in 431. How could we? Yet times change and we change with them, and from the beginning of the twentieth century onwards, times have been changing very rapidly indeed. But even in earlier centuries it was necessary to keep up to date, and although Orthodoxy recognizes a maximum of only seven Ecumenical Councils, a number of other councils have played a decisive role in the life of the Church. Two councils held in Constantinople in the fourteenth century and two other councils in the seventeenth century—the Synod of Jassy in 1642 and the Synod of Jerusalem in 1672—were particularly important. There are also a number of official documents promulgated at various times to deal with specific problems, but most of these are now only of historical interest.[7] Councils, however, are rare, especially councils involving more than one of the Orthodox Churches. Apart from other problems, they are a nightmare to organize and expensive to arrange. The Orthodox Church, therefore, like most of the other Churches, finds that it cannot really keep up with the speed of changing events, and we will look in vain for any conciliar pronouncement on (for example) the 'morning after pill' (i.e., Emergency Contraceptive Pills or ECPs), the morality of national lotteries, or cloning.

This is where Roman Catholicism has an advantage. Its centralized authority, and the principles inherent in what we have called 'primacy of jurisdiction', mean that much faster responses are possible. When it comes to making a decision, the pope is not obliged to call a council, nor is he obliged to consult his bishops, but may

---

6. Section 8 of the document which can be found on the Internet at http://www.uk-christian.net/boc/2church.htm.
7. See Ware, *The Orthodox Church*, 202-3, and the relevant entries in *The Blackwell Dictionary of Eastern Christianity*.

issue papal statements or give papal approval to other statements as and when needed with the tacit approval of the 'post-apostolic college'. A number of such statements have appeared in recent years, though not all have been well received.

For the Orthodox Churches, consultation, if not a council, remains essential, and it is the firm belief of Orthodoxy that this is how the Holy Spirit guides the Church. 'We are following', said the bishops at the Second Council of Nicaea in 787,

> the God-spoken teaching of our holy Fathers and the tradition of the universal Church, for we recognize that this [tradition] is from the Holy Spirit who dwells within her.[8]

Nothing is more important. On the other hand, the Holy Spirit does not restrict itself to Ecumenical Councils. *All* councils, it is hoped, are guided and inspired by the Holy Spirit—every council invokes the Holy Spirit at the beginning of its deliberations—and, since the Spirit is fully God and fully divine, it follows that the Church is guided by God himself. It is this fervent belief in a 'God-spoken teaching' that lay at the root of the long and bitter controversy between east and west over the *filioque*. What was this controversy, and why is it important?

To understand the problem we have to go back to the Council of Chalcedon in 451. At that council, the bishops declared (among other things) that they accepted as one of the fundamental statements of the faith what is commonly (but inaccurately) called the 'Nicene-Constantinopolitan Creed.' Sometimes, and even less accurately, it is just called the 'Nicene Creed'. It is the most widely used of all Christian creeds and will be familiar to many readers of this book. Here is a literal translation:

> We believe in one God, Father, almighty, maker of heaven and earth, and of all things visible and invisible;
> And in one Lord Jesus Christ, the only-begotten Son of God, begotten from the Father before all ages, light from light, true God from true God, begotten not made, con-

---

8. Translated from the Greek text in *Decrees of the Ecumenical Councils*, 135.

substantial with the Father, through whom all things came into being; who, for us humans and for our salvation, came down from heaven and became incarnate from the Holy Spirit and Mary the Virgin and became human, and was crucified for us under Pontius Pilate, and suffered and was buried, and rose on the third day according to the Scriptures, and ascended into heaven, and sits on the right hand of the Father; and he will come again with glory to judge the living and the dead, of whose kingdom there will be no end;

And in the Holy Spirit, the lord and life-giver, *who proceeds from the Father*, who with Father and Son is together worshipped and together glorified, who spoke through the prophets; [and] in one holy, universal, and apostolic Church.

We confess one baptism for the remission of sins; we look forward to a resurrection of the dead and the life of the world to come. Amen.[9]

According to tradition, this Creed was first formulated at the Council of Nicaea in 325, and then expanded at the Council of Constantinople in 381, but the tradition is not quite correct. In all probability, the Creed started off as a baptismal creed of the Jerusalem Church; it was then elaborated at the 381 council (that much is probably correct); and was then given canonical approval at Chalcedon in 451. But whatever its origin, the Creed stated unequivocally that the Holy Spirit proceeded from the Father alone—the passage is italicized above—and not from the Father and the Son. The additional word *filioque*—'and the Son' in English—was added to a Latin version of the Creed for the first time in 589 at the Third Council of Toledo in Spain. At that time, many Spanish Christians were Arian subordinationists (a heretical viewpoint we discussed in Chapter Two) and the additional word was intended to imply that the Son was in no way inferior to the Father, but equal to him in every respect. The addition then slowly spread through the rest of western Europe, and reached Rome in the eleventh century.

9. Translated from the Greek text in *The Oecumenical Documents of the Faith*, 64.

The eastern Churches objected to the *filioque* on two grounds, one legal, the other theological. The legal objection was simple: what had been approved by an Ecumenical Council could be changed only by another Ecumenical Council, and this had not been the case. The Third Council of Toledo was certainly not ecumenical, and neither the fifth, sixth, or seventh Ecumenical Councils had approved the change. The theological reasons, stemming primarily from the ideas of Augustine of Hippo (354-430), were much more complex, but—unfortunately—were solidly rooted in misunderstanding.

As far as the Orthodox Churches were concerned, the idea that the Holy Spirit came into being from the Father and the Son (the doctrine known technically as 'Double Procession') was incorrect for two main reasons. The first was that Double Procession implied that there were two First Principles—two Fathers, to put it crudely—who jointly brought the Holy Spirit into being. This idea was wholly unacceptable. For eastern theologians, there could be but one 'Fount of Divinity' in the Godhead, and that was the Father. The Father eternally and from eternity brings forth the Son, and, through the Son, eternally and from eternity brings forth the Holy Spirit. But the Son is the Son, not the Father, and to posit two Fathers was unbiblical, unchristian, and unorthodox.

The second reason why the east rejected the doctrine was that it seemed to imply that the Holy Spirit occupied a lower place in the Trinity than the two Persons who engendered it. The Trinity, in fact, looked rather like an old-fashioned English pawn-broker's sign with the two golden balls at the top representing Father and Son, and the golden ball below them representing the Holy Spirit. In other words, the *filioque* not only implied that there were two 'Fathers', but it also implied that the Holy Spirit was an inferior and subordinate member of the Trinity, and, by definition, not fully God. And if the Holy Spirit was not fully God (as we pointed out in Chapter Two), the Church had been guided not by God (in the Person of the Holy Spirit), but by some thing or some being less than God. The Church, in other words, was not really holy, but only sort-of-holy, and the teaching of the fathers of the Church was not really 'God-spoken', but 'slightly-less-than-God-spoken'.

Now let us state from the start that in their interpretation of Double Procession the Orthodox Churches were mistaken. It was never the intention of the west to imply two 'Founts of Divinity', nor to imply any inferiority among the Persons of the Trinity. Far from it. The idea that the Church was guided by God, 100% God, was every bit as important for the west as for the east. Indeed, even Cyril of Alexandria, whom we met in Chapter Two, had used, more than once, the phrase 'and the Son' as well as 'through the Son' when speaking of the procession of the Holy Spirit. But at the time the controversy arose, relations between west and east were severely strained, and (as we saw in Chapter Three) the situation just got worse as time went on. It will not come as a surprise, therefore, to find Michael Cerularius (whom we met in the last chapter) fiercely attacking the Roman Church in 1054 not only for its use of unleavened bread in the Eucharist, but also for insisting on the heretical and illegal use of *filioque* in the Creed. But by that time, the word had become no more than a political slogan, and few on either side understood the theological misunderstandings (and also subtle theological differences) which had engendered it.[10]

Nowadays, both east and west are aware that, from 381 (the date of the Second Ecumenical Council), there never really was any dispute on the divinity of the Holy Spirit. The west never intended an inferior Third Person of the Trinity (quite the contrary, in fact), and the east erred in its interpretation of Augustine. *Legally*, however, Orthodoxy still has a case, and it is interesting to note that in certain churches of the Anglican communion, which look to the early councils for their essential doctrines, one can sometimes hear the Creed recited without the additional 'and the Son'. It is even more interesting to note that when Pope John Paul II quoted the Creed at the beginning of his encyclical *Dominus Iesus*, issued on 6 August 2000, he quoted it *without* the *filioque*. But for Roman Catholics in general, the additional words have become part of the Tradition of the Church, and, as we shall see in due course, for both Roman Catholics and Orthodox, the concept of 'Tradition' can be both a blessing and a curse.

The recognition of the full divinity of the Holy Spirit, therefore, is essential both to Orthodoxy and to any other Christian Church, and it enables us to answer the questions we posed at the end of

10. The details may be read in Bell, *Many Mansions*, 193–207.

the last chapter. What do we mean when we say that the Orthodox Church is conciliar and spiritual? And, given the self-governing nature of its component parts, can we really speak of the Orthodox Church as *a* Church at all? The answers now are clear.

Orthodoxy is indeed one Church, just as the individual members of a board may be referred to as 'the Board', despite their differing opinions. And when we say that the Orthodox Church is conciliar and spiritual, we are not saying two things, but one. It is a Church guided (one trusts) by the Holy Spirit, who is fully God, and the Holy Spirit guides the Church most effectively by means of councils, or, at least, consultation. And even if the guidance of the Holy Spirit is not always evident, or if—which is more often the case—human beings misjudge, mishear, or misrepresent the Holy Spirit's counsel, the collegial process is probably a safer way of arriving at reasonable decisions than any other. We might say that, in general, conciliar decisions are best looked at as sign-posts pointing in approximately the right direction. The design and lettering of the various sign-posts must inevitably reflect their date and provenance, and some sign-posts are more accurate than others. A few may be pointing in quite the wrong direction, and, in the course of time, will need to be corrected. But, in general, it is better to have approximate sign-posts than no sign-posts at all, and wandering lost in a mapless waste is unquestionably perilous, both from a practical and a theological point of view.

As we have seen, many of these conciliar decisions are of fundamental importance. The early councils were right to condemn a subordinationist view of the Trinity; they were right to condemn doctrines which suggested that Christ was no more than an inspired man; and they were right to give their whole-hearted approval to icons, and to the use of icons as representations of the faith and as aids to faith. Icons, in fact, are much more than mere pictures. In themselves they enshrine some of the most important teachings of the Orthodox Tradition, and, in the next chapter, we need to look at icons and their meaning in a little more detail.

5
MORE ABOUT ICONS

LET US FIRST SUMMARIZE what we said in the previous chapter. We saw there that icons are two-dimensional representations of Christ, Mary, angels, saints, or biblical scenes. The depictions follow traditional, formal patterns, some of which we will look at in more detail here. By the fifth century icons were wide-spread and popular, but by the seventh century they were certainly being abused. From aids to faith they had become the faith itself—a sort of iconolatry—and we saw how Saint Anastasius of Sinai berated churchgoers for thinking that if they merely kissed the icons they were assured of salvation. Saint Anastasius died in about 700, and twenty-six years later the Iconoclastic Controversy erupted. This long, violent, and bitter dispute lasted almost a hundred and twenty years, and over this period countless icons were destroyed. Not many early icons now survive, but a number dating from the sixth to the ninth centuries are to be found in the Monastery of Saint Catherine at the foot of Mount Sinai.

We also saw that Orthodox do not worship icons. They venerate them, which is an entirely different matter. Furthermore, this veneration is not, in fact, directed to the wood and paint of the icon, but to what or whom is behind it. Veneration passes through the icon to its prototype, but the process is not one-way. Icons are windows looking out on heaven, and, like windows in general, they permit those inside to see out and those outside to see in. An icon is not only our contact-point with the saints, it is the saints contact-point with us. Thus, a church full of icons of saints and angels is a church full of saints and angels.

It follows from this that icons can be powerful objects. They are channels for celestial forces, and wonder-working icons are not uncommon, especially in the Russian tradition. Ivan the Terrible regarded them as 'machines generating spiritual power',[1] and they played just as important a role in his military expeditions as other, more material, weapons. This is not to say that we should emulate Ivan the Terrible; it *is* to say that icons are not merely holy pictures, though that aspect is not unimportant.

At the time of the Iconoclastic Controversy, icons played a major role in instruction. In a society in which literacy was limited and books enormously expensive (and there is little point in being able to read if one cannot afford a book), the facts of the faith were painted on the walls of the churches. If you come across pagans who are interested in knowing something of the Christian faith, said the pro-icon party, all you need do is take them into a church and show them the icons. *There* is the faith, from icons of Old Testament prophets, to an icon of the Mother of God, to an icon of the Nativity, to an icon of the Crucifixion, to an icon of Christ triumphant over death, to an icon of Pentecost, to icons of the saints and ascetics who followed in the footsteps of the apostles. Nowadays, of course, the situation is different. Most of us can read. But the fact remains that pictures can have infinitely more impact than a page of print, and although discursive meditation based on icons is not a standard part of the Orthodox tradition, there is no reason why it should not be. That is a matter we shall discuss in Chapter Eleven.

Icons are also theological statements. This is especially true of icons of Christ, but it is also true of other icons as well, particularly those depicting the Mother of God. One of the arguments of the anti-icon party was that since you cannot paint a picture of 'divinity', any representation of Christ can only be a representation of Christ in his humanity; and to represent Christ as no more than a human being, however saintly, is to deny the truth of the Incarnation. Christ was not, emphatically not, a mere man, and any portrait of Christ as a mere man is, by definition, heretical.

To this argument the pro-icon party had a simple rejoinder. It is perfectly true that you cannot paint a picture of 'divinity', but the whole point of the Incarnation was that in Jesus the Son of

---

1. Robert Payne and Nikita Romanoff, *Ivan the Terrible* (New York, 1975) 128.

Mary, God became human. The important word here is *became*. God did not merely appear to be human. He did not just seem to be human. He *was* human. When God became a man, divinity was united with humanity in an unconfused union. Divinity remained divinity, humanity remained humanity, but although the two were distinct, they were not separate. It's much like the soul and body: soul is soul and body is body, both are quite distinct. But if we separate them, we end up with a carcase, and carcases are of little use. We don't even eat them. Anybody in first-century Galilee who saw Jesus of Nazareth saw God incarnate: divinity and humanity. And if God could be manifest in the flesh, he can also be manifest in wood and paint.

We have to remember here that 'in the flesh' is a misleading term. The human body of Jesus of Nazareth was not just flesh. It was flesh, muscle, sinew, blood, bone, teeth, fingernails, entrails, digested food and drink, skin, and hair; and bones (to take but one example) are both inorganic and organic. They consist of calcium phosphate, calcium carbonate, gelatin, collagen, and a number of other things. But calcium carbonate is no more than chalk, and if Christ could be manifest as chalk, why not as paint?

Furthermore, the very fact that God became embodied (not just enfleshed) in Christ means that he sanctified bodily materials by that very act. It's like putting a spoonful of salt in a fresh-water lake: the lake is no longer fresh water. The saltiness may be too dilute for us to taste, but the fact remains that the chemical constitution of the lake has changed in kind, changed in state, not just in degree. Similarly, when God became incarnate, material stuff underwent a spiritual change of state. By becoming truly human, bones and all, Christ planted within the organic and inorganic material of the created universe the seed of his Spirit. The Word-made-matter deified matter, and matter was transformed. What does this mean? It means that the entire universe now has within it the potential to be redeemed and glorified. Redemption, therefore, is not confined to human beings: it involves dogs, seals, wasps, cats, trees, stones, water, and anything else you care to name. It follows, then, that our human business in this world is not just our own salvation, but the salvation of the planet. As we have said, you cannot be Orthodox without being an ecologist—a fact made eminently clear in many of the letters and pronouncements of the Ecumenical Patriarch, Bartholomew I.

An icon, therefore, is infinitely more than a simple devotional picture. It is a sort of incarnation in its own right. Perhaps a better term might be 'inwoodation' or 'impaintation'. But Christ is *there*, that's the point, just as his Spirit is in everything around us. The Gospel of Thomas is quite correct: 'Split some wood: I am there; lift a stone, and you will find me there.'[2]

The most common icon of Christ depicts Christ as the *Pantocrator* (or *Pantokrator*, with the accent on the third syllable), and a nineteenth-century Greek example appears as Illustration One. Pantocrator means 'All-Sovereign' or 'Ruler of All', and the term is applied to Christ in Revelation 1:8 where it is usually translated as 'the Almighty'. The icon itself depicts Christ as the severe judge. He is heavily bearded, his hair is parted in the middle and drawn back to the nape of his neck, his gaze is stern, his eyes piercing. This is not gentle Jesus, meek and mild. This is the Alpha and Omega of the Book of Revelation, 'He who is and who was and who is to come, the All-Sovereign' (Rev 1:8). In his left hand he carries a closed book (in some variants, the book is open, not always at the same verse), and his right hand is raised in a curious gesture of blessing. The upright and curved fingers actually form the Greek letters IC and XC (C and X are the Greek capital forms of s and CH): IC is I<OĒSU>S and XC is CH<RISTO>S, i.e. Jesus Christ. The same abbreviations appear to the left and right at the top of the icon. Around his head is a halo with a cross, and written in the cross, in Greek, is '<H>O ŌN', 'He who is'. This is important. It is the name which God revealed to Moses on Mount Horeb (Ex 3:14), and it is also one of the titles of Christ in Revelation 1:8. In other words, 'He who is' not only substantially identifies Father and Son, it also refutes the ideas of certain heretics (the second-century teacher Marcion is the best known) who maintained that the God of the Old Testament was not the God of the New.[3]

---

2. Gospel of Thomas, saying/*logion* 77. There are a number of editions and translations.

3. See Bell, *Cloud of Witnesses*, Chapter Seven.

Not all icons of Christ as the Pantocrator are quite as stern as this. Many Russian and Slav portrayals depict a less severe judge, and in Crete, where icon painting was deeply influenced by western, especially Venetian, art, we also tend to find less austere depictions. But if we want a really gentle Jesus, we need to go back to the Saviour's infancy and see him in the arms of his mother.

The Orthodox Church—all Orthodox Churches—have a deep devotion to the Mother of God. She is generally referred to as the *Theotokos* or 'God-bearer', a title we have already discussed and which goes back to the third century. It was given canonical approval at the Council of Ephesus—the Third Ecumenical Council—in 431, but since the Apostolic Catholic Assyrian Church of the East does not recognize this council, neither does it use this title. It still, however, maintains a deep veneration for its subject.

But for all the other Orthodox Churches, Mary is indeed the God-bearer, and whereas the saints merit veneration—*douleia* in Greek—the Mother of God deserves 'more than veneration', or *hyperdouleia*. After all, it was she who bore the Saviour of the World, and not only was she found worthy to do so, she could also have refused. Indeed, given the mores of first-century Jewish society, it would have been easier for her to refuse. It is no simple task for a pregnant woman to persuade people that she is a virgin, and even less simple to persuade the man to whom she's engaged. But Mary's answer—'be it done with me according to your word' (Lk 1:38)—is regarded as a perfect example of what, in Orthodoxy (and modern business), is referred to as synergy, our free human cooperation with the will of God. We shall say more about synergy in Chapter Seven.

In Orthodox (and Roman Catholic) belief, not only did Mary conceive as a virgin, she also retained her virginity through the birth of her Son. She is therefore called 'ever-virgin'—*aeiparthenos* in Greek—a title which goes back to at least the fourth century, when it was used by Athanasius the Great (d. 373).

But let us be controversial here, even heretical. For many contemporary Christians, the doctrine poses problems, and it may be that the problems are unnecessary. Speaking theologically, it really does not make any difference to the salvation of the world whether or not Mary retained her virginity at the birth of her son. Medieval analogies, such as a sunbeam shining through a pane of glass without breaking it, are unpersuasive to our modern mentality, and there are further difficulties with the mention in the Gospels of Jesus's brothers and sisters. He had at least four brothers—James, Joses/Joseph, Jude/Judas, and Simon—and at least two sisters (the word appears in the plural) who are not named.[4]

The standard Orthodox and Roman Catholic explanations are that these brothers and sisters are either Joseph's children by a previous marriage (which is why Joseph often appears in religious art as being much older than Mary), or that they are cousins or adopted siblings. This may or may not be true. On the other hand, there are many modern men and women who see virginity as a state of heart and mind, not necessarily a physical condition. There are, therefore, many believing Christians who see Mary as ever-virgin to God, whether or not she retained her physical virginity through the birth of Jesus, and whether or not she had other babies as well. Every week, in the Orthodox Liturgy of Saint John Chrysostom, we hear that Mary gave birth to God the Word 'without defilement' (*adiaphthorōs* in Greek), but there is more than one way of understanding that.

Indeed, there were a few second/third-century theologians—not many—who refused to accept the doctrine of Mary's perpetual virginity on the grounds that it cast doubt on the true humanity of Christ. Real human babies are not born without certain inevitable physical consequences, and to suggest that this was not the case with Mary might imply that Jesus was not a real human baby with real human flesh. Such a view, in fact, was widespread among Gnostic groups who maintained that Jesus only *appeared* to be human (the technical term for this idea is docetism, a word which derives from a Greek word meaning 'appearance'), and the Christian Church rightly condemned it. If Jesus was only an apparition or appearance, then his death on Calvary was only an appearance; and if his death on Calvary was only an appearance, so, too, is our redemption. If Jesus was not truly human, we are still in our sins. But although there is solid logic behind these objections to the doctrine of Mary's perpetual virginity, the Church decided in its favour. In the decrees promulgated by the Fifth Ecumenical Council, held at

---

4. Early Christian tradition was happy to fill the gap by calling them Mary and Salome.

Constantinople in 553, Mary is several times referred to as 'ever virgin'. How was it possible? Both the Orthodox and Roman Catholic Churches offer the same answer: it was a miracle, and that is all that need be said. But although miracles unquestionably occur (far more often than we realize), those who have difficulty accepting this one need not, I think, be too deeply troubled. That, however, is no more than a personal opinion, and is not the traditional teaching of the Orthodox Church.

It is also true that Orthodoxy has sometimes tended to elevate Mary to too high a degree. In the fourteenth century, Theophanes, archbishop of Nicaea (d. 1381), took things much too far, and ended up by referring to Mary as God, Lord, and King of Kings. He even called her the spouse of God the Father, and, in his view, if she was not actually a fourth member of the Trinity, she was certainly intimately associated with the three divine Persons.[5] This, as we have said, is indeed going too far, but it is a useful warning to us that when we venerate, or 'more-than-venerate', the virgin, we do not venerate Mary as Mary, but Mary as the God-bearer, the *Theotokos*. The title in no way implies semi-divinity on the part of the Mother of God. It implies the complete humanity of her son.

In the Roman Catholic west, Mary is also believed to have been conceived without original sin. The doctrine of the Immaculate Conception, proclaimed as an article of faith for all Roman Catholics by Pope Pius IX in 1854, states that God, by a unique grace and privilege, preserved Mary from all stain of original sin from the first moment of her conception. Orthodoxy does not generally accept this idea, though some Orthodox theologians have done so in the past. Not too surprisingly, Theophanes of Nicaea was one of them. Even in the west there were many who opposed it—not least Saint Bernard of Clairvaux and Saint Thomas Aquinas—and their view of the matter was that Mary was conceived, like everybody else, *with* original sin, but that she was cleansed of it by a special act of God's grace sometime between her conception and her birth.[6] They believed, in other words, in a doctrine of an immaculate *birth*,

---

5. See Bell, *Many Mansions*, 250–251.

6. There were also those who maintained that Mary was cleansed from original sin at the moment of the Annunciation.

but not of an immaculate *conception*. But for all that, it is now an article of faith for Roman Catholicism, though Orthodoxy has never made any definitive pronouncement on the question. Most Orthodox, as we have said, do not accept the doctrine and find it unnecessary, but if some prefer to do so, that is entirely up to them.

On the matter of Mary's bodily assumption into heaven the matter is quite different. Apocryphal texts claiming that after her death Mary was assumed into heaven soul and body first appeared in the fourth century, and in the east the Feast of the Dormition (the 'Falling Asleep') of the Virgin—the eastern equivalent of the western Feast of the Assumption—has been celebrated since the year 600. The details of exactly how the Virgin ascended to heaven differ from text to text (in the Coptic version, Jesus takes his mother's body to heaven in a fiery chariot), but neither east nor west had any doubt that that was what had happened. In the west, the doctrine was proclaimed as an article of faith for Roman Catholics by Pope Pius XII in 1950.

But, once again, let us be un-Orthodox and heretical. Not only is the doctrine based on apocryphal texts of very doubtful authority, it also reflects an earlier and simpler age. It was not, of course, without precedent. The Old Testament maintains that both Elijah and Enoch went bodily to heaven, and the doctrine of the resurrection of the body (which we will discuss in Chapter Seven) means that what happened to Elijah, Enoch, and Mary is what, eventually, will happen to us all. But not everyone nowadays is happy with the idea of a physical bodily resurrection, and the stories of Elijah, Enoch, and Mary reflect a more corporeal view of Paradise than many modern Christians are willing to accept.

There are those, therefore, who prefer to regard the doctrine of the bodily assumption of the Virgin as a symbol or allegory. They are in no doubt that the Mother of God is in Paradise, but they have serious doubts as to whether she is there in her physical body. For such as these, the doctrine is true, but allegorically true, not literally true, and, as an allegory, it may be interpreted in a number of ways. It may be seen, for example, as reinforcing the idea that there is nothing inherently evil about human bodies, and that in the Incarnation (as we saw above) Christ sanctified matter and rendered it worthy of deification. Indeed, the doctrine of the corporeal assumption may be seen as an admirable allegory of the possibility of human deification, for where one human being can go, others may go also. And there are other such interpretations. This is not, of course, Orthodox teaching. The Orthodox tradition, once again, is that when we speak of the bodily assumption of the Virgin, that is what we mean. But if one finds oneself honestly unable to accept such a physical view of heaven and the afterlife, it need not drive one either from the Orthodox or the Roman Catholic Church, though in such matters of conscience, discussion with a wise priest or bishop can often be profitable.

The icon illustrated in Illustration Two represents Mary as 'the God-bearer Showing the Way' (*Theotokos Hodegetria*). We introduced the title in the last chapter. According to tradition, this type of icon was first painted by Saint Luke, and it is certainly the most influential of all so-called 'Madonna types' in iconography. We see the Virgin robed in black and very dark blue (the colours symbolize her humility), supporting the Christ-child on her left arm. On her robe (*maphorion* is the technical term) there are three stars, one above her brow and one on each shoulder (the one on the left is hidden behind her Son). These symbolize the miracle of her threefold virginity, before, during, and after the birth of Jesus. Jesus himself wears orange-red robes (symbolizing his kingly status) and holds a rolled-up scroll in his left hand. This is the scroll of the new dispensation, but it is as yet unrolled since the boy has not yet begun his ministry. With his right hand, he gives a blessing. At the very top of the icon we see the letters M<Ē>TĒR TH<E>OU, or 'Mother of God'. Just to the left of the Virgin's halo is her title as she appears in this icon, Ē HODEGETRIA, 'She Who Shows the Way'. And Christ's name, I<ĒSOU>S CH<RISTO>S, appears to the right of his halo which, just as in the icon of Christ *Pantocrator*, contains the words <H>O ŌN, 'He who is'. This, as we have seen, is one of the names of God in the book of Exodus, and one of the titles of Christ in the book of Revelation. The *Theotokos*, therefore, points to the Being who is, at one and the same time, her truly human baby son, born in time, and the infinite and eternal Lord of the Universe.

While the God-bearer is worthy of 'more than veneration', the saints are worthy of veneration. Icons, as we have said, are windows onto another world, and a communion of icons is a communion of the saints themselves. As we said in the previous chapter, a solitary worshipper in an Orthodox church is far from being alone. There is no formal list of saints in Orthodoxy, and who is or is not a saint varies from Church to Church. Some—such as the evangelists and certain other 'universal' saints—are common to all; others are particular to a particular Orthodox Church or even to a particular locality. Some saints are easy to understand and appreciate; some are difficult; some were decidedly peculiar, not to say unpleasant, in their habits. Just as in Roman Catholicism, a number of saints are commemorated each day, some well known, some obscure. Sometimes a particular saint may have more than one feast-day: one to commemorate his or her death, one to commemorate the discovery or translation of the relics, one to commemorate the canonization, and so on. We shall shortly see an example in Saint Nicholas of Myra. But in all cases they are there to help us, and their icons may be regarded as our cyberlink with them.

We need not, of course, believe all that we are told of the saints. In many cases, their stories are, for the most part, the stuff of legend, and (from a scholarly point of view) we are justified in entertaining the gravest doubts about the factual nature of stories for which they are famed. We may doubt, for example, whether Saint Nicholas ever pieced together the pickled boys whom we shall meet in a moment, or whether Saint Mary of Egypt really was buried by a monk called Zosimus with the help of a passing lion, or whether Saint Margaret (Marina in the East) of Antioch really was swallowed by a dragon which later burst asunder, or whether Saint Pachomius really did cross the Nile on the back of a helpful crocodile. Such tales are no more than fairy-tales, but, like many fairy-tales, they may teach us things we need to know in a way to which we can easily relate. If, for example, the legend of Mary of Egypt—a harlot turned hermit—convinces us of the efficacy of repentance, all well and good; and if the story of Saint Nicholas's gift of gold to three young women who desperately needed it shows what generosity can do, then let us seek to emulate that generosity. Such stories as these (and there are hundreds of them in the pages of *The Golden Legend*) may not be literally true, but they may certainly be allegorically true, and they may well illustrate, in an unforgettable way, the heroic virtue for which the saint is venerated. We need not be disturbed, therefore, to find that saints did not do all that they are said to have done, and if we sincerely ask for their assistance, we may safely leave it to God to attend to the details.

Illustration Three is a reproduction of a late nineteenth-century Russian icon depicting Saint Nicholas, bishop of Myra in Lycia, which is now Muğla in the south-western corner of Turkey. He is one of the most popular saints in both east and west—in the course of time he would be transformed into Santa Claus—but, as we hinted above, what we know of him is almost entirely legendary. He is said to have been imprisoned during the Great Persecution (303–312) of the emperor Diocletian (which is possible), and, according to tradition, he was one of the bishops present at the Council of Nicaea in 325 (which is almost certainly not the case).

His legend, however, contains a number of charming stories, some of which are very well known, and some of which we mentioned above. On one occasion, he secretly gave three bags of gold to three young women for their marriage dowries to save them from being sold into prostitution. On another occasion, when a murderous butcher had killed three little boys and pickled them in his brine-tub (cheap and handy meat for his customers in a time of famine), Nicholas raised them back to life. Forth they came, Timothy, Mark, and John, whole and entire, praising God. And on yet other occasions, he saved from execution three men who had been unjustly condemned to death, and three sailors who were near to drowning off the coast of Turkey. He is therefore claimed as the patron of unmarried girls, children, and sailors—and also, less obviously, of merchants, apothecaries, and pawnbrokers. He is also the patron of Russia.

Since he was patron of children, it became the custom in the Low Countries to give gifts to children on Nicholas's feast-day, 6 December, and when Dutch-speaking immigrants from these areas came seeking a new life in the United States, they brought with them their 'Sante Klaas'—Saint Nicholas—and Sante Klaas, with one or two Nordic additions, became the Santa Claus of today.

After the rise of Islam, Myra and its shrine were captured by the Muslims, and in 1087 the relics of Nicholas were translated to the seaport city of Bari in southern Italy. There a new basilica was built to house them (it is still there, the Romanesque Basilica of San Nicola), and Pope Urban II himself was present at the consecration of the crypt in 1089. Nicholas, therefore, is also commemorated on 9 May, the traditional date of the translation of his relics from Myra to Bari.

The figure depicted in this icon has little in common with Santa Claus. He is far more stern and much more imposing, and his name appears in Cyrillic script to the left and right of his halo: SVYATI NI/ KOLAI CHUDOTVORETS (this last word is much abbreviated), or 'Saint Nicholas the Wonderworker'. This is his invariable title in the Orthodox Church. His high domed forehead symbolizes his intelligence and, above all, his intuition, and he wears the vestments of an Orthodox bishop. His right hand is raised in episcopal blessing, and in his left hand he holds a copy of the New Testament open at the Old Slavonic translation of Luke 6:17. This begins 'At that time, Jesus stood on a level place . . .', and leads into the Lucan version of the Beatitudes. It is the Gospel read on Nicholas's feast-day.

To the left and right of the saint are two small figures, but they are less small when you see that what they are standing on is, in fact, the world. On the left is Jesus, and on the right his Mother. According to the legend, when Nicholas was elected bishop of Myra, Christ brought to him the Gospel Book, and the Mother of God presented him with the bishop's stole. Both can clearly be seen in the icon. In the Orthodox Church, this stole is known as the *omophorion*, and corresponds to the pallium of the western Latin Church. Nowadays, it is usually made of embroidered white silk, but the omophorion worn by Nicholas in the icon is turquoise, with two brownish-red crosses.

Icons of Christ, Mary, and the saints comprise the majority of Orthodox icons, but there are also icons of the Holy Trinity, icons of angels, and scenic icons depicting characters and events from the Old and New Testaments. Of the icons of the Trinity, by far the most famous is that painted by Andrei Rublev (*c*.1370-1430) in which the Trinity is represented by the three angels who visited Abraham at Mamre.[7] It is now in the Tretyakov Gallery in Moscow, and is one of the best-known icons anywhere. A modern copy of it by the

---

7. The story appears in Genesis 18:1-15.

iconographer Eileen McGuckin appears as Illustration Four. Of the angelic icons, those depicting Michael and/or Gabriel are the most common: sometimes the two archangels appear individually; sometimes they are portrayed together. An icon of Michael, again painted by Eileen McGuckin, is reproduced as Illustration Five.

Of scenic icons, the most common depict events in the life of Christ or his Mother: primarily the Nativity of Mary, the Annunciation, the Nativity of Christ, the Purification (called in the east the Meeting in the Temple), the Baptism, the Transfiguration, the Entry into Jerusalem, the Crucifixion, the Descent from the Cross, the Resurrection, the Ascension, Pentecost, and the Dormition of the Virgin. But portrayals of Old Testament worthies and events are not uncommon, especially of Elijah, who is seen as the Old Testament prototype of Christian monasticism. In the New Testament, his mantle is taken up by John the Baptist (John the Forerunner, as he is called in the east), who is seen as the second Elijah, and is likewise a type or symbol of Christian monasticism. Indeed, we find a whole series of scenic icons relating to the monastic tradition. There is, for example, a charming icon of Saint David the Dendrite (the 'Tree-Dweller'), one of the two patron saints of the northern Greek city of Thessaloniki, which depicts the saint perched uncomfortably and precariously in the almond-tree into which he retreated for three years to escape the crowds who came to him for advice and healing.

Illustration Six is a twentieth-century Greek icon of Elijah painted by Fotis Kontoglou, a major figure in modern Greek painting (especially Orthodox hagiographic painting), who was born at Aivali (now Ayvalik in Turkey) in 1896, and died at Athens in 1965. The image depicts the events narrated in 1 Kings 17:3-6, when Elijah, at God's command, fled to the Wadi Cherith, east of the Jordan. There he drank from the wadi and was fed by ravens (one of them appears in the icon) who brought him bread and meat at morning and evening. In the icon, we see a bearded and long-haired Elijah wearing a pale green robe and (following 2 Kings 1:8) a heavy brown mantle of animal hair. It was this mantle that fell near Elisha when Elijah was taken up to heaven in the fiery chariot (2 Kings 2:13). The prophet is concealed among the rocks with the wadi at his feet, and his name appears in Greek above his halo: HO PROPH<ĒTĒS> ĒLIAS, 'The prophet Elijah'.

Further than this we cannot go, for this is not a handbook of iconography. Enough has been said to show that icons, especially icons of Christ and his Mother, are not only pictures, but theological statements, and theological statements of major importance. What, after all, can be more important to Christianity than the truth of the Incarnation? We human beings are ourselves icons of God in that we were created in his image and likeness, and the whole process of redemption is, we might say, iconographic. Our redemption, as Ernst Benz has said,

> consists in our being renewed in the image of Jesus Christ, incorporated into the image of Christ and thus through Jesus Christ experiencing the renewal of our status as images of God.[8]

In a sense, therefore, the holy icons are not so much part of Orthodoxy as Orthodoxy itself, but if that is going a little too far, there can be no doubt that they are a vital part of the Orthodox Tradition, and it is to a consideration of the meaning and content of that Tradition that we must now turn our attention.

---

8. Ernst Benz, trans. Richard and Clara Winston, *The Eastern Orthodox Church. Its Thought and Life* (New York, 1963) 19 (with minor amendments).

6
TRADITION AND TRADITIONS

TRADITION, as we said in Chapter Four, can be both a blessing and a bane. It is a two-edged sword. Positively, it permits change, development, and adaptation. Negatively, it can produce ossification, conservatism, and the idolization of the past. For the early fathers of the Church, the 'Tradition' was what had been revealed by God through his prophets and apostles; and since the Tradition had then been handed down by the apostles to the Churches they established or organized, it became known as 'Apostolic Tradition'. Whether this idea can be supported by historical fact is quite another matter. Much of the Tradition was to be found in the various Christian creeds, but, as time went on, the term came to be applied to the continuing explanation, interpretation, and elucidation of scriptural revelation. Sometimes it came to include ideas and customs which had developed slowly—sometimes imperceptibly—over the centuries, and which were legitimized by the very Tradition of which they were part. In other words, Tradition can define itself, and that is a dangerous thing.

At the time of the Protestant Reformation, the question of Scripture versus Tradition was a topic of heated controversy. But although the Reformers stressed *sola scriptura*, the authority of the biblical page alone, this was never really possible. Save for factual historical statements, such as the names of kings or the location of places, the Bible always demands interpretation. It is all very well to say 'Love your neighbour', but who is my neighbour, and what, exactly, do you mean by love? Does the injunction advocate having a torrid affair with the person next door? Or is it limited to paying the medical expenses for injured Samaritans? *Sola scriptura*, in fact, is hardly ever *sola scriptura*, but almost always *scriptura interpretata*, 'Scripture interpreted'. Nevertheless, for the Protestant reformers the interpretation of Scripture was (and is) undeniably more fluid and individual than it was (and is) for their Roman Catholic opponents; and when the Second Vatican Council stated that, for Roman Catholicism, Scripture and Tradition, 'flowing from the same divine wellspring, in a certain way merge into a unity and tend toward the same end'[1], the Council was also speaking for Orthodoxy.

The key to Tradition is, once again, the Holy Spirit. Tradition, in theory, is not merely the human interpretation of God's revelation, but human interpretation guided by God. There are cases, admittedly, when we might suspect that human beings have erred (and erred seriously) in their interpretation, or that God's guidance has been exasperatingly obscure, but the essential fact remains. Tradition may be defined as the dynamic understanding of God's Word in and through the Holy Spirit.

One of the problems, however, is that once something has become part of the Tradition, it is very difficult to change it, even if we suspect that it is wrong. A good example is the question of the ordination of women. Neither Orthodoxy nor Roman Catholicism will ordain women to the priesthood, and in this they differ from most Anglicans and Episcopalians, and virtually all the varieties of Protestantism. Within Roman Catholicism there has been much discussion of the matter, and some writers have gone to considerable lengths to demonstrate that, in earliest Christianity, there was no 'ordination' in the modern sense, no 'priesthood' in the modern sense, and that Jesus of Nazareth never at any time prohibited the appointment of women as ministers.

There were certainly women among the apostles. The unquestionably female Junia, lauded by Saint Paul as 'prominent among the apostles' (Rom 16:7), was changed by a male-dominated Church into a man, Junias. Furthermore, the fact that Jesus chose only men

---

1. Second Vatican Council, Dogmatic Constitution on Divine Revelation, §9. The document may be found on the Internet at http://www.rc.net/rcchurch/vatican2/dei.ver, and elsewhere.

to be his disciples is perfectly understandable given the social conditions of his day, and his choice is not to be seen as a theological fiat, but a sociological necessity. But such arguments are essentially irrelevant. Even if a new gospel were to be discovered which revealed that there was a thirteenth disciple called Jane, it would not change the situation. We are not talking about history here, we are talking about Tradition; and the Tradition, for both Roman Catholicism and Orthodoxy, is that priestly ordination is conferred upon males alone. Within Roman Catholicism, this was stated authoritatively by Pope John Paul II on 22 May 1994 in the encyclical *Ordinatio Sacerdotalis*, and reiterated in a document issued by the Congregation for the Doctrine of the Faith on 28 October 1995. Orthodoxy has not found it necessary to make such a statement, but discussion of the subject within Orthodoxy has not been in any way as intense as it has been within Roman Catholicism and Anglicanism.

The same is true of other matters which, in recent years, have been much discussed in Roman Catholicism: the celibacy of the clergy, for example, or certain liturgical changes. It is sometimes possible to demonstrate beyond any doubt that the Tradition of the Church does not reflect early Christian history (Saint Peter, after all, was married), but as we said above, the appeal to early Christian history is of little consequence. The Tradition of the Church is an *authoritative* Tradition, and Roman Catholicism and Orthodoxy are agreed that believing Roman Catholics and believing Orthodox are obliged to accept the content of that Tradition until and unless the Church, in and through the Holy Spirit, decides otherwise.

Thus, if we return for a moment to the ordination of women, there can be no doubt that the subject needs to be discussed, and discussed fully and comprehensively. The arguments used to support the present practice are not always convincing and are sometimes patently inadequate, and there are a growing number of Orthodox, both ordained and lay, male and female, who would like to see the question examined. As yet that has not happened, and at present only the tiniest minority of Orthodox clergy would support the ordination of women. But Orthodox Christians are obliged to accept the Tradition as it is at present, even though they may disagree with it, and it cannot be denied that although Tradition is a living and dynamic thing, and although it may be changed, it changes—if it changes at all—only very slowly. There are times when an aged and arthritic tortoise moves faster than the Orthodox Church.

Tradition can become no more than a synonym for stagnation, and too great a veneration of the past can be perilous. It's rather like dealing with a very old person: we need to distinguish utterances which enshrine decades of invaluable experience from observations which stem only from senility. Age is not always synonymous with wisdom. There is every reason to believe that the Holy Spirit is just as eager to guide human beings as he, she, or it ever was. Human beings, however, do not always wish to be guided. But the Second Vatican Council showed what *could* happen when a human being— in this case, Pope John XXIII—heard the voice of God and responded to it. To be loyal to Tradition is to be open to the Spirit, and there is still too much blind faith in the Orthodox world.

On the other hand, Tradition can protect the Church. It can protect it from change which may be too hasty, too rash, or too individualistic. It can also offer the practising Christian a rich sense of continuity with the past, and a sense of identity with the earliest Christian communities. If Tradition may be seen as the witness of the Holy Spirit in the Church, then Tradition links the believer with that astonishing experience at the first Pentecost, when the same Spirit manifested as tongues of fire on the heads of the apostles. Nowadays, it seems, things tend to happen less dramatically, but, according to Orthodoxy, it still remains true that 'no one can say "Jesus is Lord" except by the Holy Spirit' (1 Cor 12:3).

What are the sources of Orthodox Tradition? Most of them we have already mentioned: the fundamental revelation of the word of God contained in Scripture, the decisions of some or all of the seven Ecumenical Councils (depending on which branch of Orthodoxy one is talking about) and of certain other important councils, and a number of doctrinal statements which appeared from the ninth century onwards. The holy icons are also a source of Tradition as well as being part of Tradition, for, as we saw in the last chapter, their portrayal of Christ or Mary or the saints is not merely artistic, but theological. And then there are the Fathers of the Church and the Divine Liturgy. The Liturgy is something we shall look at in a later chapter; the Fathers of the Church must be considered here and now.

Who were these Fathers, when did they live, and what did they say? In essence, they were the theologians (bishops for the most part) who were instrumental in elaborating and establishing the fundamental principles of Christian theology: the doctrines of the Trinity and the Incarnation, for example, and the doctrines of the Church and the sacraments. This they did primarily through the interpretation of Scripture, though it cannot be denied that there were times when that interpretation was, to say the least, somewhat forced.

Many of these doctrines were established during the course of the fourth and fifth centuries, and some of the most important Fathers were to be found in this period: Athanasius the Great, for example, who was the adversary of Arius and the champion of the Creed of Nicaea; or the three Cappadocian Fathers—Basil the Great, Gregory of Nazianzus (or Gregory the Theologian), and Gregory of Nyssa—who played a vital role in the development of the doctrines of the Trinity and the Incarnation; or John Chrysostom, the too-outspoken patriarch of Constantinople, who was one of the greatest preachers of his day. But there are also earlier Fathers and later Fathers.

From the earlier period we have Ignatius, the highly-strung bishop of Antioch, who saw clearly the perils of docetism and who was martyred in Rome *c.* 107, or Justin Martyr, in whose writings we see the real beginnings of the doctrine of the Trinity, or the staunchly anti-Gnostic Irenaeus of Lyons, who is one of the first theologians to give real place and personality to the Holy Spirit.

Among the later Fathers are Dionysius the Pseudo-Areopagite, who was almost certainly a sixth-century Syrian, and who left behind a collection of writings which had far-reaching influence on both eastern and western spirituality and mysticism. From the sixth and seventh centuries come Maximus the Confessor, who wrote prolifically on orthodoxy, heresy, spirituality, mysticism, biblical interpretation, and the Divine Liturgy; and John of the Ladder, or John Climacus, whose *Ladder of Divine Ascent* remains a classic of eastern monastic spirituality. The eighth century is dominated by John of Damascus, one of the most effective defenders of the holy icons and the author of the *Fount of Wisdom*, a lucid and important summary of Orthodox doctrine. From the ninth century we have Photius, patriarch of Constantinople, an immensely learned bibliophile and a staunch opponent of the western understanding of the primacy of the pope. In the tenth century we find Symeon the New Theologian, one of the greatest of the Byzantine mystical writers. From the fourteenth century we have Gregory Palamas, called 'the Light of Orthodoxy', and one of the most brilliant theologians the eastern tradition ever produced. From the fifteenth comes Mark of Ephesus, who had much to say (in opposition to the west) on the nature and procession of the Holy Spirit. And from the eighteenth century we have Macarius Notaras of Corinth, a spiritual guide and writer of first importance, and Nicodemus of the Holy Mountain (i.e., Mount Athos), whom we shall meet again in a moment. But there is no official list of Fathers of the Church, and although the great majority of those normally included died before the ninth century, there is always the possibility that another might appear in our own day. The inspiration of the Holy Spirit is not circumscribed by time, and Tradition, as we have said, is (or should be) dynamic, not dead. Indeed, given the nature of modern society, we might even see a Mother of the Church, and that would be no bad thing.

In the past, women certainly played an important role in eastern spiritual life, and modern research has revealed that there were many more 'Desert Mothers' than many people suspect. But although some publishing companies now have a section devoted to Matrology as well as Patrology, eastern female theologians are rare, and women like Saint Macrina the Younger, the elder sister of Basil the Great and Gregory of Nyssa, and (as Gregory makes clear) a competent theologian in her own right, are remarkable exceptions.

Given the fact that theology demands education, this is hardly surprising. Unless a woman came from a family which had the means and inclination to provide her with a private tutor, her education was inevitably limited. Furthermore, we also have the biblical injunction which prohibits women from teaching or from having any authority over men (1 Tim 2:12), and, certainly not least in importance, we have to take into account the wholly subordinate position of women in eastern society. In the western Church, on the contrary, we see a succession of extraordinary literate women, both mystics and theologians (the great Teresa of Ávila is a Doctor of the Church), but this is not generally the case in Orthodoxy. There are a few rare exceptions (we shall speak of them in Chapter Eleven), but they are the exceptions that prove the rule.

In this area, the Roman Catholic Church has shown itself to be far more enlightened, and any Orthodox who does not or cannot see in, say, Julian of Norwich or Teresa of Ãvila a spiritual teacher of first importance is either stupidly obdurate or obdurately stupid.

It remains true, however, that the writings of the Fathers of the Church form an important part of the Orthodox Tradition, and translations of their works are not difficult to find, either in print or on the Internet. On the other hand, these writings are sometimes verbose, and the ideas they express are not always easily accessible. That is to say, the Fathers were men of their times, often deeply enmeshed in complicated theological controversies, and without a clear understanding of these controversies, their language, terminology, and philosophical background, the writings of the Fathers can sometimes be obscure.

Furthermore, almost all of them came from a monastic environment, and their lives, for the most part, were centred on the Orthodox liturgy. Monasticism, which we shall discuss in detail in a later chapter, obviously offers a way of life very different from the hustle and bustle of everyday life, and even those modern men and women who find the writings of the Fathers congenial are not always familiar with eastern liturgies, or with the theological controversies which troubled the first few centuries of the Christian Church. Does this mean, then, that the works of the Fathers are out of date? Or that their instructions can be of practical interest only to monks and nuns? Or that their writings can be understood only by ecclesiastical historians? It does not.

In 1782 there was published in Venice a Greek work called the *Philokalia*. The title means 'The Love of the Beautiful'. It was compiled by Saint Nicodemus of the Holy Mountain and Saint Macarius Notaras of Corinth, both of whom we mentioned above. It is a magnificent collection of texts selected from some of the greatest spiritual writers of the Orthodox tradition, and it covers a period of twelve centuries, from the fourth to the fifteenth.[2] Neither Nicodemus nor

2. There is an excellent annotated English translation: *The Philokalia. The Complete Text compiled by Saint Nikodimos of the Holy Mountain and Saint Makarios of Corinth*, tr. Gerald E. H. Palmer, Philip Sherrard, and Kallistos Ware (London-Boston, 1979–). Five volumes (at the time of writing, the fifth has not yet been published).

Macarius, however, were mere compilers: both were spiritual masters in their own right and both have left other important writings. But the *Philokalia* seems at first glance to be a book by monks for monks. It is solidly rooted in the eastern contemplative tradition, and some of the ideas and instructions set forth seem of little relevance to the busy people of the twenty-first century scurrying around at the beck and call of their cell-phones. But in his introduction to the work, Nicodemus stresses that 'unceasing prayer' is not just for monks. It may and should be practised by all, even though it may be easier in the regulated and quiet life of a monastery. The call to perfection is a general call, and on this matter Nicodemus is at one with his tenth-century predecessor, Symeon the New Theologian. 'Don't say it's impossible to receive the Divine Spirit', said Symeon,

> Don't say it's possible to be saved without him;
> Don't say that we can possess him without knowing it;
> Don't say that God doesn't appear to human beings;
> Don't say that human beings don't see the Divine Light,
>   or that it's impossible in this day and age.
> My friends, it's never impossible.
> On the contrary, for those who really want it, it's obviously
>   possible—
> Though only to the extent that in our lives we have
>   purified our passions and purified, too, the eye of the
>   mind.[3]

In the fourteenth century, Nicholas Cavasilas[4] said much the same thing. To live the 'life in Christ' we don't need to retreat to the desert. Generals can still command their armies, and workers can continue to work. We don't need to leave our usual employment, and we don't need to give up our possessions. What we do need to do is participate fully in the liturgical and sacramental life of the Church, and, in loving God, try our best to fulfil his will. For Cavasilas, Christianity is a living encounter with Christ in and

---

3. Symeon the New Theologian, *Hymn* 27.125–134; *Sources chrétiennes* 174: 288 (Turnholt: Brepols, 1971).
4. His name is actually spelled Cabasilas, but the B is pronounced as a V.

through the Holy Spirit, and that is not something restricted to monks, nuns, or the ordained clergy.[5]

In other words, the writings of the Fathers are part of the *living* Tradition of the Church. They are not museum pieces to be studied only by scholars. Being people of their times, not all that they say is to be heeded (we can safely ignore John Chrysostom's misogyny), and some of what they say needs to be adapted to present circumstances. But to read the *Philokalia* is to immerse oneself in some of the most effective spiritual writing to come from the Christian tradition. In browsing through its pages one may well come across some very odd plants, that is true, but one may also find a very great deal of spiritual nourishment.

Such, then, are the sources of the Orthodox Tradition. That it is a rich Tradition is not in doubt. That it is a dynamic Tradition is also true, though it is not, perhaps, as dynamic as it should be. But in addition to Tradition, Orthodoxy also has traditions. Customs might be a better word. Here we are talking about a multitude of things, ranging from the way Orthodox cross themselves (up, down, right and left; not, as in the west, up, down, left and right) to how they take the Eucharist (usually on a spoon, as we mentioned in Chapter One). Such customs may vary from Church to Church, and in the Oriental Orthodox Churches we see a great many unique traditions unknown to the Greek-Russian-Slav majority. But this is inevitable in a system of self-governing Churches, and simply adds to the richness of Orthodox life. On the other hand, we cannot say that everything is rosy in the garden of ecclesiastical custom. In the past, conflicts of traditions have been exceedingly violent, and few conflicts were more violent than the so-called Schism of the Old Believers in seventeenth-century Russia.

The origins of this schism lay in a question of first importance for the Church in Russia: should Russian Orthodoxy be truly Russian, consonant with the Russian character and its own Russian traditions, or should it accommodate itself to the Greek Orthodoxy from which it sprang, and follow Greek liturgical customs? In other words, should Orthodoxy in Russia be true 'Russian Orthodoxy', or should it be 'Greek Orthodoxy in Russia'?

5. For a brief account of Cabasilas's ideas, see Bell, *Many Mansions*, 184–190.

Both sides could boast formidable champions, and a sure sign of which side you supported could be seen in the way you crossed yourself. If you used two fingers, which was the older, Russian custom, you supported 'Russian Orthodoxy'. If you used three fingers, as the Greeks were then doing, you supported 'Greek Orthodoxy in Russia'. The former group came to be known as the Old Believers, and they were excommunicated in 1667 and violently persecuted. They were persecuted again in the nineteenth century, but survived the Revolution and are still to be found in Russia today—and, as immigrants, in Canada and the United States. The excommunication of 1667 was lifted by the Russian Orthodox Church in 1971, but the schism still exists.

In this case, what may seem to us today to be a minor divergence in custom—two fingers as opposed to three—was of major importance. It was a ritual gesture which, like all ritual gestures, could embody and reveal a person's entire religious, social, and political position. Try giving a Nazi salute at a meeting of the B'nai B'rith. Religion, in any case, thrives on ritual gestures, and they have always played a major role in Orthodoxy. We shall be saying more about them a little later.

A more contemporary, and, from the point of view of modern Orthodoxy, more relevant conflict of custom involves the calendar, and here, too, what appears to be no more than unnecessary archaism must also be seen in its own light. We are once again in the realms of religious symbolism.

The story begins in 46 BC when the Roman emperor Julius Caesar introduced a revised calendar based on certain mathematical calculations which provided an almost—but not quite—accurate figure for the length of the year. It came to be referred to as the Julian Calendar, and the length of the Julian year was a little bit shorter than the astronomical year. It took more than sixteen centuries for a more accurate calendar to be introduced, but in 1582, under the auspices of Pope Gregory XIII, ten days were omitted from the year to correct an accumulated error, and new rules were devised for leap years. The result, the Gregorian Calendar, was much more accurate, and was slowly adopted by most of the Christian world and the world that used the Christian calendar.

Orthodoxy, bound to its ancient traditions, resisted the change, and until the end of the First World War used the old Julian Calendar. At an Orthodox Congress in 1923, the decision was made to introduce a revised version of the Julian Calendar, a version which was almost identical to the Gregorian Calendar, and, in the long run, slightly more accurate. The decision, however, was controversial, and several Orthodox Churches refused to accept it. The result was that Orthodoxy still uses two calendars: the unrevised Julian, referred to as the Old Calendar, and the revised Julian, which is, effectively, the Gregorian, and which is referred to as the New Calendar. The Old Calendar is thirteen days behind the New. The Churches which use a Greek liturgy *tend* to follow the New Calendar; the Churches which use a Russian or Slav liturgy (except for Bulgaria and Romania) *tend* to follow the Old Calendar; but there are many exceptions to both. The situation becomes more confused when we take into consideration the Oriental Orthodox Churches, and yet more confused when we find Russian Orthodox parishes in the west following the New Calendar, while their parent parishes in Russia remain staunchly dedicated to the Old. And while one might expect to find the Orthodox Church in America following the New Calendar, this is not always the case. Many OCA parishes do; many do not.

How can we defend this confusion? Or is it simply a case of Orthodox obscurantism: the past for the sake of the past, tradition for the sake of tradition? For some, there is no doubt that this is true. But for others, what is at stake is much more significant. It is the question of the extent to which Orthodoxy should be influenced by the west, and it involves controversial matters which we will discuss later in this book: Church union and ecumenism. There are many conservative Orthodox who see in the old unrevised Julian Calendar an important symbol of 'true Orthodoxy', whatever that may mean. Again, there are some revised western Orthodox who wish to keep the feasts and festivals at the same time as their unrevised brothers and sisters in, say, Russia. Yet other revised western Orthodox see the unrevised calendar—the Old Calendar—as no more than a symbol of that unfortunate ethnicity which, as we shall see, is one of the major problems with the Orthodox tradition in a global society. But the fact remains: there are two calendars in use: Old and New. Many find this confusing and many find it unnecessary, but it does illustrate how tradition can sometimes be a heavy burden.

For all that, Tradition and, to a lesser extent, traditions, are the basis of Orthodox life, but a basis is something to be built upon. A house without a foundation may be unstable, but a foundation without a house is useless. So what is the goal of Orthodoxy? What is the point of all this Tradition? To what end does the Tradition point? What is the purpose of the 'life in Christ'? What are we supposed to build on this traditional foundation? The answer to these questions will be the subject of our next chapter.

7
BECOMING LIKE GOD

THE GOAL OF ORTHODOXY is the goal of Christianity: salvation, or, more precisely, redemption. In other words, the Orthodox hope is the Christian hope, which is hardly surprising. For Christians, redemption is to be found in the incarnation, crucifixion, and resurrection of Jesus of Nazareth, but before we can discuss that, we need to say a few words about why we need redemption and why we cannot redeem ourselves.

Orthodoxy is at one with the rest of the Christian tradition in maintaining that something went wrong in the Garden of Eden. Many Christians, Orthodox and otherwise, do not now accept the story of the Fall as literal truth, but rather as a myth designed to explain why, in general, we prefer sin to virtue, and why 'being good' is so intolerably difficult. The traditional story also explains why we are susceptible to disease, and why we grow old and die. If Adam and Eve had not sinned (so the story goes), death and disease would have had no dominion in Paradise; but sin they did, and the consequences of that sin have been handed on to us. In theological terms, what we are talking about here is Original Sin, but we are not talking about Original Guilt. What is the difference?

To understand the difference we need to go back to the fourth century and the Pelagian Controversy. The protagonists in the controversy were, on the one hand, a British theologian named Pelagius (c. 354–c. 420?) and his followers, and on the other hand, Saint Augustine of Hippo (354–430). Augustine was the most important single formative influence on western Christianity, but despite his undoubted genius, his views could be decidedly idiosyncratic. Pelagius and his followers rejected the idea—standard at that time in both east and west—that Adam and Eve's descendants (i.e., the human race) had somehow inherited the stain and corruption of Adam and Eve's sin. Human souls, said Pelagius, were created by a perfectly good God, and since a perfectly good God would not deliberately create anything evil, human souls were, by definition, also good. It is true that we might have inherited mortality from our first parents (though Pelagius was not sure of that), but we did *not* inherit either their sin or their guilt. If we sin (as sin we do), it is through imitation—putting it in modern terms, we are socialized into sinning—and if, by a supreme exercise of our will, we decide to do good, we can do so.

To these ideas Augustine was wholly and adamantly opposed. His own view, based to some extent on a misreading of Romans 5:12,[1] was that not only did we inherit the sin of Adam and Eve, we also inherited their guilt. The human race—and, in consequence, every child who comes into this world—is *una massa peccati*, 'one lump of sin'; and since we are totally, utterly, 100% corrupt, we can no more do a single good act than absolute darkness can put forth a beam of light. Only by the gift of God's grace can we do good, and since we can never earn or merit or deserve grace by good actions, it follows that the only people who can and will do good are those whom God selects to receive his grace as a free gift. And who are these? Augustine has no idea of their personal identity, but by his own logic he is forced into the position of maintaining that only those predestined to receive God's grace will receive it, use it, and achieve salvation. The rest of us are doomed to eternal darkness, everlasting torment, and the worm that dieth not.

This pessimistic view of the total depravity of the human race, with predestination as its corollary, became the official teaching of the western Church from the fifth century onwards. With John Calvin in the sixteenth century, it also became the official view of Calvinistic Protestantism, though other varieties of Protestantism questioned the idea or downright rejected it. Modern Roman Catholicism is still technically Augustinian, though it skilfully skirts round some of the more problematical features. Modern Anglicanism, for the most part, rejects the idea of predestination. Modern

---

1. See Bell, *A Cloud of Witnesses*, 147.

Protestantism displays an astonishing variety of opinions from one extreme to the other. What, then, of Orthodoxy?

Pelagianism was condemned at a number of Church councils in the fifth century, including the Third Ecumenical Council held at Ephesus in 431. Orthodoxy, therefore, concurs in this condemnation, but—and the *but* is important—although the Orthodox Churches agree that Pelagius was wrong, they do not agree that Augustine was right. Pelagius, say the Orthodox, was indeed wrong in thinking that, at birth, human beings have a perfectly free choice between sinning and not sinning. On the contrary. Something did happen in the course of evolution to make us more susceptible to vice than to virtue—perhaps it stems simply from an instinct for pleasure and self-preservation—but whatever happened, it did not remove *entirely* our capacity for good. The free gift of redemption must be *freely* accepted. On this point, then, Augustine (according to Orthodoxy) was wrong: we are not simply *una massa peccati*, and none of the Orthodox Churches has ever acknowledged the doctrine of absolute and total human depravity consequent upon the first sin.

It follows from this that we *can* do good, though it may not be easy, but Orthodoxy is at one with the other Christian Churches in maintaining that without God's grace we cannot, of our own accord, do enough good to achieve salvation. In other words, as human beings, we retain our free will, but grace remains essential. If, by our own will, we perform one good act, God will respond to this by making his grace available to us; then, in cooperation with this grace (and only in cooperation with this grace), we may do further good acts to which God will further respond by making further grace available, and so on. In Orthodoxy, this cooperation of human free-will and divine grace is called synergy. We introduced the word in Chapter Four. It means our cooperation with the Creator in the on-going process of redemption: both our own redemption and that of the planet on which we live. Which brings us back to the question of just what is redemption.

That we cannot redeem ourselves is clear. Human beings may indeed be images of God, only a little lower than the angels, but they are flawed images of God. Depending on how you look at it, the sin of Adam and Eve in the Garden of Eden, or some quirk in the course of evolution, has so weakened our will that we cannot, of our own power, do enough good to save ourselves. Grace, therefore, is essential, and grace is inseparable from Christ. 'Grace to you and peace', says Saint Paul at the beginning of the letter to the Romans, 'from God our Father and the Lord Jesus Christ' (Rom 1:7). Both as a greeting and as a blessing, 'the grace of Our Lord Jesus Christ' is an important phrase in the Christian liturgy and an essential part of the Christian hope.

The Incarnation was a consequence of human sin. While it is true that a number of western theologians and one or two easterners maintained that Christ would have become incarnate even if human beings had not sinned,[2] that is not the general teaching of the Christian tradition, nor is it part of the earliest Christian preaching. 'I have handed on to you', says Saint Paul, 'what I in turn received, and it is of first importance: Christ died for our sins in accordance with the scriptures' (1 Cor 15:3). Exactly how the death of Christ atoned for our sins was a matter of theological speculation, some of it excessively legalistic, but the Fathers of the Church were unanimous in believing that, as a consequence of the crucifixion, the hitherto unbridgeable gap between God and the human race—a gap created by human sin—had been bridged. As the God-Man, Christ had brought about an atonement, an 'at-one-ment', between the divine and the human, and the flow of grace, which had been cut off by human sin, was, in and through him, reestablished.

The crucifixion demands the resurrection. Indeed, without the resurrection the crucifixion might be no more than the execution of yet another Judaean rabble-rouser. Not only did Jesus of Nazareth come to teach us the way to salvation, not only did he come to take upon himself the sins of the world, not only did he come to wash away those sins with his own blood, he also came to triumph over death, which was the result of sin. In the dramatic events of Calvary, Christ the Saving Victim becomes Christ the Triumphant Victor, and while western Christianity tends to emphasize the former while recognizing the latter, eastern Christianity tends to emphasize the latter while recognizing the former. But the difference is only one of emphasis. The suffering servant is also God, and God is also the suffering servant.

2. The matter is discussed in Bell, *Many Mansions*, 217–220.

In the fact of the resurrection, death has been swallowed up in victory. The entire fifteenth chapter of Paul's first letter to the Corinthians hinges upon this fact, and the apostle leaves us in no doubt on the matter: 'If Christ has not been raised, your faith is futile and you are still in your sins' (1 Cor 15:17). Christ's resurrection is the guarantee of our own resurrection (we need not think of this in purely bodily terms), and in his immortality we, too, may become immortal. Putting it another way, in the events of Calvary, Christ not only offers us the grace of forgiveness of sins, he also offers us the grace of eternal life. Indeed, he offers us even more than that. As Saint Athanasius said, 'God became human that in him humans might become god'.[3] We quoted the sentence in Chapter Two. In other words, what we are offered is nothing less than the grace of divinity. But this, if misunderstood, can be a dangerous doctrine, and we must understand clearly just what Athanasius is and is not saying.

What he is *not* saying is that human beings can become God. That, according to Isaiah, is what Satan wanted to do, and he came to a bad end. The twelfth-century western writer William of Saint-Thierry put it neatly: we may not become God (*Deus*), he said, but *quod Deus est*, 'what God is'.[4] What we are talking about here is what Orthodox Christians call deification. We introduced the term in Chapter Two and it is now time to talk about it in a little more detail.

To begin with, let us go back to Athanasius's own words: 'God became human that in him humans might become god'. What does Athanasius mean? What he means is rooted in Platonic philosophy, but there is no need to elaborate on that here. The essential meaning is that in the atonement, the whole of humanity was reconnected with the whole of divinity, and, as a consequence of this re-connection, we human beings are able to share or participate in the divine attributes. To some extent we already participate naturally

---

3. Athanasius, *Ad Adelphium*, 4; cf. *De incarnatione*, 54.
4. William of Saint-Thierry, *Epistola ad Fratres de Monte Dei* (*Epistola aurea*) §258 (Sources chrétiennes 223 [1975] 348–350). English translation by Theodore Berkeley, *The Golden Epistle. A Letter to the Brethren at Mont Dieu* (Cistercian Fathers Series 12; Spencer, 1971) 94.

in these attributes. We exist by participation in God's being; we live by participation in his life; we think by participation in his reason. God, in short, is the essential foundation of our human existence. We may use our God-given reason, in cooperation with God-given grace, to fulfil God's will, and if we do this we become good in his goodness. That is to say, we participate in his perfection; and by participating in his perfection, we may also participate in his perfect joy; and, once this life is over, we may also participate in his eternity. This is deification: our participation in the attributes of God, whatever those attributes may be. If God is (for example) good, wise, joyous, merciful, perfect, and eternal, we—so far as is possible for human weakness—may participate in his goodness, wisdom, joy, mercy, perfection, and eternity, and become, in our turn, good, wise, joyful, and so on. The process begins here and now; it finds its culmination only after death.

For Orthodox Christians, this life is not merely a threshold to the life to come. It is not like the departure lounge in some worldly airport where we merely pass the time with magazines and drinks before boarding the flight to Eternity. Our business here involves more than sitting on our backsides watching television, surfing the net, or playing computer games. As we said above, the process of deification begins here and now. How? Well, we might start by being a little more courteous to people and a little more caring to animals. We might even begin by caring a little more for the planet on which we live. Deification takes place in community—not just the human community, but the planetary community of all living things from soil to saints—and ecology is part of deification. As we said in Chapter Four, you cannot be Orthodox without being an ecologist.

It is true that 'doing good' is difficult and we may not be very proficient at it, but that is no excuse for not trying. God does not always expect us to succeed, but he does expect us to try. Deification, therefore, is not only for professional athletes in the spiritual Olympics; it is not only for saints and mystics; and it is not solitary. If deification is indeed to become not God but God-like—to become 'what God is'—then it necessarily involves caring for God's creation. God did not bring the universes into being, check that they were working properly, and then retire to a celestial armchair with his cat and a cigar. On the contrary, the process of creation is an on-going process, and our business as human beings is to cooperate with God in the work of creation. It is an awesome responsibility. Deification cannot be completed here on earth. Adam and Eve might have been immortal before the Fall (*pace* Pelagius), but eternal life is no longer an earthly prerogative. Our participation in eternity comes after death, and whether we inherit eternal life in heaven or hell depends on our own free-will. Let us say a word or two about these ultimate ends.

The traditional teaching of the Orthodox Church is that immediately after death the soul is judged by God, and one's eternal destiny is decided at that moment. But this judgement is, as it were, a proleptic, an anticipatory, judgement, for the soul does not experience the fullness of either joy or despair—indeed, according to some theologians, the soul experiences neither joy nor despair—until the time of the Last Judgement when Christ shall return in glory to judge both the living and the dead. At that time, the dead shall rise again in transfigured, spiritual bodies, and shall then inherit the plenitude of eternal bliss or eternal punishment.

There is no place in this scheme for purgatory (though we do find the doctrine in the writings of some seventeenth-century Orthodox theologians), and there is no place for limbo. Limbo, in older Roman Catholic theology, was the name given primarily to the abode of the souls of unbaptized babies who, having died, were excluded from the full bliss of the Beatific Vision because they had not undergone baptism. They were not subjected to any punishment, and, in limbo, they experienced the fullness of natural happiness. They did not, however, experience that supernatural happiness which comes only with the vision of God. Neither limbo nor purgatory form part of Orthodox belief.

Orthodoxy, in fact, speaks of our post-mortal conditions with what Sergius Bulgakov calls a 'wise uncertainty'.[5] Many people today, for example, would object that infinite punishment for finite sins is neither equitable nor just. Many others think that the very idea of an eternal hell is contrary to the concept of an all-merciful God. Yet others find the idea of the resurrection of the body, transfigured or not, old-fashioned, crude, and unnecessary, and there are

5. Sergius Bulgakov, *The Orthodox Church* (New York-London, [1935]) 208.

not a few who regard the promise of the Second Coming much as the story of the First Sin, namely, as a myth which conceals a more subtle reality.

The fact that Orthodox Christians pray for those who have died certainly implies that the dead may profit from our prayers, but precisely how they profit, and in what condition they exist, are both alike unknown to us. What *is* important is that Orthodox believe that our prayers can not only help a soul in torment, but release it from torment entirely. In other words, we may envisage hell as serving just the same purpose as purgatory—i.e., a place of temporary purging in order to prepare one for Paradise—even though we do not call it that. Indeed, we may go even further and join Gregory of Nyssa, Maximus the Confessor, and certain nineteenth- and twentieth-century Russian Orthodox theologians who see no place for either a permanent hell or permanent evil. At the end of time, says Gregory, even the 'introducer of evil', the Devil himself, will be healed and restored to God.[6]

It is true that ideas such as these were condemned at a synod held at Constantinople in 543, but that was not an Ecumenical Council, and the assembled bishops might have been wrong. The idea of a final and universal restoration—the technical term in Greek is *apokatastasis* (with the accent on the fourth, not the fifth, syllable)—is certainly not standard Orthodox teaching, but there are many Christians, Orthodox and other, who prefer to believe it.

In matters such as these one cannot help being reminded of Saint Antony who, on one occasion, was asking God all sorts of difficult questions: why do some people die young? why are some people poor and some rich? why do the wicked prosper? A celestial voice answered him and told him to mind his own business.[7] That the dead benefit from the prayers of the living is an important part of Orthodox belief; the answer to the question of how they do so is 'God knows'. That there is a hell and a heaven is likewise an important part of Orthodox belief; their precise nature and duration will be made known to us in due course.

---

6. Gregory of Nyssa, *Oratio catechetica magna*, 26.
7. *The Sayings of the Desert Fathers: The Alphabetical Collection*, tr. Benedicta Ward (Oxford-Kalamazoo-London, 1975) 1 (Anthony, #2).

Reincarnation is not part of the Orthodox tradition, just as it is not part of the Christian tradition. This is not to say that many Christians do not accept the idea, and many, likewise, maintain that it can play a role in Christianity without destroying the essence of the faith. In the ancient world, it was generally accepted by later Platonists and a number of Gnostic groups, and the fact that it was frequently attacked may indicate that not all Christians were averse to the idea. It is certainly at variance with the ancient tradition of the resurrection of the body, but, as we have seen, many modern Christians are doubtful about the idea of bodily resurrection, and have no sympathy at all with the idea of an eternal hell. For them, a process of deification which lasts not one life but many offers a far more satisfactory solution, and they find no need to maintain that Hindus, Buddhists, Jains, and Jewish Qabbalists are all wrong. The doctrine also provides a helpful answer to Saint Antony's questions. But the fact remains: rightly or wrongly, reincarnation plays no role in Orthodox Christianity. One thing alone is certain: in due course all our questions about what happens after death will be answered, and there is no doubt that many of us are going to be surprised.

It is time, then, to come back to earth. Those who are reading this book are, presumably, still alive, and if they are alive, they are, like all of us, all too enmeshed in this all too solid flesh. What does Orthodoxy have to say about the flesh? Many of the western Churches have problems with the flesh and sexuality, primarily because of the idiosyncratic opinions of Saint Augustine of Hippo. For many years, Augustine was a Manichaean or Manichee, a follower of a dualistic sect founded in third-century Persia by one Mani, which believed that created matter in general, and flesh in particular, was inherently evil. Once Augustine became Christian, he wholly rejected this viewpoint, but its emotional impact never wholly left him, and it is not difficult to find in his writings a grave distrust of the flesh. And when we add to this his idea that original sin was most probably transmitted by the actual act of sexual intercourse, which, being devoted to pleasure, was, by definition, sinful in itself, the consequences for the Augustinian tradition were profound. Many of the western Churches have viewed the flesh with deep suspicion, if not fear, for more than fifteen hundred years.

The situation in the east was and is rather different, primarily as the result of a violent controversy which ravaged the Orthodox world in the fourteenth century. At the heart of the dispute was a practice known as hesychasm. This was a mystical technique which involved a particular bodily posture, semi-yogic breathing exercises, prayer, and concentration. We shall say more about it in Chapter Twelve, but we must introduce its principles here. The hesychasts were convinced that, by means of these techniques, it was possible for them to experience the uncreated light of God. At the basis of this idea is the straightforward statement in the first letter of Saint John that 'God is light'; and if God is light, then to experience that light is to experience God. We are not talking here about *created* light—not sunlight or starlight or moonlight—but the *uncreated* light which is a true revelation of God's own being. It is certainly not the whole of God's being—that, after all, is infinite—but if Saint John is correct (and what Christian could deny that?), then the experience of the uncreated light is, by definition, a true experience of God.

This idea did not sit at all well with a fourteenth-century professor at the University of Constantinople named Barlaam, and Barlaam attacked hesychasm and the hesychasts on two main grounds. First of all, he maintained that the Divine Light seen or experienced by the hesychasts in their mystical practices could not be the uncreated light of God. Why not? Because God is unknowable, and when Moses, in an impertinent moment, asked God to show him His glory, he was told that no one could see the face of God and live (Ex 33:18-23). If, then, God and his uncreated light were one and the same, to experience the fullness of that light was certain death. Barlaam did not deny that the hesychasts had experienced what we would now call an altered state of consciousness, nor did he deny that they had had a vision. But the light they saw could only have been created light—much like sunlight, only brighter—and it was certainly not God. The hesychasts, after all, were still alive.

Secondly, Barlaam maintained that worship is a matter for the spirit, not the body, and he, too, had no less an authority than Saint John to back him up. 'God is spirit', said the Evangelist, 'and those who worship him worship him in spirit and in truth' (Jn 4:24). If, therefore, God is to be worshipped *in spirit*, the bodily contortions and navel-gazing of the hesychasts have no place in Christian devotion. The hesychasts, in other words, were wrong in their interpretation of what they had experienced, and wrong in the way in which they went about seeking that experience.

The chief opponent of Barlaam and the chief defender of the hesychasts was Saint Gregory Palamas (1296–1359), a monk of Mount Athos and brilliant theologian who, in 1347, was consecrated archbishop of Thessaloniki in northern Greece. To both of Barlaam's criticisms Palamas had effective replies. His answer to Barlaam's first argument led him to distinguish between God's 'essence', which is what God is in himself, and God's 'energies' or attributes, which are the ways by which God reveals himself to us. We can never know God 'in himself', for God in himself is known only to God, but we *can* know God as creator, redeemer, and comforter, as well as God as compassion, love, mercy, light, and a host of other manifestations or 'energies'. And just as my right hand is truly part of me, yet not all of me, so God's light is truly part of God, yet not all of God. If someone holds my hand, it really is me they are holding, though not all of me; if the mystics experienced the Divine Light, it really was God they were experiencing, though not God in himself, in his totality. In Palamite terms, deification involves our participation in God's energies, not his essence, and by participating in and experiencing these energies we become *quod Deus est*, or 'what God is'. But we never become God.

As to Barlaam's second argument, Gregory pointed out that when God became incarnate he took on real human flesh, that human flesh really suffered and died at the crucifixion, that when Christ rose again he rose again in the flesh, and that when he ascended into Heaven he ascended into Heaven soul *and fleshly body*. He did not leave a soul-less carcase lying around on earth. The crucial importance of all this is that in the Incarnation, Christ redeemed not only our souls, but also our bodies. After all, the consequences of the Fall were not confined to the human soul: they also affected the human body, which, as we have seen, became liable to colds, flu, beri-beri, and AIDS, as well as losing its God-given immortality. But Christ, in redeeming humanity, redeemed the whole of humanity, not just the human soul; and by spiritualizing human flesh in the resurrection and ascension, he rendered it once again capable of incorruption and immortality.

For Palamas, therefore, redemption was a holistic process, and to use the redeemed flesh of our bodies in the worship of the Saviour was to commemorate the glory of the Incarnation and Christ's triumph over death. Barlaam's Christianity was only half a Christianity, and to accept the old Platonic idea that the body was simply a tomb for the soul was short-sighted, mistaken, immoral, and wrong.

For the hesychasts, their bodily postures were a wholly appropriate commemoration of the Incarnation, the 'enfleshment', of Christ. For us, Gregory's ideas have wider ramifications. Given the fundamental principle of the redemption of the flesh, *any* ritual bodily gesture may be regarded as a commemoration of the Incarnation. During the Divine Liturgy, for example, Orthodox continually cross themselves (my wife, on first attending the Liturgy, suggested that you could tell Orthodox Christians by the muscular development of their right arm), but given the ideas of Palamas, we see that these gestures are not merely incidental to Orthodox worship: they *are* Orthodox worship. Similarly, if one goes into a church, bows before an icon and kisses it, this, too, is a modern equivalent of the bodily postures of the hesychasts, and this, too, may be regarded as worship incarnate. But the same principle may be taken much further. Depending on our intention, it can apply to everything from washing our face or the dishes to using the computer. It is an important and far-reaching idea.

Without grace, however, none of this is possible. 'Of our own power', said Augustine, 'we can only fall.'[8] Not according to Orthodoxy. Of our own power, we ourselves can indeed take the first hesitant steps towards deification, but, equally certainly, of our own power we cannot complete the process. What, then, is the source of grace, and where does it operate? As to its source, that is easily answered: grace is from God alone. As to where it operates, that is more tricky. Grace cannot be confined, and it certainly cannot be confined to the Christian Church, much less to Orthodoxy. Only a fool or a bigot would say that the grace of God did not operate in and through the leaders of all the great religious traditions, or that the communion of the saints is restricted to Christians. But if

---

8. Augustine of Hippo, *Enarratio in Ps.* 129.1.

one happens to be Christian, and if one happens to be Orthodox, it is only natural that one would seek the grace of God in a church rather than in a mosque, and in the Christian sacraments rather than in, say, the rich and effective rituals of Japanese Tendai Buddhism. Let us move on, then, to talk about Orthodox churches, describe what they look like and what they contain, and say something more than we said in our first chapter about what goes on inside them.

8
GOING TO CHURCH

WHAT DOES an Orthodox church look like? It is really impossible to say. An Ethiopian Orthodox church is very different from a Byzantine Orthodox church, and the onion domes of Russia will not be seen in Syria. And in the United States and Canada, where the Orthodox Church in America has often bought churches previously belonging to other Christian traditions, an Orthodox church may look exactly like an Episcopalian or Anglican church, simply because that is what it was.

Speaking very generally, there are two basic plans which predominate in church architecture: the basilica plan and the centralized plan. In both cases the axis of the church normally runs east-west, and the altar will be at the east end. The pre-Christian roots of this lie in the pagan custom of praying towards the rising sun, and it was not difficult to adapt this to a Christian context. For Christians, Christ is the Sun of Righteousness (Mal 4:2), and it is from the east that he will appear at the Second Coming.

A basilica is essentially a rectangular structure with a door at one end and an altar at the other. Larger basilicas commonly have two wings—transepts—opening off the main body of the rectangle near the altar end, thus producing a floor-plan in the form of a Latin cross where the upright is longer than the cross-piece. A tower or spire is commonly built over the crossing where the transepts meet the main body of the church.

In the centralized plan, we have a large central expanse, either circular or polygonal, usually with a dome over the central area, and there are normally one or more projecting wings. If the wings are of equal length, we have a floor-plan in the form of a Greek cross. If one wing is lengthened and becomes a nave, we have a floor-plan—once again—in the form of a Latin cross. Most Orthodox churches in the Byzantine east are centralized churches, based on the plan of the Greek cross, but, in Orthodoxy, tradition is as important in architecture as it is elsewhere. Ethiopian churches, therefore, do not look much like the Cathedral of the Virgin of Kazan in Saint Petersburg. Why should they? Ethiopia is far different geographically, historically, climatically, and culturally from Russia. Within Ethiopia, the Ethiopian tradition dominates, as it should. But nowhere in Orthodoxy do we see the innovative, imaginative, and sometimes daring ecclesiastical architecture which can be seen in the non-Orthodox west.

Speaking of crosses, many Chalcedonian churches (and all those belonging to the Russian and Slav jurisdictions) will display on and/or in their buildings the Orthodox cross, which looks like this:

The uppermost of the three bars is the *titulus* or 'inscription' which identified the criminal. In Jesus's case it read 'Jesus of Nazareth, the King of the Jews' in Latin, Greek, and Hebrew. The long central bar is that to which he was nailed through the wrists. The oblique bar at the bottom probably represents a piece of wood which sometimes (though not always) projected from the cross either at crotch level or at foot level, and provided the victim with some support. It was not there for comfort: it was intended to prolong the agony of crucifixion. A person hanging by the arms with no support dies quickly, certainly in a few hours. If the body has even minimal support, death by crucifixion can take days. The oblique angle of this lower bar may possibly be an early attempt at three-dimensional representation, though there are also other explanations, none of them entirely satisfactory. Coptic and Ethiopic crosses are very different, but to go into details would take us too far from our present course.

Once inside an Orthodox church, the visitor is often struck by two things we mentioned in our first chapter: the presence of icons and the absence of seats. Icons are everywhere. In some churches they cover every surface (including the ceiling), but much depends on the popularity and wealth of the church and the generosity of donors. But at the very least, the visitor will always see an iconostasis, an icon-screen, which divides the sanctuary, where the clergy officiate, from the rest of the church, which is the domain of the laity.

Originally the iconostasis was merely a sort of low wall on which stood columns joined at the top by a decorated parapet. This can still be seen in some old churches in Rome. But by the late Middle Ages, the space between the columns had been filled in, and the iconostasis had taken the form it continues to have: a solid wooden screen, covered with icons, and pierced by three doors. The door on the right (or south) corresponds to the sacristy or vestry in a western church. Here are kept the clerical vestments, sacred vessels, and service-books used in the Divine Liturgy. The door on the left (or north) leads to a room in which stands a table on which the priest and deacon prepare the bread and wine to be used in the Eucharist. The central door is called the Holy Door, Royal Door, or Beautiful Gate and it opens onto the altar. It consists of two half-doors, behind which is a curtain. Sometimes, in the course of the liturgy, the doors (and curtain) are closed, sometimes they are open. Precisely when they are open or closed depends on the custom of the individual church. Indeed, in some Orthodox churches, especially in Greek parishes, neither gates nor curtain are ever closed, and in other parishes, the gates are there, but the curtain has been removed. But it is still common to see both gates and curtain, and to see both closed at certain points during the liturgy. The altar itself is called the Holy Table, and, unlike the western Roman Catholic tradition, there is normally only one altar in each church. It stands free of the eastern wall, thereby allowing the clergy to walk round it.

To the right of the Royal Door there will be an icon of Christ; to the left will be an icon of the Mother of God. To the right of the icon of Christ there is often an icon of John the Baptist, and to the left of the icon of the Mother of God there is frequently an icon of the saint to whom the church is dedicated. On the two other doors are icons of the archangel Michael (to the south) and the archangel Gabriel (to the north). Along the top of the iconostasis there is commonly a series of twelve icons depicting the twelve most important events in the life of Christ. In Greek Orthodox churches, the iconostasis tends to be fairly low—it stops short of the ceiling—and just two or three tiers of icons are common. In Russian and Slav Orthodoxy, the iconostasis often towers the full height of the building, and may have six or seven rows of icons. One of the largest and most imposing examples was once to be seen in the Cathedral of the Dormition in Vladimir. It was painted by the greatest of Russian icon-painters, Andrei Rublev (*c*.1360–*c*.1430), and some of the icons were ten feet in height. This icon-screen no longer exists *in situ*, but parts of it have been preserved in museums in Moscow and Saint Petersburg.

In front of the iconostasis there will sometimes be a row of large candles in large candle-sticks, and there will always be a table covered by a cloth on which stand (among other things) a cross and, if possible, an icon of the feast or the saint of the day. On 15 August, for example, there would be an icon depicting the death of the Virgin, since 15 August is the Feast of the Dormition, or, in western terms, the Assumption of the Mother of God. On 2 May there would be an icon of Saint Athanasius. But if the church does not possess such an icon (and many do not, being too small or too poor), then its place will be taken by some other appropriate icon.

On entering a church, as we said in Chapter One, the first thing Orthodox Christians do is buy a candle or candles, go up to one or more of the icons, kiss it, light a candle, and stand it in front of the icon. While doing this they will cross themselves one or more times. We said in the last chapter that such a ritual gesture is an integral part of Orthodox worship, and is no more idolatrous than the genuflexion of a believing Roman Catholic in front of the reserved sacrament. In any case, veneration is not worship, and every icon is regarded as a meeting-place of heaven and earth.

This act of veneration may take place either before or during the liturgy, for one of the things that often strikes non-Orthodox Christians as peculiar is the freedom of movement within an Orthodox congregation. As we shall see in a moment, Orthodox liturgy tends to take longer than is usual in the west, and people do not always come at the beginning and do not always stay until the end. This freedom of movement is made much easier in Orthodoxy by the fact that the churches (generally) do not have pews or seats. In this, they are at one with the practice of the early Church, and, we might add, with the western Church until the late Middle Ages. There may be benches or seats along the walls for the aged or infirm, or sometimes a series of semi-stalls designed to give some support to a standing person, but in the majority of Orthodox churches, the area outside the iconostasis is pewless. In the case of what we might call second-hand churches—previously non-Orthodox churches bought by Orthodox congregations—the original pews are, naturally, still in evidence, but even there, the congregation remains standing for most of the liturgy.

This lack of seating obviously makes it easier for people to come and go and move around at will, and there is not the slightest problem in coming to the Divine Liturgy after it has begun, discreetly making one's way to the front of the church, lighting a candle before the icon of the Mother of God, and then mingling with the rest of the congregation. Worship is more informal than in the many western denominations—in Orthodox churches, you sometimes have to step over the youngsters playing on the floor—but in the view of Orthodox Christianity, worship should be no more (or no less) than a sanctified form of everyday life.

As we said a moment ago, Orthodox liturgy tends to be longer than in most non-Orthodox churches, though it can appear short when compared with the preaching marathons in some fundamentalist denominations. It rarely takes less than an hour and a quarter but rarely takes more than two hours, and if one decides to stay for the whole celebration, one can find oneself sinking down into what one might call Sacred Time. Sacred time moves at a slower pace than clock time, and it has a different quality and a different rhythm. It is meditative rather than active, and the measured, repetitive cadences of Orthodox liturgy (which contains lots of litanies) and the unhurried choreography of the officiating celebrants can have a remarkable effect on those of us accustomed to running our lives by our watches. The world outside the doors of the church is an instant world, with demands ranging from instant coffee to instant information on the Internet. Within the church, time has a different quality and moves at a different speed. On the other hand, if one really does have only twenty minutes to spare, then there is no problem in attending the liturgy for that length of time and then quietly disappearing. There'll be no looks of disapproval, and one need not feel in the least embarrassed.

In general, the Orthodox name for what, in other Churches, is called the Mass, Eucharist, Lord's Supper, or Holy Communion, is the Divine Liturgy, Holy Liturgy, or simply the Liturgy. It is normally celebrated only on Sundays and major feast days. The only other services ordinarily attended by the average Orthodox Christian are Matins and Vespers. Matins is the morning service which precedes the Liturgy and merges with it, and it consists of psalms, a reading from the Gospel, hymns, and a doxology. Vespers is said on Saturday evening (or the evening before an important feast), and, like Matins, consists of hymns and biblical readings. Orthodox priests say Matins and Vespers every day, but for Orthodox laity, Vespers, Matins, and Liturgy are a weekly celebration.

Whatever the office, it is always sung, and it is almost always unaccompanied. Traditionally, it was always unaccompanied, but here and there in North America one may nowadays find an un-Orthodox organ. But whether unaccompanied or not, no services are said or spoken in the Orthodox tradition. The singing, however, cannot really be called congregational singing. It is true that in some parishes, especially in the west and in parishes of the Orthodox Church in America, the congregation will join in singing some parts of the service, but most of the offices and liturgy are a dialogue between priest, deacon, and choir—and sometimes just between priest and deacon.

The nature of the music naturally varies from church to church, and for westerners accustomed to western music it is not always easy to appreciate. This, as we said in our first chapter, is especially true of the Oriental Orthodox Churches, but the old Byzantine plain-chant used in Greek Orthodoxy can also sound strange to someone unused to its curious intervals. The music of the Russian Orthodox Church is probably the most accessible to westerners, for much of it has been deeply influenced by western Romanticism. There are settings of the liturgy by very well-known composers such as Tchaikovsky and Rachmaninov, by (unjustly) less well-known composers such as Gretchaninov, Bortniansky and Shvedov, and by a very great number of composers known only to lovers of Russian Orthodox liturgy. This is not to say that Russian Orthodox music is any better (or worse) than, say, the music of the Ethiopian Orthodox Church. It is simply a matter of taste, familiarity, or upbringing. Much the same is true of the Latin Church in the west: some people prefer plain-chant to Berlioz, and some people prefer Berlioz to folk Masses. But nowhere in Orthodoxy will one hear folk Masses or modern avant-garde church music, for Orthodox music, like Orthodox art, is firmly rooted—some would say hidebound—in Tradition.

The liturgy itself follows the same essential pattern as any eucharistic liturgy. All such liturgies have two parts: an opening section, usually, in Orthodoxy, called the synaxis, which culminates in a reading from the Gospels, and a concluding section, the Eucharist, which culminates in the consecration of the bread and wine, and communion by the congregation. Synaxis is a Greek word which literally means 'congregation', but the term has been borrowed by most of the Orthodox Churches. In English it is often called the Ministry of the Word, and the Ministry of the Word is what it says it is: a celebration of the Word of God in litanies, prayers, and readings from Scripture. In Orthodoxy, the climax of this first part of the liturgy is the Little (or Lesser) Entrance, when a copy of the Gospel Book is carried in procession round the church before the reading of the Epistle and Gospel. Following the reading from the Gospel, there may be a sermon, though this is often moved to the end of the liturgy. Unlike the Protestant tradition, the sermon does not play a major role in modern Orthodoxy (the situation in the early Church was quite different), and Orthodox sermons are usually short.

The second part of the liturgy, the Eucharist, normally begins with further litanies which lead to the Great Entrance. Like the Little Entrance, this involves a procession round the church, but this time it is not the Gospel Book that is taken in procession, but the bread and wine which, in due course, will be consecrated by the priest and changed, by the power of the Holy Spirit, into the body and blood of Christ. Both bread and wine have previously been prepared by the priest and deacon in the small room to the north of the sanctuary. There, before the liturgy begins, the priest cuts a loaf of leavened bread into small pieces, and arranges the individual pieces in a certain pattern on a round plate which stands on a central foot. In the west, this plate is called the paten; in the Byzantine east, it is called the discus or *diskos*. Wine and water are poured into the chalice by the deacon, everything is then covered with a veil, and paten and chalice are left on the table until the drama of the Great Entrance.

When the procession has reached the altar and the bread and wine have been placed upon it, there normally follows another litany and the recitation of the Creed. The priest then begins the rite which culminates in the consecration. He commences with prayers and thanksgiving, and these lead into the narrative of the Last Supper. This, in turn, is followed by a commemoration of Christ's death, burial, resurrection, ascension, enthronement on the right hand of God, and Second Coming. And then, at the climactic moment of this second part of the liturgy, the priest calls down the Holy Spirit onto the bread and wine that it may be transformed into the body and blood of the sacrificed Redeemer.

In Orthodoxy, this invocation of the Spirit is the true moment of consecration. Western churches generally have a different view. For those who believe that a real change takes place in the bread and wine, this change occurs at the moment the priest says the Words of Institution—'This is my body . . .' and 'This is my blood . . .'—but in the Orthodox world the change occurs a little later. This 'calling down' of the Holy Spirit is generally known as the *epiclesis* (or *epiklesis*) and it has a long, complicated, and controversial history both in east and west. But Orthodoxy once again relies on Tradition, and the Orthodox Tradition holds that when the priest prays that the Holy Spirit may descend upon the gifts of bread and wine (and, in some liturgies, on the congregation as well) and change them into the true body and blood of Christ, that is what happens and that is when it happens. There then follows a commemoration of all the members of the Church alive and dead (who comprise the mystical Body of Christ), a number of other prayers, and, finally, communion. The liturgy concludes with thanksgiving and a final blessing.

In all Orthodox Churches, Chalcedonian and non-Chalcedonian alike, the eucharistic liturgy follows this same basic pattern of synaxis and Eucharist, but the actual liturgies used naturally differ from

Church to Church. Sometimes there are overlaps; sometimes not. The Liturgy of Saint Basil, for example, exists in two forms. The shorter (and older) version is the normal liturgy of the non-Chalcedonian Coptic Orthodox Church; the longer (and later) form is used on ten days each year by the Chalcedonian Churches. Similarly, the Liturgy of Saint James (Jesus's brother) is an ancient liturgy found in both Greek and Syriac, and it came to be widely used in Egypt, Ethiopia, Armenia, Syria, and Georgia. But it is also used once a year in some of the Chalcedonian Churches on the anniversary of the death of Saint James (23 October), and at Jerusalem on the first Sunday after Christmas. The Liturgy of Saint Mark, on the other hand, was the traditional liturgy of the Church of Alexandria, and it began as an even more ancient local Egyptian rite. Some fragments of this liturgy have been discovered on pieces of papyrus. In a modified Coptic form, it is still used in the Coptic and Ethiopic Orthodox Churches, but not by any of the Chalcedonian branch.

The most common liturgy, and certainly the most widespread, is the Liturgy of Saint John Chrysostom. This is the normal eucharistic liturgy of the Chalcedonian Churches and is used on almost all Sundays of the year. Its actual connection with Saint John Chrysostom, the patriarch of Constantinople who died in 407, is disputed (though he certainly did not compose it), and it seems to have come into prominence in the Middle Ages when it was the liturgy used at Constantinople, the imperial capital. It assimilated large parts of the older liturgies of Saint James and Saint Mark, and by the thirteenth century had almost entirely superseded them. It also superseded the Liturgy of Saint Basil, which, earlier, had been the chief liturgy of Constantinople, but the liturgies of Saint Basil and Saint John Chrysostom are actually very similar.

The only other liturgy we need mention is the Liturgy of the Presanctified Gifts. This is used only on certain days in Lent and the first three days of Holy Week, and it differs from the other liturgies in being considerably shorter and having no consecration. Communion, for those who wish to receive it, is given from the consecrated bread and wine reserved from the previous Sunday, i.e., the Presanctified Gifts. The Mass of the Presanctified is also used in the Roman Catholic and Anglican Churches, but only on Good Friday.

Now that we are familiar with the Orthodox liturgy, let us turn our attention to the Orthodox priest. What does he look like? Much like any other human being, obviously, but a western visitor at an Orthodox liturgy might be struck by three things: the priest's beard, his headgear, and his vestments.

In the early Church, both eastern and western clerics wore beards, but the situation began to change in the fifth century. From then on, the west moved to a clean-shaven clergy (as we said in Chapter One, it seems that clean-shaven monks influenced the matter), and by the ninth century the question of beard versus no beard had become one of the numerous points of contention between the eastern and western Churches. Generally speaking, modern Orthodox priests are still bearded—sometimes dramatically so—and, traditionally, they also let their hair grow long and bind it up on top of their head where it is covered by some sort of headcovering. This is not always the case with Orthodox clergy in the west, but it is still very common elsewhere.

The question of headgear is no more than cultural. In the past, both in east and west, one did not appear in public without some sort of head covering, and, in the east, to appear in the presence of a superior with one's head uncovered constituted an unforgivable insult. The western practice tended to be the opposite: a man took off his hat to show respect. In the Orthodox tradition, the clergy still cover their heads, though how they do so depends on their own cultural traditions. In the Oriental Orthodox Churches, for example, monastic clergy wear a sort of close-fitting cap ornamented with crosses; in Greek and Russian Orthodoxy, priests wear a *kamelavchion* (or *kalymmavchion*, both spellings are used), a sort of black top-hat without a brim, though the Russian form differs slightly from the Greek. In the Orthodox Church in America we often see no hat at all. In the western Church, too, we see skull-caps and birettas, but whereas an ordinary Roman Catholic or Anglican priest celebrating the liturgy does so bare-headed, Orthodox priests sometimes have their hat on and sometimes off: it all depends on where they are in the course of the liturgy.

All clerical vestments, in fact, are no more than a fossilized remnant of the standard, everyday, walking-about-town dress of a late Roman gentleman. Only after the fourth century do we see the development of a specific priestly form of dress, when clerics retained the long tunics and cloaks which were being discarded by laymen in favour of shorter and more convenient garments. By the Middle Ages the form of most of the standard vestments had been fixed, and, naturally, there is a considerable overlap between east and west. A few vestments are uniquely eastern or western, but in general, and allowing for obvious cultural differences in, say, Ethiopian Orthodoxy, a Roman Catholic priest and an Orthodox priest at the altar have obviously been dressed by much the same tailor. As to the artistic designs on the materials, they tend, in Orthodoxy, to be more conservative and traditional (though the materials themselves may be sumptuous), and the contemporary and often very attractive abstract designs one sees on the vestments of some Roman Catholic and Anglican priests will not be seen in an Orthodox church.

Let us now turn our attention to what goes on in the church. We have already spoken of the Divine Liturgy and will speak of it again a little later, but if we are to begin at the beginning, we must begin with the moment a child becomes a member of the Church and a member of the Christian community. All else follows from that. If we have not been baptized into the Body of Christ, if we have not been raised with him into what Nicholas Cavasilas would call the new 'life in Christ', then what actually happens in church has little relevance. Let us therefore look at the sacraments of baptism and chrismation and see just how one becomes an Orthodox Christian.

9
BECOMING ORTHODOX

APART FROM A FEW Protestant denominations (the Salvation Army, for example), all Christian Churches see baptism as the fundamental sacrament by which a person is initiated into the Christian Church. But what do we mean by a sacrament? The word itself comes from the Latin term *sacramentum*, and *sacramentum*, in turn, was a translation of the Greek word *mystērion* or 'mystery'. The sacraments, therefore, were considered the means by which human beings participated in the 'mystery' of the Incarnation; and, conversely, the sacraments were the channels by which the grace of God, restored to us in the Incarnation, flowed into the faithful.

For more than a thousand years there was no formal list of sacraments. The recitation of the Lord's Prayer, if it were done devoutly, might be called a sacrament, and the same was true of the recitation of the Creed. Anything, in fact, which could communicate grace and render us more *sacer* or 'holy' might be termed a sacrament, and lists of sacraments ranged from two to thirty. The first time we find the formal list of seven, which, in the west, would become traditional—baptism, confirmation, eucharist, penance, marriage, holy orders, and extreme unction—is in an anonymous Latin document dating from about 1145 called the *Sententiae divinitatis* or 'Sentences on Divinity'. The same list then appeared in the work of Peter Lombard (d. 1160) and Thomas Aquinas (d. 1274), and was formally affirmed by the Council of Florence in 1439 and the Council of Trent in 1545–1563.

The Orthodox world had no such list, and it was not until the seventeenth century that Russian Orthodoxy borrowed the formal list of seven from Roman Catholicism. Other Orthodox Churches followed suit, but more for convenience than theological conviction. In theory, all seven sacraments were instituted either by Christ or his apostles, but in some cases this is hard to demonstrate. There is no doubt about baptism and the Eucharist (they are sometimes called the 'evangelical' or 'dominical' sacraments), but when we come to consider, say, unction or holy orders, the situation is much more dubious. But for Orthodoxy, as for Roman Catholicism, it is the Tradition of the Church that defines the nature and number of the sacraments, not the scholarly details of early Christian history.

Any sacrament is 'a visible form of invisible grace'. The definition is a good one, even if it has a curious history. The person responsible for its formulation seems to have been an eleventh-century theologian called Berengar of Tours who was actually condemned for heresy; but by a series of misunderstandings, the definition came to be attributed to Augustine of Hippo, who, in the west, was regarded as the very incarnation of dogmatic truth. Whatever its source, the expression is useful and accurate, and as Saint John Chrysostom pointed out, what we see and what we believe are two different things.[1] The visible form of baptism is a child taking a bath; the invisible grace is the washing off of sins. The visible form of the Eucharist is a very light snack of bread and wine; the invisible grace is our participation in the body and blood of Christ. Not all the sacraments are of equal importance, and not all apply to everyone. Baptism and the Eucharist are certainly pre-eminent and can apply to all. Holy orders and marriage apply only to some. The *Sententiae divinitatis*, in fact, specifically divided the seven into two groups: those which are common to all Christians (baptism, confirmation, eucharist, penance, and unction), and those which are not (holy orders and matrimony).

Apart from the sacraments, there are also things called sacramentals. The term is actually Roman Catholic, not Orthodox, but the idea is the same in both east and west. Sacramentals are a sort of semi-sacraments which also have a visible form and which also communicate invisible grace, but not quite in the same way or to the same extent as the sacraments. The blessing of the water for

---

1. John Chrysostom, *In epistolam I ad Corinthios, homilia* 7.1.

baptism is a sacramental; the blessing of the ring or rings in the marriage ceremony is a sacramental; saying grace at meals is a sacramental; the ritual of monastic profession is a sacramental; the burial service is a sacramental. And there are many others, but there is no formal or definitive list. If an action communicates grace and renders the actor or actors more 'holy', it may justly be called a sacramental.

In a certain sense, the sacraments have nothing to do with the priest, and they certainly have nothing to do with whether the priest is or is not a blatant sinner. In a long drawn out and violent controversy in the fourth and fifth centuries, a certain group of puritanical North African Christians—the Donatists—maintained that sacraments celebrated by ministers who were in a state of serious sin were invalid. Their rigorist views were rightly challenged first by Optatus, a fourth-century North African bishop, and then, more formidably, by Saint Augustine. Both Optatus and Augustine asserted that it is *God* who effects the sacraments, and the officiating priest or minister is no more than a channel. Saint John Chrysostom was of exactly the same opinion. It is the Father, Son, and Holy Spirit who act, he said: the priest simply 'lends his tongue and provides his hand.'[2] It is rather like someone dying of thirst in the desert. What they need is water, and whether the water be brought by someone who has just had a shower or someone who hasn't bathed for years is irrelevant. The latter may not smell too good, but the water he brings will save your life. And the mention of water brings us back to baptism.

In the Orthodox Church, baptism cannot be separated from what, in the west, is called confirmation and first communion. In this, Orthodoxy is at one with the practice of the early Church, and the early Fathers were unanimous in maintaining that in baptism four things happened. First, baptismal immersion, which was (and is) performed three times in the name of the three persons of the Trinity, symbolized a candidate's dying and rising with Christ. It also symbolized the three days Christ spent in the tomb, and the candidate's final 'resurrection' from the baptismal water was a resurrection to a new life in Christ. Secondly, in baptism the candidate

2. Idem, *In Joannem, homilia* 86.4.

formally and willingly accepted Christ as his or her personal Saviour. In the case of an infant, this acceptance was (and is) done vicariously by the godparents. Thirdly, in the course of baptismal immersion, one's sins—original and otherwise—are washed away. And fourthly, anointing with oil and laying on of hands (something we'll talk about in a moment) symbolizes the communication of the grace of the Holy Spirit.

The death and resurrection symbolism of baptism demands that baptismal immersion should be total immersion, and that is the invariable practice of almost all the Orthodox Churches. A very few Orthodox Churches in the west use the western rite of *affusion*, in which the water is poured only on the head of the child, but this is not normal Orthodox practice. We are 'buried' in the waters as Christ was buried in the tomb, and we rise from the waters as he also rose. This applies both to children and adults, though if there are health problems, the priest will simply substitute affusion. The purpose of baptism is not infanticide. Sometimes, depending on the Church, an infant is not actually plunged into the baptismal water. In some traditions, for example, the priest places a receptacle on the floor or a table, holds the child in his left arm, and pours water over the whole of the child's body. But here, too, it is done three times, from feet to head, and the essential symbolism of the ancient rite is thereby preserved. Baptism is normally performed by a priest or bishop, though in an emergency it can be performed by any baptized Christian, Orthodox or otherwise. But in the Orthodox tradition (unlike Roman Catholicism), it cannot be performed by a person who has not himself or herself been baptized.

Immersion, however, is only one part of the baptismal rite. The complete ritual involves exorcisms (four of them in Greek Orthodoxy), a formal renunciation of Satan, a profession of faith, the blessing of the water and oil, anointing, immersion, chrismation, a reading from the Epistles and Gospel, symbolic tonsure (just a few hairs are cut to symbolize the candidate being dedicated to God), first communion, and final dismissal by the officiating priest. What infants cannot do is done on their behalf by their godparents, and in the Orthodox tradition, the relationship of child and godparents is much closer and much more important than it often is in the west. Of the names given to the child at baptism (or, more precisely, at a naming service associated with baptism), one will be the name of a saint, and a person's name day—which is more important than one's actual birthday—is the day of the feast of the saint. A girl called Melanie, for example, would celebrate her name day on 31 December; a boy called John on any one of a variety of days, depending on which Saint John we're talking about. Converts to Orthodoxy also take a baptismal name, although, as we shall see, they may not need to be baptized.

As we said a moment ago, baptism involves more than simple immersion, and one of the things it involves is chrismation, which is a form of anointing. But what is chrismation, what part does it play in the ceremony, and how does it differ from the other anointing which precedes immersion?

For the first anointing, the priest blesses the holy oil (it is simply very pure olive oil with a variety of added perfumes) and then both priest and godparent—godfather or godmother—anoint various parts of the candidate's body from the head to the feet. To some extent, this first anointing echoes the practice of ancient athletes who anointed themselves before competition, and if, with Saint Paul and the author of the letter to the Hebrews, we may see the Christian life as a sort of spiritual athletics, anointing at baptism is a psychological preparation for the trials that lie ahead.

Chrismation is different. First of all, the oil used—chrism—is not blessed by the priest, but by the patriarch of an autocephalous Church. Until recently, in the Chalcedonian tradition, it was blessed by the Ecumenical Patriarch, but this is no longer considered necessary. Nevertheless, a small number of autocephalous Orthodox Churches still prefer to use chrism blessed by the Ecumenical Patriarch as a sign of Orthodox union and loyalty to the Ecumenical Patriarchate.

Secondly, whereas the initial anointing by priest and godparent is considered to be part of the sacrament of baptism, the anointing which occurs at chrismation, after the baptismal immersion, is a sacrament in its own right. In the west, it is called confirmation, and the name tells us what it does. The Latin verb *confirmare* means 'to strengthen' or 'reinforce', and that is exactly what happens: the grace which comes with baptismal immersion is here strengthened or reinforced, and with chrismation/confirmation, the child (or adult) receives the full gift of the Holy Spirit. As we might expect, the way in which chrismation is carried out is different in the Chalcedonian and non-Chalcedonian Churches, but the principle and symbolism are identical. In Byzantine—Greek, Russian, and Slav—Orthodoxy, the candidate is chrismated with the sign of the cross on the forehead, eyes, nostrils, mouth, ears, chest, hands, and feet: thirteen places in all. In the Coptic Orthodox tradition, there are thirty-six anointings: eight on the head, two on the front of the body, two on the back, twelve on the arms, and twelve on the legs.

In the Roman Catholic and Anglican/Episcopalian west, baptismal immersion and confirmation became separated. This was simply for practical, not theological, reasons, and followed from the fact that in the early Church it was the responsibility of the bishop alone—not the local priest— both to baptize and confirm new Christians. But as the number of new Christians increased, especially from the fourth century onwards, it became logistically impossible for a single bishop to fulfil all the demands, and east and west solved the problem in different ways.

In the east, as we have seen, both baptism and chrismation were delegated by the bishop to the local priest. In the west, only the rite of baptism was so delegated, and confirmation remained the prerogative of the bishop. And since bishops were busy people and dioceses were large, it was never possible for bishops to attend all baptisms. Normally, therefore, there was an interval of time between baptism and confirmation, though the length of the interval varied considerably. It might be days, it might be years, and in the Middle Ages confirmation was conferred very erratically. By the later Middle Ages, however, it had become customary for the rite to be performed as soon as possible after a child's seventh birthday, but since 1971 a later age is more usual. Roman Catholicism still uses chrism in confirmation; in Anglicanism its use was dropped in 1549, but has since been reintroduced as optional in recent liturgical reforms.

How, then, does all this apply to converts to Orthodoxy? Do they need to be baptized and chrismated? The general principle is that Christian sacramental baptism is not repeated, but chrismation may well be required. In other words, if Roman Catholics or Anglicans-Episcopalians decide to convert to Orthodoxy, the Orthodox Church will normally (though not always) recognize the validity of their baptism. The situation is trickier in the case of members of the Protestant denominations. Strictly speaking, if baptism is *not* regarded as a sacrament by the convert's original church, then it should be repeated *as* a sacrament, but it is not always quite clear whether the rite is regarded as sacramental or not. The question must therefore be discussed between the prospective convert and the local Orthodox priest or bishop.

Chrismation is the usual way by which a convert is accepted into the Orthodox tradition, but practices vary with the different autocephalous Churches. Russian Orthodoxy, for example, generally recognizes the validity of Roman Catholic confirmation because (as we saw above) it retains the use of chrism and sacramental anointing. The Russian Orthodox Church, therefore, will often, though not always, receive Roman Catholic converts simply by a profession of faith. The other Chalcedonian Churches normally require chrismation, and in the case of non-Roman Catholic Christians, this is regularly the case. Chrismation is also normally required by the Oriental Orthodox Churches, though once again, the matter must be discussed between convert, priest, and bishop.

The point is that there really are no formulae in these matters. Non-Christians, as we might expect, are always received into Orthodoxy by both baptism and chrismation, but, when dealing with Christians, we cannot simply look down a list under 'From non-Orthodox Church X to Orthodox Church Y' and read the instructions. That may have been the case once, but it is not so now. Much depends on the disposition of the converts and what they really believe in their heart. Do they honestly believe that, in baptism, whether by total immersion or not, their sins were washed away and that they were raised up into a new life in Christ? Do they honestly believe that in Anglican confirmation, without anointing, they truly received the fullness of the gift of the Holy Spirit? And so on. The Orthodox Church in America wisely lays great stress on this question of interior disposition, but it is not difficult to find other Orthodox Churches—especially those with strong ties to their homelands—being unnecessarily sticky and unpleasantly pharisaic.

On the other hand, the Orthodox Church does have a rite of conditional performance of a sacrament. If converts are not sure whether or how they were baptized, the priest may rebaptize them, but he will precede the baptismal rite by saying 'If not yet baptized, be baptized now. . .'. The same is true of chrismation. But in all such matters, full and honest discussion is essential, and if either convert or priest is unsure, then they should consult the bishop. That's what bishops are for, and there's nothing like passing the theological buck.

Baptism and confirmation are then followed by first communion, and in the Orthodox world this is as easy for a baby as it is for an adult. But to understand why, we need to examine the actual practice of holy communion in a little more detail, and that is a matter for a later chapter.

For the moment, let us return to baptism. Nowadays, save for adult non-Christians converting to Orthodoxy (something of more consequence in the east than in the west), baptism usually means infant baptism. It is true, says the Church, that in baptismal immersion the infant's sins are washed away, and it is equally true that in chrismation or confirmation, the same infant receives the grace of the Holy Spirit. But infants still sin. So do adults, sometimes quite spectacularly. How, then, do we deal with the problem of post-baptismal sin? How can we prevent ourselves from meeting death and our Maker utterly corrupted by dozens of years of continual sinning and worthy only of well-deserved condemnation? The answer lies in the sacrament of confession and repentance which, in the early Church, was sometimes referred to as 'second baptism'. Its history is interesting.

The penitential system dates back to at least the fourth century, and in the works of the three fourth-century Cappadocian Fathers—Basil the Great, Gregory of Nazianzus, and Gregory of Nyssa—there is a great deal of material on the grievous nature of sin and the length and severity of penance. Unlike Roman Catholicism, however, the Orthodox Churches have never made a formal distinction between mortal sin (which is so serious that it cuts one off entirely from the grace of God) and venial sin (which is anything less), but the Church naturally distinguishes between grave sins, such as premeditated murder, and trifling sins, such as having one too many beers or an extra helping of dessert. Sin, however, is sin, and being a sinner is rather like being pregnant: you either are or you aren't. You can't be a little bit pregnant. And since sin—post-baptismal sin—was an unavoidable reality for everyone save Christ, the Church had to do something about it. What it did was to institute penance, but penance in the early Church was very different from what it is today.

For a start, it was public. Sinners had to ask for penance from the bishop, and if it were granted, they were immediately excluded from receiving communion, and had to undergo a gruelling course of prayer, fasting, and almsgiving for as long as the bishop thought necessary. For serious sins this could last for years. And even when it was all over and one had been publicly restored to communion, one had to spend the rest of one's days in chastity and continence, whether one were married or not.

Furthermore, this penitential 'second baptism', like the first baptism, could be performed only once. It was therefore expedient to delay it as long as possible, preferably to the very end of one's life, though this called for delicate timing. You could never be sure when you were going to have a heart attack or be run down by a chariot.

Such a system was just too severe to last, and in the late sixth century it began to break down. Penance changed from being public to private; it could be repeated; and the demand for life-long continence was quietly forgotten. The actual penances, however, could still be long-lasting and severe, but this too changed with changing times. By the Middle Ages, the penitential system was much as it is today, both in east and west, with private confession, formal absolution, and a token penance.

In the Orthodox Church there was always a tendency to emphasize repentance rather than penance, and it was also emphasized that forgiveness was a matter between the penitent and God. Furthermore, hardly any of the early Fathers maintain that formal sacramental absolution is necessary, and if formal sacramental absolution is not necessary, it is not necessary to confess to a priest. Why should it be? Only God truly knows the heart of the penitent, and only God can forgive sins. From the Middle Ages onwards, it was not unusual for Orthodox Christians to confess to non-ordained monks, and, in Russia, confession to a *starets* or spiritual father was common. We shall say much more about these *startsy* (the plural of *starets*) in Chapter Eleven. Confession could also be made to a nun or even to a saintly lay-person, male or female, though this was rare. Nowadays it is the invariable practice for Orthodox laity to confess to a priest. The situation is reflected in the formula generally used in Orthodoxy for absolution. The person to whom the penitent has confessed does not normally say 'I absolve you', but 'May God absolve you'—the contrast, in theological jargon, is between an *indicative* and *precatory* formula—though in the eighteenth century, the Latin version with 'I absolve you' was adopted by Russian Orthodoxy.

But if sacramental absolution is not necessary, is it necessary to confess to anyone at all? The answer, theologically, is No. If you wish to talk to God, talk to God. If God recognizes your repentance and forgives you, you are forgiven, and that is all there is to it. As we said above, Orthodoxy, unlike Roman Catholicism, does not distinguish mortal sins from venial sins, and that is important. In Roman Catholic teaching, if one is consciously in a state of mortal sin (and one cannot be in a state of mortal sin without being conscious of it), and if one dies before the sin has been confessed to a priest, then one dies wholly without grace and must, inevitably, go to hell. If, on the other hand, one is not in a state of mortal sin, one need not actually go to confession ever. In Roman Catholic teaching, the guilt of those who die in venial sin is forgiven immediately after death by God, though the punishment for having committed the sins must be suffered in purgatory. It's rather like a youngster throwing a stone through a neighbour's window. The aggrieved neighbour may like the boy (or girl), realize that it was no more than a prank, dare, or accident, and forgive him for having thrown the stone—but he will still require him to contribute something from his weekly allowance to pay for the broken glass. Even purgatorial pain, however, may be avoided by means of an indulgence, but the doctrine of indulgences must be left for a text-book on Roman Catholicism. They play no part in Orthodox Christianity.

This distinction between guilt (which is forgiven) and punishment (which is still to be endured) is not accepted by any of the Orthodox Churches. If God forgives a sin, he forgives the whole of the sin, and once the sin has been wholly forgiven, there is nothing left to deserve punishment. Nor does Orthodoxy accept the doctrine of purgatory—a matter we discussed in Chapter Seven.

Illustration 1

Christ as the Pantocrator, Christ the 'All-Sovereign' or 'Ruler of All'. This Greek icon from the second half of the nineteenth century is fully described on page 62.

Location: Private collection.

Photo: Terryl N. Kinder.

Illustration 2

Mary as Theotokos Hodegetria, 'the God-bearer Showing the Way'. The Way (to salvation) is Christ, and Mary points to him with her right hand. This is a late twentieth-century Greek icon and is fully described on page 67.

Location: Private collection.

Photo: Terryl N. Kinder.

Illustration 3

A late nineteenth-century Russian icon of Saint Nicholas the Wonderworker. Nicholas was a fourth-century bishop of Myra—now Mugla in south-western Turkey—and over the course of the centuries he would be transformed into Santa Claus. The icon is fully described on pages 69–70.

Location: Private collection.

Photo: Terryl N. Kinder.

Illustration 4

A copy of a famous icon by the Russian iconographer Andrei Rublev (c.1370–1430). The Trinity is represented by the three angels who visited Abraham at Mamre (Genesis 18:1-8). It is sometimes called the Old Testament Trinity. The original is now in the Tretyakov Gallery in Moscow; this is a contemporary copy by the American iconographer Eileen McGuckin.

Icon by Eileen McGuckin.

Location: The Icon Studio, New York <www.sgtt.org>

Photo: Eileen McGuckin.

Illustration 5

Icon of the archangel Michael. He holds in his right hand the rod of a messenger—in this case an archangelic messenger—and in his left hand he holds a jewelled orb in which are three Greek letters. They are the initial letters of 'Christ the Righteous Judge'. The way in which Michael appears in this contemporary icon is wholly traditional.

Icon by Eileen McGuckin.

Location: The Icon Studio, New York <www.sgtt.org>

Photo: Eileen McGuckin.

Illustration 6

Icon of the prophet Elijah by Fotis Kontoglou (1896–1965). Kontoglou was a major figure in Greek icon-painting, and this icon—which is fully described on page 71—is a superb example of his work.

Location: Private collection.

Photo: Terryl N. Kinder.

Furthermore, since Orthodoxy does not make the formal distinction between mortal and venial sin, the idea that unconfessed mortal sin leads ineluctably to hell can have no place in the Orthodox tradition. *Any* sin may lead to hell if that is what God wills, but, conversely, any sin may be forgiven by God if the sinner is truly repentant—which leads us back to the point we were making earlier. From a theoretical and theological point of view, Orthodox Christians do not need to make sacramental confession ever, and they do not need to receive sacramental absolution. But theory and practice are not the same, and the Orthodox Church, like the Roman Catholic Church, strongly advises regular confession on the part of its members. Some Orthodox jurisdictions—the Copts, for example—demand it, and in Russian Orthodoxy, confession and absolution are normally required before a person can take communion. Confession is, after all, a sacrament, and the sacraments are channels of grace. What does this mean?

It means that if an Orthodox Christian decides to go to confession, he or she is doing something more than making a visit to a psychological counsellor, social worker, or amateur psychiatrist. True, an experienced confessor can be an invaluable help, and confession may be psychologically cathartic, but there is more to it than that. The grace which comes through the sacrament of repentance may be presumed to bring about an interior change in a person—provided, of course, the person concerned is open to such change. True repentance itself is no more than a change of heart, but a true change of heart may not be possible without help. It is the simplest thing in the world to vow to go on diet twenty minutes after over-eating at Christmas dinner; it is quite another thing to keep to one's resolution.

On the other hand, neither grace nor its results are predictable. If we ask God for grace, we might well get it; but when God gives us his grace, he gives us what we *need*, not necessarily what we *want*. Indeed, the two are sometimes quite opposite, and it is a dangerous thing to ask for grace. It demands courage and responsibility. Too often we think of grace as gentle, cosy, warm, fluffy, and nice. It might, however, come as a whirlwind, and to be on the receiving end of grace can be very uncomfortable. Ask Saul of Tarsus. Grace is effective, we may be sure of that, but we human beings are often so obtuse, bloody-minded, and stiff-necked, that little short of a bomb up our backsides will have much effect. If, then, we truly ask God for help in the sacrament of repentance, we may hope to receive that help. We may not, however, receive it in the way we ourselves would like. Grace may come as honey to the soul, as balm to Gilead; it may also come as a flame of fire.

The actual practice of the sacrament follows much the same pattern in all the Orthodox Churches. There is no confessional box such as we used to find (and can still find) in Roman Catholic churches, and confession may take place at any convenient location in the church. Sometimes there is a special room set aside for confession such as we also find nowadays in some Roman Catholic churches, for since 1973 Roman Catholicism—like Orthodoxy—has emphasized the importance of open dialogue between confessor and penitent. In both Churches, the seal of the confessional is absolute: what is said to the priest remains with the priest, and he can never ever, under any circumstances, reveal the content of a sacramental confession.

The rite usually begins with the confessor asserting that he is merely a witness to the confession (the penitent is confessing to Christ himself), and then, after the confession, he may ask questions and give advice. Following that, the penitent bows his or her head or kneels, the priest places his stole over the penitent's head, lays his hand on the stole (or makes the sign of the cross on it), and asks God for absolution. A token penance may be given, but that is not common. The precise details of the rite vary with the different Orthodox Churches—in Coptic Orthodoxy, for example, the priest does not place his stole on the head of the penitent, but touches his or her head with a cross—but the general principles remain constant.

How often one goes to confession is a personal matter. Some people go frequently; some do not. In general, it is rare for Orthodox Christians to confess as regularly as Roman Catholic Christians, but some Orthodox Churches—and, indeed, some priests—are more insistent than others. The sacrament is there: whether, when, and how we avail ourselves of it is up to us.

Let us now turn our attention to another sacrament, that of marriage. After all, both baptism and chrismation assume that there is someone there to be baptized and chrismated, and that usually means babies. And since babies are normally produced by the pleasurable process of human reproduction, we cannot deal with marriage without dealing with sex. That will be the subject of our next chapter. But since neither marriage nor sex are chosen by all, we must also say something about Orthodox ordination and the question of clerical celibacy.

10

SEX, MARRIAGE, AND CELIBACY

AS WE MIGHT EXPECT, Orthodoxy maintains the early and traditional stand of the Christian Church that sexual intercourse should be confined to marriage. That this, in practice, is frequently not the case is neither here nor there. Attitudes to the question differ radically from culture to culture, and, within any one culture, they may differ even more radically between urban and rural areas. But that, as we have said, is beside the point. Human beings have been sinning since the Garden of Eden, the Church recognizes the fact, and Orthodoxy, as we have just seen, has ways of dealing with the problem of post-baptismal sin.

The Orthodox Church prefers that Orthodox Christians marry other Orthodox Christians, but does not insist upon it. There is nothing peculiar about this, and the same preference exists in most other religions, Christian and non-Christian alike. Sometimes a person of one faith *cannot* legally marry a person who is not of that faith—Islam is a good example—but that is not the Orthodox way. If, however, the non-Orthodox is not a Christian, then Orthodoxy requires that he or she be baptized before being married in an Orthodox church. But if the non-Orthodox person is Christian, and has been baptized in the name of the Father, Son, and Holy Spirit,[1] then there is no problem. Marriage to an Orthodox Christian

---

1. Acts 2:38, 10:48, and 19:5 appear to testify to baptism 'in the name of Jesus Christ' or 'in the name of the Lord Jesus', but even if this did indeed occur (and that is not certain), a modern baptism using this formula is not considered valid by any of the Orthodox churches.

in an Orthodox church, however, does not automatically make the non-Orthodox spouse Orthodox. The non-Orthodox husband or wife still cannot receive Holy Communion or any of the other sacraments, and they cannot be accorded an Orthodox funeral. As we saw in the last chapter, to become Orthodox, the non-Orthodox partner must usually be chrismated.

So what if two people—one Orthodox and one not—decide to marry in a non-Orthodox church, Anglican, Catholic, Methodist, or whatever? Generally speaking, Orthodoxy will not recognize the validity of the marriage, and, in most Orthodox Churches, the Orthodox bride or groom's full sacramental membership of the Orthodox Church goes into a sort of holding pattern until the marriage has been celebrated once again in an Orthodox church. During the intervening period, the unorthodoxly-married Orthodox cannot receive any of the Orthodox sacraments. Whether this is just or, indeed, particularly Christian is another matter, but it is the Tradition of the Church. We might also note that until very recently the Chalcedonian and non-Chalcedonian Churches did not recognize the validity of each other's marriages. It was not until the year 2000 that Syrian Orthodox, Coptic Orthodox, and Greek Orthodox agreed to such mutual recognition, but it is still not universal.[2]

In the case of mixed marriages—Orthodox to non-Orthodox—the Orthodox Church requires from the husband and wife an undertaking to bring up their children within the Orthodox tradition. Some Orthodox Churches require this undertaking in writing; some ask only for a verbal declaration.

Same-sex marriages cannot take place in Orthodoxy, and if they have been performed in another, non-Orthodox church, their validity is not recognized. Many Orthodox, especially in North America, are prepared to recognize the legality of civil unions, in which both partners have appropriate legal rights and responsibilities, but no Orthodox priest will bless a same-sex marriage. Indeed, the attitude of Orthodoxy to homosexuality in general tends to be conservative,

---

2. The Fourth Meeting of the Heads of the Oriental Orthodox Churches in the Middle East, Cairo, March 15-17, 2001, §II.3. The document is available on the Internet at http://www.copticpope.org/news/The_Forth (sic)_Meeting/body_the_forth_meeting.html.

and, some would say, old-fashioned, though the advice given to a homosexual couple by an old priest in a small Middle Eastern town may well differ from the advice given to a similar couple by a young priest in Chicago. Orthodoxy, however, would not call itself old-fashioned in this matter, but simply traditional. It maintains the principles found in certain passages in the New Testament[3] which undoubtedly regard homosexuality as a serious sin, and the Orthodox Churches would agree with the view expressed at the 1998 Lambeth Conference by Archbishop George Carey of the Church of England. The archbishop saw 'no room in Holy Scripture or the entire Christian tradition for any sexual activity outside matrimony of husband and wife.'[4] At the same conference the Anglican bishops voted 526 to 70, with 45 abstentions, that homosexuality is 'incompatible with Scripture'.[5] Orthodoxy would agree.

On the other hand, the Lambeth Conference recognized that there were balanced and healthy people of true homosexual orientation, and emphasized that if gays and lesbians were baptized, believing, and faithful Christians, then—regardless of their sexual orientation—they are full members of the mystical Body of Christ. But the bishops could not advise either the legitimizing or blessing of same-sex unions, and it could not support the ordination of those involved in such unions. Once again, Orthodoxy would agree, but the open and important discussion of the question which occurred at Lambeth, and which has occurred elsewhere, especially in the churches of the Protestant family, has not yet occurred in Orthodoxy. That is a pity, for gays and lesbians are obviously to be found within the Orthodox community just as in any community, and recent developments in Greece have revealed an indefensible hypocrisy in this matter which does no credit whatever either to Orthodoxy in general or to Greek Orthodoxy in particular. In 2005 the Greek Orthodox Church was rocked by a number of serious scandals, one of which involved rampant homosexual activities—

---

3. Primarily Romans 1:26-27, 1 Corinthians 6:9-10, and 1 Timothy 1:9-10. There are also a number of relevant passages in the Old Testament.
4. See *Christianity Today* for 7 September 1998, available on the Internet at http://www/christianitytoday.com/ct/8ta/8ta032.html.
5. *Ibid.*

activities which, in theory, the Church condemned—within its highest echelons. This, clearly, demands open investigation and discussion, though we have heard, regrettably, little of either. Questions of sex and sexuality are very much in the public eye at the moment—they cannot and must not be ignored—but, for the most part, the Orthodox Church has avoided any serious discussion of the matter, and can too easily be likened to an Orthodox ostrich. Christianity, in theory, regards all human beings as images of God, and we must remember that Jesus Christ did not come into this world to call the righteous to repentance. He also had a number of dubious friends—tax-collectors and sinners[6]—though the Christian Church sometimes finds that fact unpleasantly uncomfortable.

Within marriage, then, sexual activity is right and proper, but should sexual activity always have the potential for pregnancy and childbirth? Putting it another way, what does Orthodoxy have to say about birth control? In the past, artificial means of birth control were strongly condemned, though there has never been any authoritative statement on the matter such as we find in Roman Catholicism. Nowadays the situation is different, and, in general, Orthodoxy recognizes that sex plays a vital role in human relationships, and that it does not exist only for the purpose of procreation. As a consequence, the decision whether or not to use contraceptives is usually left to individual couples. If they wish to consult their parish priest or spiritual advisor on the matter, they may do so, though it must be admitted that not all parish priests or spiritual advisors are up to the task. They may also expect to get different answers from, say, a Coptic Orthodox priest and a priest of the Orthodox Church in America. But an unwanted child can all too often remain unwanted, and there is not the slightest doubt that contraception in any form can be vital for a happy and fulfilling relationship.

Abortion, on the other hand, is not contraception, and the Orthodox Churches regard abortion as murder. This, indeed, was the ruling of a number of early Church councils, though modern Orthodoxy tacitly condones abortion if the life of the mother is at

---

6. See Mt 9:10-13, and synoptic parallels. First-century tax-collectors were hated as rapacious individuals who lined their own pockets as well as the pockets of the equally hated government.

stake. On the other hand, there are many Orthodox women who have abortions for other reasons, though the availability of the procedure varies widely from country to country. All Orthodox Churches regard this as a grievous sin—they can hardly do other—and an Orthodox priest will not knowingly allow a woman who has chosen to have an abortion to receive Holy Communion. The question of her confession and restoration to full sacramental membership of her church is a matter for discussion between the woman and her parish priest. Personal situations differ dramatically, and there is no universal formula. But there has been little discussion of the question within the Orthodox tradition, even though such discussion was called for in 1990 by the Joint Commission for the Reunification of the Chalcedonian and non-Chalcedonian Churches. And so far as I am aware, there has been no discussion at all of such modern medical developments as Emergency Contraceptive Pills (ECPs), sometimes called 'morning-after pills', which some would regard as abortifacients.

The question of whether an unmarried mother (a mother who was never married, not a mother who has been divorced) may receive Holy Communion is delicate, and the answer may differ not only from Church to Church—the Russians, for example, may not say the same thing as the Copts—but from parish to parish, and even from priest to priest. In general, if an unwed mother recognizes that what she willingly did was contrary to the teachings of the Church, if she is truly sorry for having done it and has asked God for forgiveness, and if she is determined not to do it again, then there can be little objection to her receiving Communion. If, on the other hand, she sees nothing at all wrong with her actions and is perfectly happy with her situation, it would be logical for the Church to refuse her Communion. It is true that one might find hard-liners in any Church who would refuse her Communion under any circumstances, but such an attitude could hardly be called Christian.

In the Orthodox tradition, marriage, as we have said, is a sacrament. That is to say, it is not regarded simply as a sociological convenience for legitimizing one's children or reducing one's taxes. It is also just as much a gift of the Holy Spirit as celibacy, and it can demand just as much hard work and dedication. In the past, the marriage ceremony comprised two separate rituals held at different times, but the two rituals are now performed successively in the course of a single service. The first part of the rite is the Betrothal or Engagement, when the priest blesses the rings and places them on the fingers of bride and groom. In some parts of Europe and much of the Christian east, the ring is worn on the right hand; in other parts of Europe and in North America, it is usually worn on the left hand. It's simply a matter of custom. The exchange of rings is a symbol of the mutual commitment and free mutual consent of the parties involved.

The second part of the ceremony is the Crowning. It begins with prayers and proceeds to the point when the priest takes the hands of bride and groom and prays that Christ may join them together, and, by the grace of his Holy Spirit, empower them to live a Christian life pleasing to God. The bride and groom are then crowned either with crowns or wreaths (the custom differs in the different Churches), and at the end of the service the newly-married couple share a cup of wine which symbolizes that sharing which is a necessary and essential part of any successful marriage. It is the 'common cup of joys and sorrows', but it is not the wine of Holy Communion. Bride and groom are normally expected to have received Holy Communion before the day of their wedding. The priest then leads the couple three times round the sacramental table (here acting as a temporary altar) in a procession called the Dance of Isaiah, and the ceremony ends with the removal of the crowns or wreaths, a final blessing, and a tumultuous scene when all assembled wish the newly-married couple many years of blessings. Exactly when the ceremony becomes sacramental is not quite clear. Some theologians consider it to be the moment when the priest takes the hands of the bride and groom and prays that they may be empowered to live a Christian life. Others consider it to be the moment of crowning. The question is technical and irrelevant: at the end of the ceremony, the couple are sacramentally married, and that is what counts. Intriguing questions such as whether a bride is truly married if the groom has a heart-attack and dies just before being crowned can safely be left to the local bishop. Send him an e-mail and let him worry about it.

There are, of course, variations in the details of the marriage ceremony depending on which of the Orthodox Churches we're talking about, but, in general, they all follow much the same pattern.

As to who can marry whom, Orthodoxy, like the other Christian Churches, forbids the marriage of close relatives. Just who is considered a close relative varies, again, from Church to Church, and if two people who want to get married are related in any way, they should check out the situation with their local priest or bishop. In general, Orthodoxy does not permit parents to marry their children, foster-parents to marry their foster-children, brothers to marry sisters, brothers-in-law to marry sisters-in-law, aunts and uncles to marry nieces and nephews, and first cousins to marry first cousins. These are fairly obvious, and the number of parents (or grandparents) wishing to marry their children (or grandchildren) is, I suspect, limited. But Orthodoxy also forbids godparents from marrying either their godchildren or the parents of their godchildren, even though there may be no blood relationship at all.

Not every marriage is a success. Many fail. Indeed, it is rare in North America to find people who do not have at least one divorce under their belt. The situation differs in other countries, and, again, in rural and urban areas, but marriage breakdown is not uncommon and Orthodoxy acknowledges the fact. It may regret divorce, but it recognizes its reality. In the past, and in theory, the Orthodox Churches maintained the New Testament principle, reiterated by a number of Church councils, that the only reason for divorce was adultery. Nowadays, and in practice, most of the Chalcedonian Orthodox Churches normally accept the decision of the state in the matter. That is to say, if a couple is granted a civil divorce, the Church will usually accept the legal decision and issue its own ecclesiastical decree dissolving the marriage. This is not automatic—the case must still be examined by an ecclesiastical court—but it is rare to withhold the ecclesiastical decree. Divorce may be a result of our fallen human condition and it may be regrettable, but it is often a very terrible experience, and the Orthodox Church, rightly, does not wish to cause its members further suffering. If a marriage has really ceased to be a reality, the Church will recognize the fact and act appropriately. Giving people a second chance can be a true and real blessing.

In the Christian east, especially for Orthodox Christians living in Muslim countries, the situation can be much more complicated, and the attitude to divorce of the Coptic Orthodox Church shows how views can change. In the nineteenth century, adultery was still seen as the fundamental reason for divorce, but the Church also acknowledged other reasons: life imprisonment, for example, or conversion to another religion (Islam being the obvious choice). In 1938 a variety of other causes were added to these, ranging from impotence to incompatibility, but in 1945 the Coptic Pope Macarius III denounced the 1938 code as being too liberal, and, in accordance with the Gospels, the Holy Synod restricted the grounds for divorce to adultery alone. This restriction was confirmed by Pope Cyril VI in 1962 and again by Pope Shenouda III in 1971. Pope Shenouda also issued a decree which prohibited a woman who had been divorced for adultery from remarrying in an Orthodox church. But what has been changed once may be changed again, and the story may not yet be finished.

Although, as we have just seen, the legal regulations for divorce and remarriage differ in different countries, if an ecclesiastical divorce has been granted, a man or woman may remarry in an Orthodox church. They may not remarry in church on the basis of a civil divorce alone. There is, in theory, a slightly different form of wedding ceremony for a second marriage—it has less joy and more penitence—but it is not always used. If this second marriage breaks down, the parties involved may divorce a second time, and if the divorce is recognized by the ecclesiastical authorities, the individuals concerned may marry for a third time in an Orthodox church. But that's it. Orthodoxy does not approve of serial monogamy, and if you want to marry four or more men or women in succession, you'll have to do so in another church or in a series of civil ceremonies.

We might add here that the Roman Catholic principle of annulment normally plays no part in Orthodoxy. The difference between divorce and annulment is simple. Divorce recognizes that a valid, sacramental marriage once existed, but now, for various reasons, has ceased to exist. There is no longer a flow of grace. Annulment seeks to demonstrate that, despite cohabitation, the sharing of bed and board, and (often) the procreation of children, a valid, sacramental marriage never existed from the start, and that the parties involved were never truly married (in a sacramental sense) in the first place. Roman Catholicism, therefore, will not recognize an Orthodox divorce. Indeed, it will not recognize any divorce, save for the unusual case of the so-called 'Pauline Privilege'.[7] It follows, then, that if an Orthodox Christian has been married sacramentally in an Orthodox rite, has then divorced, converted to Roman Catholicism, and now wishes to remarry in a Roman Catholic church, he or she would first need to have the previous marriage annulled. Whether this is sensible, just, or scriptural is a matter of dispute.

So what happens if a Roman Catholic has been granted a civil divorce, but not an annulment, and wishes to marry an Orthodox Christian in an Orthodox ceremony? From a Roman Catholic point of view, the person is still married, but most Orthodox jurisdictions will approve the civil divorce and permit remarriage in an Orthodox church. There are, however, some Orthodox jurisdictions which may require a decree of annulment, and any men or women who find themselves in this situation will need to discuss the question with their local Orthodox priest or bishop.

Let us now turn to the question of marriage and the priesthood. As most people are aware, Roman Catholicism insists on a celibate priesthood, though this insistence is proving a seriously divisive factor in the Roman Catholic Church of today. Orthodoxy does not insist on celibacy, but willingly recognizes that it is a particular calling for some people. Orthodox clergy may be married or unmarried, though there are certain rules which apply. Orthodoxy, like Roman Catholicism and Anglicanism, recognizes Major Orders and Minor Orders. Major Orders are subdeacon, deacon, priest, and bishop. The only important Minor Order is that of reader, though 'chanter' would be a better term since no Orthodox liturgy is ever said. A reader is authorized by the bishop to read the Epistle and certain other biblical passages, but not the Gospel, which can be read only by a deacon, priest, or bishop. Subdeacons can do rather more than readers and rather less than deacons, but the details need not concern us.[8]

---

7. This is based on 1 Corinthians 7:15. If two non-Christians are married and one of them decides to convert to Christianity, and if the non-Christian spouse then either wishes to separate or prevents (or seriously hinders) the new convert from practising his or her faith, the two may separate and the new Christian may contract a new marriage. The Pauline Privilege is set forth in the Roman Catholic *Codex Iuris Canonici* (1983), canons 1143-1149.

8. In the Roman Catholic Church the subdiaconate was suppressed in 1972. In the Anglican Church it can still be found in a few missionary dioceses.

The relation of all this to marriage is that, in Orthodoxy, the state in which one enters a Major (not Minor) Order is the state in which one remains. If, therefore, a man wishes to be a married priest, he must marry before he becomes a subdeacon. If he is ordained as a subdeacon while he is unmarried, he cannot then change his mind and marry. Bishops, on the other hand, are always unmarried, though some have been consecrated bishop after their wife's death. If a man does marry before ordination and his wife then dies, he cannot marry again. Once again, the question of whether all this is sensible is another matter, and the sight of Orthodox seminarians scrabbling to find a wife between the end of their studies and their ordination is not always edifying. It may certainly be challenged theologically, but it is—for the moment—the Tradition of the Church.

Within Orthodoxy, it is expected (though it is not always the case) that celibate clergy will take monastic vows. What does this mean? It means that most celibate priests are also monks, and monasticism, as we shall see in our next chapter, has had a long and important history within the Orthodox tradition. Bishops always take monastic vows, though in the case of a widower, he may take these vows late in life. It is worth mentioning, however, that this was not always the case. Up to about the sixth century, married bishops were not uncommon, but the increasingly high esteem accorded to monks, and certain legal problems relating to a bishop's property and possessions (did they belong to him or to the Church, and who inherited them?), led to an insistence on celibate bishops, though they did not at that time have to take monastic vows. That provision dates from the Middle Ages. There is no doubt that this produces problems. The great majority of Orthodox clergy are married, and that means that the pool from which a bishop can be elected tends to be small. There is also no necessary connection between celibacy and administrative competence, and the election of some Orthodox bishops in recent years has turned out to be nothing short of disastrous. One can therefore make a very strong case for removing the restriction of celibacy from the election of bishops, but given the speed at which the Orthodox Church moves in these matters, it would be unwise to hold one's breath. How bishops are elected or appointed, and who participates in the process, differs among the different autocephalous Churches, and those interested in the details must pursue their researches elsewhere.

Deacons, we might add, are rather more important in Orthodoxy than in Roman Catholicism or Anglicanism. In these Churches, the diaconate, until quite recently, tended to be seen simply as a stepping-stone to the priesthood, though the Second Vatican Council (1962-1965) restored a permanent diaconate, which certainly existed in the early Church. According to the same council, deacons (under the authority of the bishop) were authorized to baptize, administer Communion, assist at weddings, give Communion to the dying, instruct the people, and officiate at funerals. Orthodoxy, on the other hand, never lost the principle of a permanent diaconate, and Orthodox deacons do all the things listed by the Second Vatican Council and more besides. But there is still a tendency for the diaconate to be seen as a temporary state, and permanent deacons are fairly rare. Indeed, deacons of any sort are not common, and some Orthodox parishes have considerable difficulty in finding them. So what about female deacons or deaconesses?

Here we have a problem. There is not the slightest doubt that deaconesses played an important role in the early Church, and there is equally no doubt that they have a long history. Phoebe was a deaconess of the church at Cenchreae (the east port of Corinth) at the time Paul wrote his letter to the Romans (Rom 16:1). The role of deaconesses, however, was seen primarily in relation to other women, especially during the rite of baptism. Baptism, in the early Church, often involved adult converts to Christianity, and since (as we know) it also involved total immersion, it was considered inappropriate for male deacons to be in attendance. But the deaconesses also acted as chaperones for women who had business with male clergy, and they also ministered to the poor and sick of their own sex.

In the Byzantine Church, deaconesses were ordained to their position by the bishop, they wore a tunic (the *sticharion*) and stole, and, in precedence, ranked immediately after male deacons. Unlike deacons, however, deaconesses were not permitted to give Communion (save to sick women), and they could not substitute for a deacon in the performance of the other sacraments. Nevertheless, their position was an important one—it was no sinecure—but with changing times, the female diaconate faded away in the later Middle Ages, though there is good evidence that it still existed in the thirteenth century. But in Orthodoxy, the female diaconate was never formally abolished. In theory, therefore, it could be revived, and in recent years there have been serious moves within the Orthodox tradition to do just that. In 1988 an Inter-Orthodox Consultation Meeting on the ordination of women took place in Rhodes, and the delegates unanimously welcomed the idea of the restoration of the female diaconate. As yet, little has been done officially in the matter, except in the case of some monasteries where deaconesses may now be seen at work, but a wider ordination of women to the diaconate is a real possibility, unlike the ordination of women to the priesthood which, as we saw in Chapter Six, can be regarded at present as no more than a theological pipe-dream.

Apart from deacons, priests, and bishops we also find other titles used within the Orthodox tradition. There are archdeacons, archpriests, and archbishops, for example, all of whom have a certain seniority, whether honorific or administrative. There are also archimandrites, a title of honour given to senior unmarried priests, just as archpriest is a title of honour given to priests who are married. There are still other designations to be found, and the Oriental Orthodox Churches have their own terminology. But to examine in detail the names of all ecclesiastical positions in, say, Syrian or Ethiopian Orthodoxy, is not the purpose of this book, and those interested must seek the information in more specialized works.

We mentioned above that Orthodox bishops always take monastic vows, and that monasticism has played an important role in Orthodox history. This is true, and the role it has played has been so important that it deserves a chapter to itself. The way of the monk or nun has been described as the 'way of the angels', the *via angelica*, in both east and west, and there is no doubt that it is a hard and demanding path. Many who think they are called to it are not truly called; and many of those who are called are not chosen. Monasteries nowadays are extremely careful about whom they admit, both for the sake of the community and for the sake of those who seek to enter, though this was not always the case. The monastic movement, however, has existed for almost as long as Christianity. Some would trace it back to the Christian community mentioned in the Acts of the Apostles, which (we are told) had but one heart and one soul and possessed all things in common (Acts 4:32), though quite what was going on there is a matter of scholarly dispute. What is certainly true is that the monastic movement blossomed in the course of the third century, and that is the date we shall take as our starting-point for our next chapter.

11

THE WAY
OF THE ANGELS

IT IS CUSTOMARY, if not wholly accurate, to begin the story of monasticism with a young man named Antony. He was born in Upper Egypt around 250 or 251 and, according to tradition, was in his late teens when he happened to hear a reading from the gospel of Saint Matthew: 'If you want to be perfect, go, sell your possessions and give to the poor, and you will have treasure in heaven' (Mt 19:21). Antony did precisely this. He gave away all that he had and devoted himself to a life of unremitting austerity. Then, in about 285, he retreated to the solitude of the Egyptian desert, where his holiness and asceticism attracted a number of disciples and imitators. There were so many of them that Antony was forced to come out of his beloved solitude and organize his followers into a loosely-knit community, though some years later, in about 310, he retreated once again into the desert and settled on a mountain, the 'Inner Mountain', Mount Clysma, near the Red Sea. After his death his disciples established a monastery here—Dair Anbâ Antûnîûs, the 'Monastery of Father Antony'—which still exists and is well worth visiting. The churches within the monastic compound have some fine icons and wall-paintings.

Antony was certainly not the first to seek the solitary life, but he was undoubtedly the most famous, and a Greek account of his life—the *Vita Antonii* or 'Life of Antony'—circulated under the name of one of the most celebrated Church leaders of the fourth century, Athanasius the Great (d. 373). If the book was not written by Athanasius himself (which is possible), it certainly came from an Athanasian milieu, and it proved extremely popular and was very widely read. It is still a good read, and translations in most modern European languages are easily available.[1]

Antony, however, was a hermit, and although, for a time, he was the leader of a community of ascetics, that was not where his heart lay. His was an austere, individualistic, and independent spirituality, and the eremitic path—the way of the hermit—is not an easy path to follow. It is harsh and unforgiving, and can all too easily lead to delusion and despair. Less heroic souls found they needed, or at least preferred, the support of a community with an established rule, together with a spiritual father and guide to whom they could go for encouragement, counsel, direction, and good common-sense advice.

Once again according to tradition, the founder of communal monasticism was another Egyptian called Pachomius. He was born about 290 in Upper Egypt, and served as a conscript in the Roman army. After his release from military service, he was converted to Christianity, and spent some three years as the disciple of a hermit. After that, in about 320, he built a monastery at Tabennisi near ancient Thebes, and his reputation for what we might call solid sanctity attracted large numbers of monks. Tabennisi grew rapidly both in size and importance, other foundations followed, and by the time of Pachomius's death in 346, there were eleven Pachomian monasteries in Egypt. Nine were for men, and two, discreetly located across the Nile, were for women.

A Pachomian monastery was truly communal—the technical term is cenobitic[2]—and some were very large. Within an enclosing wall there was a church, refectory, guest-house, and infirmary, and a series of simple houses for the monks. Each house lodged about twenty monks under the direction of a prior, and the whole complex could house up to a thousand. The monks (and, in their separate communities, the nuns) worshipped and ate together, and all were bound by total and absolute obedience to the will of their

---

1. For an excellent English translation, see *The Life of Antony by Athanasius of Alexandria*, trans. Tim Vivian and Apostolos N. Athanassakis. Cistercian Studies Series 202 (Kalamazoo, 2003). The volume contains translations of the Greek and Coptic Lives of Antony, the *Encomium on Antony* by John of Shmūn, and Serapion of Thmuis' *Letter to the Disciples of Antony*.

2. The term derives from *coenobium*, the Latin word for community.

superior. They were also expected to work, not only because the products of their labours—primarily baskets, mats, ropes, and linen cloth—could be sold to support the monastery, but also because manual work was a sure remedy against the insidious attacks of the devil. Idleness and temptation have always been congenial bedfellows, and the Pachomian rules ensured that the only time monks and nuns were unoccupied was when they were asleep.

Cenobitic monasticism, for a variety of reasons, became immensely popular, and the more popular it became, the more nervous grew the local bishops. The loyalty of monks was first and foremost to their abbot, to whom they were bound by holy obedience, and if abbot and bishop disagreed, either ecclesiastically or politically, the situation could become very tense. That they did on occasion disagree is not in doubt, and a political abbot who could draw upon a large and loyal strike-force of several hundred devoted monks was clearly a power to be reckoned with. One bishop who was deeply concerned about this problem was Basil the Great, Basil of Caesarea, whom we mentioned briefly in Chapter Six. He was born about 330, received a fine education in Caesarea, Constantinople, and Athens, and was known and respected for his learning, holiness, and administrative ability. He had always been drawn to the monastic life, and in 357–358 visited a number of monastic communities in Palestine and Egypt, including the Pachomian monasteries. These made a deep and favourable impression on him, but when he returned to Cappadocia (in the east of modern Turkey) he first lived the life of a hermit before deciding that the cenobitic way was better. Sometime during this period—between 358 and 364—he composed two important monastic works, the *Moral Rules* and the *Asceticon*, but in about 364 he was called forth from his monastic refuge to defend the orthodox tradition against heresy. A few years later, in 370, he was consecrated bishop of Caesarea, and governed his diocese ably and intelligently until his death about nine years later.

The *Asceticon* is the more important of the two rules, and it exists in more than one form. It is not, in fact, a rule in any systematic sense, but rather a series of questions and answers on a variety of ascetic and spiritual topics, but the principles it enunciates have remained the standard for eastern cenobitic monasticism. The form in which the *Asceticon* usually appears was actually compiled some two centuries after Basil's death, and it includes the *Moral Rules* (eighty of them, each endorsed by quotations from the New Testament), the questions and answers of the *Asceticon* proper (here divided into fifty-five 'detailed rules' and 313 'short rules'), additional regulations pertaining to appropriate punishments for monastic offences, and a series of prologues, most of which are indeed from Basil's pen. This work, usually called the *Great Asceticon*, was further expanded in the course of the Middle Ages, and Basil's rules form the basis, directly or indirectly, for virtually all Orthodox monastic rules. One of the most important of these was that compiled by Theodore of Studios, a monastic reformer, brilliant theologian, anti-iconoclast, and true spiritual father who died in 826.

As we might expect, Basil advocates the *coenobium*, the community, but not the huge monastic legionary camps of Pachomius. A small, workable group is what is needed for the development of a true community spirit, for only in community can one practise the christian virtues of mercy, charity, and love of one's neighbour. Monks and nuns were also required to be poor, chaste, and, above all, obedient—but obedient to the local bishop as well as the superior of their own monastery. Basil, as we might expect, is insistent on this point.

The life of these communal religious consisted of a strict round of liturgy, prayer, work, eating, and sleeping. But although Basil himself was in no doubt that the celibate, ordered, ascetic life—the way of the angels—was the most effective way to God, he was also convinced that true asceticism had to be balanced asceticism. He had no time for the excessive and sometimes outlandish mortifications practised by many of the desert hermits, especially those in Syria.

Basil's expanded *Asceticon* came to be the standard for eastern monasticism. The minutiae of daily life certainly differed, sometimes quite significantly, from monastery to monastery, but the Basilean rules were never intended to furnish detailed instructions for the hour by hour or day to day running of a community. Nevertheless, the principles set forth by Basil provided a theological and practical foundation for Orthodox monasticism in general, and Orthodox monasticism today is still solidly rooted in Basil's ideas, ideals, and regulations.

In the course of time, this Basilean basis led to a number of significant differences between eastern and western monasticism. The first, and most obvious, is that in the Orthodox east, monasticism never divided and subdivided, as it did in the west, into a variety of Orders, each with its distinctive dress, regulations, practices, and ideals. Some western Orders have been entirely enclosed and contemplative, some more or less so, some (in modern times) actively involved with 'the world'. Some have specialized in teaching, some in combatting heresy, some in ministering to the sick and the poor, some in missionary work, some in education. They have covered the entire sociological spectrum, from uneducated lay-brothers to aristocratic members of such chivalric Orders as the Knights Hospitaller, who still exist today as the Knights of Malta and, in England, as the Saint John Ambulance Brigade. All wore their own distinctive clothing, and even now, when the monastic habit has been simplified and, one might say, streamlined, you cannot mistake a Cistercian in black and white for a brown-habited Franciscan. This is not the case in Orthodoxy. For the most part, Orthodox monasticism remained (and still remains) one Order, and all the monks and nuns (with slight variations) wear one distinctive habit which we will describe in a moment.

A second area in which Orthodox monasticism differs from its western counterpart lies in the percentage of monks who have been ordained as priests. Pachomius did not want clerics in his monasteries 'for fear of jealousy and vainglory,'[3] and the earliest monks were virtually all laymen. In Pachomius's view, ordination could be 'an occasion for strife, envy, jealousy, and then schisms to arise in a large community of monks.'[4] Basil, however, introduced a formal liturgical ceremony by which a man became a monk or a woman a nun, and, as a consequence of this, a monk occupied a sort of middle ground between laity and clergy. He was more than a layman, yet less than a priest. There were and are, of course, monks who were and are priests—they are referred to as hieromonks, and

---

3. *Pachomian Koinonia I: The Life of Saint Pachomius and His Disciples*, trans. Armand Veilleux. Cistercian Studies Series 45 (Kalamazoo, 1980), 47–48 (Bohairic Life §25).
4. *Ibid.*, 314 (First Greek Life §27).

are essential for the celebration of the sacraments—but they are very much a minority. Western organizations such as the Canons Regular or Augustinian Canons, all of whose members were ordained clergy, had no parallel in the Orthodox East.

A third area of difference is to be found in the attitude of the monastic movement to learning and scholarship. That there were learned Orthodox monks is not in doubt. Some of them were very learned indeed, theologians of the first rank whose laser-like minds were essential in dealing with complicated, dangerous, and all too persuasive heretical ideas. But unlike, say, the Benedictines or Dominicans in the West, Orthodox monasteries have not generally been centres of scholarship, and they have not fostered what we might call a culture of learning. At the heart of Orthodox monasticism lies the communal liturgy, the life of balanced asceticism, and the pursuit of the contemplative experience of God. This is not to say, of course, that the same principles cannot be seen in western monasticism—they can, and clearly—but the brilliant scholarly treatises produced by (for example) the Benedictine Congregation of Saint-Maur in the seventeenth and eighteenth centuries have no counterpart in the Orthodox East. Monk-scholars of real genius have not been uncommon in the West, but they have been far less common in the East. Orthodox monasticism never produced scholars like the Maurists Jean Mabillon (1632–1707) and Edmond Martène (1654–1739). It did, however, produce a number of spiritual guides and writers of great wisdom and discernment. The *Philokalia*, which we mentioned in Chapter Six and which we will have cause to mention again, remains an impressive and invaluable compendium of Orthodox spirituality, and much of its teaching is as useful today as when it was first published more than two centuries ago.

The final area in which we see a significant difference between eastern and western monasticism lies in the contribution made by women. There are Orthodox nuns, of course, and there have been since the days of Pachomius. The Desert Mothers were fewer in number than the Desert Fathers, but their contributions to what may be called 'desert spirituality'—it has a temper all of its own—were just as telling and just as important as those of their male counterparts. In the early Church there were women like Macrina the Younger (*c.* 327–380), the elder sister of Basil the Great, who shared her brother's organizational abilities and who, as we said in Chapter Six, was a competent theologian in her own right. But once we advance into the Middle Ages and beyond, such women tend to fade from the picture. In the west, the monastic Orders produced a variety of outstanding spiritual and mystical writers, especially from the twelfth century (though there were many Anglo-Saxon nuns of no mean ability), but women like Hildegard of Bingen, Angela of Foligno, Julian of Norwich, Catherine of Genoa, Catherine of Siena, Teresa of Jesus, Jeanne de Chantal, Marie of the Incarnation, Elizabeth of the Trinity, Thérèse of Lisieux, Faustina Kowalska, and others more recent, have hardly any parallels in the Orthodox world. One of the rare exceptions was Thaisia (1840–1915), abbess of Leushino for over thirty years, and one of the most famous nuns in Russia. She was renowned for her spiritual insight, but—unusually—she also left an extraordinarily interesting autobiography and a series of eminently sensible *Letters to a Beginner on Giving One's Life to God* which remain a standard guide to the religious life for Russian female monastics. Both are now available in English translation.[5] There were undoubtedly other Orthodox religious women whose experiences were just as profound as those of abbess Thaisia, but, if we may quote George Eliot, they 'lived faithfully a hidden life, and rest in unvisited tombs'.[6]

Orthodox monasticism flourished in the Byzantine empire, especially in and around Constantinople, and the monks played an active and important role in the theological controversies of their day. Two of these controversies were of major importance: the earlier was the iconoclastic controversy of the eighth and ninth centuries; the later was the hesychast controversy which ravaged the eastern church in the fourteenth century, especially the first half of the fourteenth century. We discussed the iconoclastic controversy in Chapter Four and the hesychast controversy in Chapter Seven.

    5. *Abbess Thaisia of Leushino: The Autobiography of a Spiritual Daughter of Saint John of Kronstadt* (Platina: Saint Herman of Alaska Brotherhood Press, 1989), and *Letters to a Beginner on Giving One's Life to God* (Platina: Saint Herman of Alaska Brotherhood Press, 1993).
    6. George Eliot, *Middlemarch* (first published 1871–72), the very end of the last chapter.

When Orthodoxy spread from the Greek world to the East Slavic lands, it took monasticism with it. In fact, monasticism had existed there even before the conversion of Russia in the late tenth century, for Greek monks fleeing the persecution of the iconoclasts (most monks were staunch supporters of the holy icons) made their way to Ukraine and southern Russia and settled there. Some of them settled in caves, either natural or artificial, and thus instituted cave monasticism. Over the course of the centuries, more and more caves were excavated, and some of the cave monasteries came to be miles long. After their deaths, the monks were laid to rest in burial caves linked to the main caves, and in some cases, since the subterranean atmosphere tends to produce natural mummification rather than decay, they are still there.[7]

Not all monks, of course, were troglodytes. Many lived above ground in small huts, leading their own ascetic lives according to their own regimen, but being subject to a single abbot. This type of organization dated back to early fourth-century Palestine and was called, in Greek, a *lavra*. The word literally means a street. In Russia it came to be known as skete monasticism, *skete* being an abbreviated Slavonic form of the Greek word *askētērion*, or 'community of ascetics'. There was, in fact, rather more interaction among the inhabitants of the skete than there had been in the old lavras, but they were far from being truly cenobitic.

In the early eleventh century, however, a new type of monastery developed in and around Kiev. They were called Founders' Monasteries because they were founded primarily by the princes of Kiev. The most important (and most dangerous) feature of these new institutions was that the prince or founder had the right to appoint the abbot, and founders also kept a careful eye on the way in which the monastic lands and properties were administered. Founders' monasteries were more classically cenobitic than the sketes—their monks were much more of a true community and less a loosely-connected collection of more or less independent

---

7. The best known example is the Monastery of the Caves in Kiev. In the lower lavra, the mummified bodies of more than a hundred monks, shrouded in white linen and lying in glass coffins, are still to be seen. Photographs of the monastery may be found on numerous Websites.

hermits—and there was no love lost between the two different traditions. The skete monks generally despised politics, especially ecclesiastical politics, and they had no time for those who pandered to the ruling classes or the governing aristocracy. They were also adamantly opposed to monks owning property, and they abhorred the efforts of the monks of the cenobitic foundations to augment their wealth, despite the fact that this wealth was often used to feed the poor and assist the local population in times of famine and hardship.

The two groups are usually referred to as Possessors and Non-Possessors, and although the distinction between them was not quite as black-and-white as is often suggested, there were certainly clashes between them—clashes which became ever more violent, reaching a head in the sixteenth century. The unpleasant details of the conflict need not concern us, but the end result was the triumph of the Possessors and the annihilation of the Non-Possessor skete system in Russia. This was unfortunate, for it left Russian Orthodoxy at the mercy of an anti-monastic state-controlled church; the elimination of Russian Orthodox monasticism under Communism had a long previous history.

As we shall see in a moment, the sketes did not entirely disappear. They vanished in Russia, that is true, but they survived, or were resurrected, elsewhere. Despite this, it remains the case that, for the most part, Orthodox monasticism today is cenobitic monasticism, and the heart of Orthodox monasticism in the Byzantine-Slav tradition is, without doubt, that rocky peninsula in northern Greece, just south-east of Thessaloniki, called Mount Athos or, in Greek, the Holy Mountain. What are we talking about here?

The peninsula in question, fifty-six kilometres long and rarely more than eight kilometres wide, is an independent self-governing part of the Greek state from which women are totally excluded. The first monastic settlement for which there is reliable evidence dates from 961, and there are now twenty ruling monasteries on the peninsula belonging to the Greek, Russian, Serbian, and Bulgarian Orthodox Churches. They are called ruling monasteries because at present the Holy Mountain is governed by a council of twenty monks, each monk being elected for one year (though re-election is possible) from one of these twenty monasteries. There is also an executive committee of four members. The ruling monasteries suffered a serious decline in numbers after the First World War, and by the early 1970s there were only about eleven hundred monks, most of them elderly. But the 1980s witnessed an astonishing revitalization of monastic life on Mount Athos, not so much in numbers, but in the small and important influx of younger, well-educated, and devout recruits to the monastic life. There are still problems, to be sure, not least in an unhealthy ultra-Orthodox fanaticism (such as that shown by the zealot monks of the Esphigmenou monastery), but spiritual and intellectual life on the Holy Mountain, once dead or moribund, has, like Lazarus, been resurrected.[8]

Much the same story can be told of Coptic monasticism. The Nitrian desert, lying between Alexandria and Cairo, was one of the great centres of early monasticism, and of all the many monastic establishments, the four monasteries of the Wadi Natroun (Wâdî al-Natrûn) were and are the most important. Their isolation was severely compromised in 1936 with the construction of the Cairo-Alexandria highway, though the new road has opened up the monasteries to visitors both male and female, save for the Monastery of the Syrians (Dair al-Suryân) which does not allow women within its walls. As with Athonite monasticism, Coptic monasticism has also experienced a renaissance in recent decades and, at the same time, Coptic spirituality has benefited from a number of popular writings by the Coptic Pope Cyril VI (who died in 1971), Father Matta el-Meskeen (Matthew the Poor), and the present pope, Shenouda III. These writings reveal a solidly scriptural spirituality, sometimes curiously influenced by Evangelical Protestantism.

Whether Greek, Slav, or Coptic, the monks of these monasteries live, as we have said, a common and communal life. They worship, eat, and (so far as is practical) work together, and what is true for the men is equally true for the women. There is, in fact, no difference whatever between the monastic life of a monk and that of a nun, and they enter the monastery and progress through the various stages of monastic profession in just the same way.

8. The whole story can now be read in the excellent and beautifully illustrated study by Graham Speake, *Mount Athos: Renewal in Paradise* (New Haven-London, 2002).

The Way of the Angels

A man or woman begins as a postulant and then, after a few months, becomes a novice. At that point they begin to wear part of the monastic habit: a black under-tunic and belt together with a head covering which is slightly different for men and women. After some years, usually between three and five (it depends on when the abbot or abbess thinks the novice is ready), he or she becomes formally a part of the monastery—a true monk or nun—and, in a formal liturgical ceremony, is permitted to wear the outer robe, a long black garment with wide sleeves reaching from neck to ankles, and a different head covering with a veil down the sides and back. Sometime later, he or she will also be given a long black hoodless cloak, which falls in pleats to the ground and which is worn only in church. The new monk or nun will also be given a new name—his or her monastic name—by the hieromonk officiating at the liturgy of profession. This name is not normally a matter of choice: the new religious accepts it as a first act of formal obedience. A number of years later (there is no set time) a religious may (or may not: it all depends on his or her capacity) move on to a further stage which is symbolized by adding other small pieces to the habit. Practically, this involves a more intense prayer life, greater asceticism, and greater responsibility. The names and duration of these successive stages vary in the different Orthodox traditions, as do the names given to the various garments—Greek, after all, is not Armenian—but what I have outlined (and simplified) here is generally the case in all forms of Orthodox monasticism.

In the past, not all cenobitic monasteries were truly cenobitic. There were some which were communal on the surface, but which were, in fact, really communities of hermits following their own spiritual paths. Apart from meeting for common worship on Sundays and feast days, they had little or no contact with each other. Such 'communities', if we may stretch the word, were described technically as idiorrhythmic—'living according to one's own rhythm'—and their original intention was to maintain a formal monastic framework while allowing almost total freedom for individual asceticism. Unfortunately, the system (which dates back to the sixth century) was always beset by problems, not least a lack of discipline. During the heyday of the movement—primarily when Greece was being ruled by the Turks—many idiorrhythmic monks lived in well-appointed apartments and were looked after by their own servants. They sometimes owned a considerable amount of private property and owed no obedience to any abbot. This, clearly, was not quite what the monastic life was all about, and more than one Ecumenical Patriarch fulminated against its undoubted excesses. On the other hand, the adaptability offered by the idiorrhythmic system unquestionably helped Orthodox monasticism survive Turkish pressure or persecution—Graham Speake has referred to it as a 'necessary evil'[9]—and by the end of the sixteenth century all the monasteries on Mount Athos were idiorrhythmic.

The movement lasted until the 1980s when, as we mentioned above, there was a dramatic revival in monasticism on the Holy Mountain. Those who now sought entry into the monastic communities sought an ordered and regular life, dedicated to the service of God, in holy obedience to an informed and discerning abbot. Since the idiorrhythmic movement no longer served a purpose, and since *laissez-faire* spirituality was not what the new aspirants were seeking, the monasteries, one by one, abandoned it. In many cases, the change proved astonishingly beneficial, and great houses like Vatopedi and Iviron enjoyed and are still enjoying a new and vibrant revival of the pure cenobitic life. The last monastery to change was Pantokrator in 1992, though it did so unwillingly. One might say that the Ecumenical Patriarchate made it an offer it couldn't refuse. But after its reluctant transformation, it, too, found itself heading for a new and dynamic renaissance in its religious life.

The principle of the idiorrhythmic system did not, however, entirely disappear. It may still be seen in the Athonite sketes, which, much like their Russian forebears, are small monastic villages grouped around a central church, each skete being dependent on one of the twenty ruling monasteries on the Holy Mountain. Each house in the 'village' is governed by an elder who is responsible for its discipline and ascetic regime (which is usually extremely austere), and each house contains between two and five other monks. The whole skete is administered by a prior, usually a hieromonk, who is assisted by two or three counsellors and an assembly of elders.

---

9. *Ibid.*, 123.

The elders also elect the prior, who holds office for one year.[10] The monks of the sketes generally have a stronger calling to the eremitic life than other religious, and seek a path more arduously ascetic. Sometimes, too, they are disciples of an elder or prior who is truly charismatic, a true spiritual master and father of great holiness, and what we see here is a continuation of a much older movement in Orthodoxy, particularly Russian Orthodoxy: that of the *startsy*. Who or what are these remarkable people?

Startsy is the plural of the Russian word *starets*. It means, literally, an elder, but a *starets* is more than just old. Indeed, he or she (for there have been *startsy* of both sexes) may be comparatively young, for it is not age which is the key here, but spiritual gifts and charisma. That charisma is manifested most importantly in the ability of the *starets* to provide individual spiritual direction, exactly tempered to the needs of a particular person at a particular time. This, clearly, means that the *starets* must be aware of what that person needs at that time, and this requires spiritual discernment of a very high order. Some *startsy* were said to know the thoughts and secrets of those who came to them before they had said a word, and many *startsy* were also thought to have powers of healing, clairvoyance, and prophecy. This, in fact, does appear to have been the case, even allowing for exaggeration in the tales told of them.

The movement may be traced back to the earliest times—some see Saint Antony, the traditional founder of the monastic movement, as the first *starets*—but it was in Russia that it achieved its greatest renown. The first of the great Russian *startsy* was Saint Sergius (Sergei) of Radonezh (*c*.1314–1392), who lived at a time when Russia had been conquered by the Mongol Tartars and the church was being repressed. But repression inevitably brings reaction, reaction often brings renewal, and that renewal may clearly be seen in the achievements of those who, like Sergius, withdrew into the Russian equivalent of the Egyptian desert—the vast untamed depths of the northern forests—and brought about a new burgeoning of Orthodox monasticism and spirituality.

Sergius himself lived for many years as a forest hermit near Radonezh, about forty miles northwest of Moscow, and counted

---

10. For further details on the sketes and their operation, see *ibid.*, 123–127.

among his disciples animals as well as humans. One animal in particular, a great Russian bear, would visit him regularly for food and company, and on more than one occasion, when Sergius had only a single piece of bread with which to sustain himself, he gave it to his ursine friend on the grounds that the bear also had to eat and Sergius did not wish to disappoint him.[11] Gradually he became renowned as a *starets*, more and more disciples gathered around him in his forest hermitage, and eventually he was forced to transform what had slowly become a skete into a regular monastery, the Monastery of the Holy Trinity, which would be the greatest religious house in fourteenth-century Russia. Other foundations followed, and by the end of his life, Sergius was the spiritual father of dozens of monasteries covering much of the northern part of the country. The two centuries after his death have been called a golden age of Russian spirituality—and also of icon painting, which, in Orthodoxy, cannot be separated from spirituality—but the seed from which it all sprang was undoubtedly sown by Sergius.

The *startsy* movement neither began nor ended with Sergius, and many (myself included) would say that it reached its zenith in the eighteenth and nineteenth centuries, which was also a time of repression in Russian Orthodoxy. The period from 1700 to 1917 is referred to as the Synodical Period, for in 1721 Tsar Peter the Great abolished the patriarchate and set up in its place the Holy Synod or Spiritual College. The twelve members of this institution were appointed or, if they proved awkward or obstinate, 'retired' by Peter, and they were not always particularly holy nor particularly spiritual. The church, in fact, became no more than a department of the centralized state, but, once again, repression brought about reaction, and reaction brought about revival.

The revival is especially associated with the work of Paisius (Paissy) Velichkovsky (1722–94), who had been a monk on Mount Athos before moving to Romania and becoming abbot of the monastery of Neametz/Niamets. While on the Holy Mountain, Paisius had discovered hesychasm, the Jesus Prayer, and the *Philokalia*, and was so impressed with the latter that, after he had left the

---

11. *A Treasury of Russian Spirituality*, ed. George P. Fedotov (New York, 1948; rpt. Gloucester, Massachusetts, 1969) 61.

mountain, he translated it into Slavonic. The Slavonic translation was published in 1793, and Russian spirituality was never the same again.

During the eighteenth and nineteenth centuries, the *startsy* movement flourished, and produced some of the most beloved teachers and guides ever to come out of Russia. Saint Seraphim of Sarov (1759–1833) is undoubtedly the most popular (as with Saint Sergius, one of his best friends was a bear), and he was known and esteemed for his discernment, telepathy, visions, healings (both physical and mental), levitation, clairvoyance, and prophecies. On at least one occasion he was also transfigured, and his face (said the young nobleman who witnessed it) 'became brighter than the sun'. All you could see, he said, was

> a blinding light spreading far around for several yards and illuminating with its glaring sheen both the snow blanket which covered the forest glade and the snowflakes which besprinkled me and the great Elder.[12]

Another revered *starets*, this time a woman, was Anastasia/Athanasia Logacheva (1809–1875), who was guided and instructed by Saint Seraphim himself. She, too, lived in harmony with the animals (though when the bears were eating too much from her little garden, she ordered them away), and was celebrated for her asceticism, foreknowledge, and, of course, spiritual discernment. She ended her days as the beloved abbess of the monastery of Saint Nicholas the Wonderworker in Siberia, and when she died in 1875 her grave became a centre of pilgrimage. It was said that if one mixed a little earth from her grave with water and then drank it, it could cure every illness.[13]

It is tempting to tell more tales of these remarkable men and women, but those interested must seek the stories elsewhere.[14] More

---

12. *Little Russian Philokalia, Vol. I: Saint Seraphim of Sarov* (Platina: Saint Herman of Alaska Brotherhood Press, 1996), 99–100.
13. For details of her life, see Alexander Priklonsky, *Blessed Athanasia and the Desert Ideal* (Platina: Saint Herman of Alaska Brotherhood Press, 1993 [2nd ed.]).
14. In, for example, Fedotov's *Treasury* cited in n. 11 above, or Sergius Bolshakoff, *Russian Mystics* (Kalamazoo, 1980).

important for our present purposes is Paisius Velichkoksy's translation of the *Philokalia* into Slavonic, and its later translation into contemporary Russian, which made it accessible to any Russian who wanted to read it. One of those who did read it was the author of a little book called *The Way of a Pilgrim* or *The Pilgrim's Tale*, first published in Russian in 1884, which describes the journey of its anonymous peasant author as he made his way from place to place in nineteenth-century Russia. The first English version of the work was published in 1930, but in 1999 a better translation appeared with an invaluable introduction discussing the history of the text and its authorship.[15] The pilgrim's spiritual odyssey began when he heard Saint Paul's instruction to 'pray without ceasing' or 'pray constantly' (1 Thess 5:17). But what did this mean? And was it, in fact, possible? He decided to seek an answer from any who might be able to provide it—teachers, preachers, ecclesiastics, government officials, devout laypeople, anyone who might help—but time after time the answers they offered were inadequate and disappointing. Then, finally, he came upon a *starets* who was not in the least surprised at the pilgrim's failure to find an answer, but who was finally able to tell him what he needed to know. The key, said the *starets*, was the Jesus Prayer—'Lord Jesus Christ, Son of God, have mercy upon me' (or 'have mercy upon me, a sinner')—and if the pilgrim wished to know all that was needful to know about this prayer, he would find it in the pages of the *Philokalia*. The rest of the book is then dominated by two themes: the practice of the Jesus Prayer and its remarkable effects, and the importance of the *Philokalia*, which the pilgrim recommended to everyone he met. The pilgrim's view of the effects of the Jesus Prayer is perhaps a little extreme—among other things, it appears as a cure for cold, hunger, fatigue, and rheumatism—but this 'sophisticatedly unsophisticated'[16] little book has had immense influence, and the Jesus Prayer plays an important role in contemporary Christian spirituality, Orthodox and otherwise. The pilgrim himself, however, was no monk or *starets*, only a

---

15. *The Pilgrim's Tale*, ed. with intro. by Aleksei Pentkovsky, trans. T. Allan Smith (New York-Mahwah, 1999).

16. *The Study of Spirituality*, edd. Cheslyn Jones, Geoffrey Wainwright, Edward Yarnold (Oxford/New York, 1986) 272.

simple layman, and what he teaches in his book is a much simplified, yet clearly effective, form of monastic—more accurately, hesychastic—spirituality intended for any man or any woman who desires to pursue it. What he teaches, in fact, is lay spirituality, one way of doing your own thing; but doing your own thing is an important topic, and we must give it our full attention in the next chapter.

12

DOING YOUR OWN THING

THE ORTHODOX CHURCH is a Church, and a Church is more than a collection of individuals. The Church is a meeting-place of heaven and earth and a vessel of grace, though grace can never be confined and is certainly not limited to Orthodoxy. The Church is also the body of Christ, and just as the members of our own physical body are interconnected, so the individual members of Christ's mystical body—*viz.*, all baptized Christians—are also interconnected. When one suffers, all suffer—or should. Our participation in the sacramental life of the Church is a true sharing of grace, and my salvation is not only a personal, private matter between me and my God, it is also (whether I like it or not) a matter between me and my neighbour. But who is my neighbour? In the most general sense everyone and everything from the trees in the garden to the cats in the local animal shelter to a Buddhist friend in Tokyo. As we said earlier, we are created to be co-workers with the Creator in the process of creation, and one cannot be truly Orthodox without also being an ecologist. But from a more specific point of view, my neighbours are the other members of the body of Christ, and to separate myself from them is to separate myself from Christ.

This is not a particularly comfortable idea. All too often, we human beings are not very nice. The Seven Deadly Sins—pride, covetousness, lust, envy, gluttony, anger, and sloth—are alive and well in every one of us, and every one of us, to a greater or lesser extent, is guilty of every one of them. We also grow old, catch various diseases, and develop irritating habits, and the idea of having to associate with other people is, for many of us, wholly depressing.

We prefer to keep to our own friends—our own kind, even—and the idea that X or Y (whom we can't stand) is an image of God who shares in the Divine Nature is obviously wrong. *I* may share in the Divine Nature, but Old Joe downtown, who panhandles, drinks Lysol, and hasn't bathed for a year certainly doesn't. When Saint John tells us to love one another, he can't really mean that. What he really means is that we should love one another in an *abstract* sort of way, with a sort of universal benevolence and good will, an intangible and theoretical Christian charity. Saint John didn't mean that we actually have to associate with people, and when he tells us to *love* them, he doesn't mean that we have to *like* them. Certainly not.

Unfortunately, this is not the view of the Orthodox Church. The Church is not a society of saints but a school for sinners, and the Church is a microcosm of the world. Not only do we find in the Church good and bad, honest and hypocritical, rich and poor, clean and dirty, and anything else we care to think of, but that is what we are supposed to find. If there is an inner, invisible Church of the saints, then God alone knows who is part of it, and it is not our business to speculate. The only sure thing is that if any one of us thinks we belong to this saintly group, we are almost certainly wrong.

The Church, therefore, provides us with a sort of training ground in which we learn to love. It is not an easy task, not always a pleasant task, and all of us need lots of practice. Furthermore, just as charity begins at home, love begins with what or whom is near at hand. A truly universal love might have been possible for some of the saints, but for those of us who are not saints, it can all too easily masquerade as a warm and fuzzy feeling of generalized goodwill mingled with magnanimity. In a remarkable unpublished sermon, John Henry Newman once said

> to attempt to be guided by love alone, would be like attempting to walk in a straight line by steadily gazing on some star. It is too high—we must take nearer objects to steady our course.[1]

---

1. *John Henry Newman: Sermons 1824–1843*, ed. Placid Murray (Oxford, 1991) 1:133.

Newman could not have been more correct. When we are commanded to love our neighbour, the neighbour we are commanded to love is not a Platonic neighbour in the abstract, but, very specifically, the nearer objects of Susie or Vladimir or Fatima or Old Joe. This is not necessarily an easy task and it cannot be learned in isolation. Learning to love is like practising competitive sports: some things we can and should practise on our own, but we can perfect our golf or tennis or football or whatever only on the course or court or field, and only with someone or some ones who can give us a run for our money. In the matter of loving, meditation on the Parable of the Good Samaritan might indeed be eminently useful, but *being* a good Samaritan is a wholly different matter. Knowing the rules of karate is no substitute for being in the ring and learning the art by (often painful) practice. In the case of karate, I speak from experience.

Learning to love, then, is not easy. It takes lots of effort, and it is not something we can hope to achieve by our own power alone. We need help. Who's help? God's help of course, though God's help may sometimes be mediated by angelic messengers.

Orthodoxy, like Roman Catholicism, has never doubted the existence of angels. They are to be found in a variety of forms in both the Old and New Testaments, and a great deal of further information about them may be found in the writings of the early Christian Fathers. They are essentially incorporeal, immortal, rational, spiritual powers—cosmic forces if you prefer—who offer us their aid as part of the on-going process of deification—not just our own deification, but the evolving deification of the universe itself. Those bodiless beings who oppose and, where possible, hinder the process of universal deification may be termed demons, and Orthodoxy is in no doubt of their existence either. We are not speaking here of angels as the humanoid things with wings which decorate nineteenth-century graves, nor are we talking of demons as red-cloaked imps with horns and cloven feet. Angels and demons are far more serious, just as lightning or nuclear fission is serious. On the other hand, the way in which angels and demons decide to manifest is up to them. When the archangel Raphael appeared to Tobias, he looked just like another young man, another traveller on the road (Tobit 5). Whatever it was that Ezekiel saw was something very different (Ezk 1).

Orthodoxy, again like Roman Catholicism, also believes that certain of these bodiless powers are intimately associated with specific individuals. We are speaking here of guardian angels, though guardian angels may also guard specific places, homes, churches, and nations. Guardian angels are in no way mediators between us and God (Christ is our only mediator), but they are there to help and protect us. That we are protected is not in doubt, and what so often we attribute to luck, Orthodoxy would attribute to cosmic intervention. Nowadays many people would agree, for since the 1990s angels have undergone a startling renaissance. In the Middle Ages, they were everywhere. In the wake of the so-called Enlightenment, they got overlooked. They have now been rediscovered, and to see the extent of this rediscovery all you need do is type 'angels' on any Internet search-engine. Orthodoxy, on the other hand, never lost sight of its angels, and in Russia icons of guardian angels are fairly common. But you do not need an icon to contact an angel: thoughts work just as well.

The four principal archangels are Michael, Gabriel, Raphael, and Uriel. Michael and Gabriel appear in the book of Daniel, and Raphael (as we saw above) in the book of Tobit. For Uriel we have to turn to a (mainly) second-century work called the *Sybilline Oracles*. Other archangels are less well known: Salathiel, Barachiel and others are venerated in the Chalcedonian tradition; Surael, Sakakael, Sarathael and Ananael by the Copts; and yet others in other traditions. As to common or garden angels, as distinct from archangels, they are innumerable, and, in the view of all the Orthodox Churches, there are quite enough of them to go round for all those who need their aid.

Ultimately, however, all supernatural aid comes from God, who alone is the source of grace, and the help we seek and the grace we need is normally to be found in the vessel of grace, which is the Church. This is not to say that grace is not to be found elsewhere (grace is actually all around us), but it is, as it were, localized—made local and present—in the Church. And nowhere is it made more local and present than in the Eucharist, which we will discuss in detail in our next chapter. In the Eucharist, the grace which was restored to us in and through Jesus Christ flows into us and transforms us into temples of the living God.

It follows from all of this that (from an Orthodox point of view) our spiritual development inevitably involves our sacramental participation, in communion with the angels and saints, in the life of the Church. And since the main source of the help that we need is to be found in the Eucharist, it also follows that Orthodox spirituality is primarily liturgical spirituality. This is not, of course, unique to Orthodoxy. It is also a western idea, and nowhere is it clearer than in the western and eastern monastic tradition where the regular round of offices—the *opus Dei*, 'God's work'—is a manifestation of our human dependence on God, our human need for his help, and our human recognition of his majesty. The liturgy, wrote Mother Bernard Payne, a Cistercian nun,

> is essentially a collective, social prayer. It would be difficult to exaggerate the importance of this as a factor in the work of sanctification. During those hours when she is engaged in the 'Work of God,' the choral Office, the religious is not praying as a mere individual; she is praying in and with the entire Mystical Body of Christ, both those members of it who are still on earth, and those already in eternity, and the entire Mystical Body is praying in and through her. It is easy to see how such a prayer, rightly understood, emancipates the soul from the little world of its own individual spiritual life, introducing it into the incomparably vaster and fuller life of the Church; again, how it demands the sacrifice of egoism in entire self-devotion to the community act of praising God. We are far removed here from sentimental pietism.[2]

If we change 'sanctification' to 'deification', and see the 'community' not as one's fellow nuns but as the members of one's local church, there are few more accurate descriptions of the heart of Orthodox spirituality.

---

2. *La Trappe in England. Chronicles of an Unknown Monastery. By a Religious of Holy Cross Abbey, Stapehill, Dorset* (London, 1935; rpt. Louisville, 1946), 188. As we mention in the text, the anonymous author was Mother Bernard Payne, abbess of Stapehill, who died in 1968.

Yet each one of us does have our own individual spiritual life, and some of us would like to pay it some attention. How? One of the ways is obviously by private prayer, and compilations of such prayers can be found in all Orthodox traditions. On the other hand, most of these prayers are either taken from or adapted from liturgical prayers, so that even in our own personal devotions, even in solitude (as Georges Florovsky says) 'a Christian prays as a member of the redeemed community, of the Church.'[3]

The best known of all private Orthodox prayers is, of course, the Jesus Prayer. This is something we introduced in the last chapter, and, as we saw there, the prayer is very simple: 'Lord Jesus Christ, Son of God, have mercy upon me' (or 'have mercy upon me, a sinner'). The prayer was intimately associated with hesychasm, the mystical movement we introduced in Chapter Seven, and we need to say a little more about hesychasm in the present context. It is not something of merely historical interest.

While the actual physical techniques of late medieval hesychasm may wisely be discouraged, the essential principles of the tradition remain valid. The term hesychasm comes from the Greek word *hēsychia* which means 'quietness' or 'stillness', and the techniques developed by the hesychasts were designed to quieten down the whole distracting bodily organism so as to make the mind receptive to God. For most of the time, our minds are racing with a multitude of thoughts, ideas, feelings, emotions, intentions, likes, and dislikes, and it is rare that we think of one thing for more than a moment. It's much like the surface of a lake: if there's no wind, the surface will act as a mirror and reflect whatever is above it. If there's a gale blowing, it will reflect nothing at all. The mind is no different. The gale of thoughts and ideas continually whips up its surface, and until the gale diminishes to at least a light breeze, we can have no hope of seeing what it can and should reflect. And what should it reflect? That, naturally, of which it is the image: God. Hesychasm, as we have said, is designed to quieten down body and mind, and thereby allow the created spirit to come into immediate contact with its uncreated Creator. How is this to be achieved?

---

3. Quoted in Ware, *The Orthodox Church*, 303.

The old hesychast tradition demanded that one should first adopt a curious and uncomfortable posture. You sit on a low stool (about nine inches high), draw up your knees, bend your back, and rest your head and hands on your knees.

Secondly, you slow down and regulate your breathing so that inhalation and exhalation coincide with the two phrases of the Jesus Prayer: 'Lord Jesus Christ, Son of God' is normally said (or thought) while breathing in; 'have mercy on me, a sinner' while breathing out.

Thirdly, you imagine—visualize is a more accurate term—your breath flowing down into your heart, thereby merging heart and head, love and reason, and leaving you ready for divine illumination. At this stage you do not think in thoughts, images, words, or concepts. In fact, you don't think at all. The intellect is emptied of all forms, and whenever a thought intrudes, it is driven out with the Jesus Prayer.

Finally, when utter stillness has been achieved and head and heart contain nothing but the Jesus Prayer, the soul of the hesychast may be flooded by Divine Light. This is the uncreated Light of God, the dazzling darkness of Pseudo-Dionysius, and those whom it illumines it also transforms. In fact, it deifies them, and the hesychasts identified it with the light of the Transfiguration.

The origin of these ideas is not here our concern, but we are clearly dealing with advanced mystical techniques. The hesychasts themselves were well aware of this, and insisted that no one should even attempt the practice without an experienced, personal, spiritual teacher, and experienced, personal, spiritual teachers were and are rare.

I am not, therefore, proposing that readers of this book should attempt the practice of fourteenth-century hesychasm—at least, not unless they can find a Saint Seraphim of Sarov to guide them. In any case, the bodily posture and breathing exercises are generally discouraged in modern Orthodoxy. But the essential principles of the tradition—the quietening of the mind and the repetition of the Jesus Prayer—may still prove useful and effective. Such indeed is the view of the Coptic Bishop Moussa, who has provided instruction on what he calls 'The Exercise of the Arrow-Like Prayer'—the Jesus Prayer—on the website of the Coptic Orthodox Patriarchate,

Bishopric of Youth.[4] This is not hesychasm for fourteenth-century monks: it is hesychasm for twenty-first century laypeople, and is an admirable example of the continuing vitality of traditional Orthodox spirituality.

The bishop recommends that we should choose a regular time for the exercise, and warns us that at first it will be boring and monotonous. He points out that we begin by actually saying the prayer out loud, but that it gradually becomes internalized; and he specifies that its object is not for us to become 'spiritual heros', but to unite us with Christ in the hope that he will forgive us our sins, sanctify our life, and comfort our spirit. The prayer is a sort of spiritual arrow, he says, which penetrates the thick veil between us and God, 'rises to the pinnacle of heaven and enters the sanctuary of the Lord.' Those interested may read the details of the method for themselves, but for our purposes it is important to note that the information is practical and up-to-date, and that it comes from a member of one of the non-Chalcedonian Churches. Nor is it restricted to Orthodoxy. I was recently visiting a Cistercian monastery in the United States and saw in the gift shop instruction tapes on the practice of the Jesus Prayer for Roman Catholics.

In fact, the exercise of the Jesus Prayer is for everyone, and each of us can devise our own particular method of applying it. It demands a certain relaxation of body, it demands dedication, it demands repetition, repetition, and more repetition, but there is no doubt that it can be effective. Ultimately, the prayer may become so internalized that it goes on all the time—this is Saint Paul's 'unceasing prayer' (1 Thess 5:17)—but that is a high level to which few of us will attain. It is certainly not impossible. It's rather like driving a car: we can steer, brake, accelerate, note the traffic signals, avoid accidents, and stay in lane while having a conversation with our passengers or enjoying the music. Similarly, when the prayer has truly become part of us, it forms a basis for the rest of our activities. We no more have to stop it in order to eat than we have to stop the car in order to talk. Nor is the practice confined to Christianity: we find examples of just the same technique in Sufism, Pure Land

---

4. At http://www.geocities.com/athens/delphi/7261/arrowprayer.htm. If the website has changed, just type 'arrow-like prayer' into your search engine.

Buddhism, and other non-Christian traditions. The Japanese Buddhist saint Hōnen (1133–1212) used to repeat his equivalent of the Jesus Prayer, *Namu Amida Butsu* ('Homage to the Buddha Amitābha') 60,000 times a day,[5] and this could only be possible if he were praying internally and unceasingly. But few of us are Hōnens.

There is also another way in which an Orthodox Christian—or any Christian for that matter—may pursue his or her private devotions, and although it is not a method customarily used within the Orthodox tradition, there is no reason why it should not be. I am speaking here about discursive meditation on icons. Once again, we need to quieten down body and mind. The voice of the Spirit is a still, small voice, and it cannot be heard if our minds are clattering with noisy thoughts. Indeed, if one reads the minutes of the councils of the Church (and fascinating reading they are) one cannot avoid the impression that the bishops were often so busy with ecclesiastical politics that the only way they could have heard the voice of the Spirit would be if the latter had come not as a dove, but as an eagle with a loud hailer.

We need, then, to learn to relax the body and clear the mind (we can actually use the exercise of the Jesus Prayer to do it). We can sit on a comfortable chair (not too comfortable: meditation easily sends one to sleep), place an icon in front of us where we can easily see it, and *let it talk to us*. If icons are indeed windows onto another world, gateways to the transfigured cosmos, they are not only powerful things in themselves, but transmitters of power—divine power—to us. The important thing is not to impose ourselves on the icon, but to let the icon impose itself upon us. We don't look at it as art historians, as specialists in, say, Alexandrian iconography, and our business is not to dwell on the interesting arguments of the Iconoclastic Controversy. The icon has to speak to us, and if we allow it to do so, it can produce some remarkable insights. It's a good thing to write down these insights immediately after such a meditation—they have a curious tenuousness, and are all too easily forgotten—and then it is also a good thing to ground oneself with something to eat or drink. Walking about in an elevated state of inspiration leads to unfortunate accidents. Much more

5. Charles Eliot, *Japanese Buddhism* (London, 1935) 263.

could be said of the practical details of this exercise, but this is not a textbook of Do It Yourself Spirituality.[6]

Traditional Orthodox spirituality is solidly biblical, particularly so in the non-Chalcedonian Churches. The Bible itself may be viewed as an icon of the Word of God, and meditation on biblical passages is a standard form of monastic spirituality both eastern and western. In this context, meditation often means repeating the biblical text in a low voice and ruminating on it. Rumination is what cows, sheep, goats, and giraffes do. They chew, swallow, and regurgitate their food, and then chew it all over again. Rumination on biblical texts works in the same way, and in the west it is called *lectio divina* or 'sacred reading'. We read the text, swallow it down, regurgitate it, and chew it over again, opening ourselves up to a spiritual—i.e., Spirit-ual—experience of the depth of its meanings. Monastic reading, says Mother Bernard Payne,

> is not the rapid perusal of one spiritual treatise after another, but the attentive rumination of the sacred texts, allowing the Word of God to sink deep into the soul—a kind of spiritual communion with the Divine Word hidden beneath the written text. Such reading is in itself a meditation.[7]

When the pilgrim of *The Pilgrim's Tale* asked a young priest how he might attain interior spiritual enlightenment, the priest told him to take one text of Scripture and direct his attention and meditation on this single text for as long as possible. Otherwise (he said) you can do the same thing with a short prayer (the Jesus Prayer is the obvious example), and 'the light of understanding will be revealed to you'.[8]

Much, naturally, depends on the text. One might not glean a great deal, for example, from some of the verses in the books of Chronicles (though medieval exegetes would have had no problem); one may glean very much indeed from rumination on the first letter of Saint

---

6. There are numerous books now available on 'praying with icons', mostly by Anglicans. Two of them—*The Dwelling of the Light: Praying with Icons of Christ* (2003) and *Ponder These Things: Praying with Icons of the Virgin* (2006)—are by the present archbishop of Canterbury, Rowan Williams.
7. *La Trappe in England*, 195 (with minor amendments).
8. *The Pilgrim's Tale*, 134.

John. Once again, we must be careful not to impose ourselves on the text (*lectio divina* is not a synonym for biblical literary criticism), but to let the text speak to us. It is not particularly easy, and what the text says is often uncomfortable, but it can be rewarding.

One can do the same thing, of course, with other spiritual literature. In Chapter Six we mentioned the *Philokalia*, that remarkable collection of ascetic and devotional material compiled by Saint Nicodemus of the Holy Mountain and Saint Macarius Notaras of Corinth, and the *Philokalia* can certainly be used for *lectio divina*. The pilgrim of *The Pilgrim's Tale* used it all the time, and it has much to say on the Jesus Prayer. The long discussion by the fourteenth-century Patriarch of Constantinople, Kallistos (Callistus) of Xanthopoulos, and his friend and fellow-worker Ignatios (Ignatius) of Xanthopoulos is of particular importance, and what they have to say deals not only with the Jesus Prayer itself, but its context: baptism, grace, blessings, obedience, virtue, the gifts of the Holy Spirit, renunciation, faith, humility, temptations, diet, the Tradition of the Church, genuflexions, judgement, repentance, the nature and varieties of prayer, silence, manual labour, joy and sorrow, true and false illumination, the use of the imagination, divine sweetness, sin and repentance, purity of heart, *apatheia*, the Eucharist, and deification. There is an astonishing wealth of material here which well repays ruminative reading.[9]

Saint Nicodemus himself emphasized that the *Philokalia* was not just for monks and nuns, and that is certainly the case. True, one must use discretion (the mother of the virtues) in selecting appropriate texts, but that should be obvious. Orthodox theologians were men of their times, and their views and suggestions are not always relevant to modern men and women. Sometimes they are just plain wrong. We need not heed Saint Nicodemus, for example, when he tells men that if they have to speak to women (and the whole business is best avoided), they should not look them in the face. If you have to talk to them, he says, you do so either looking down at the ground or with your eyes closed.[10] On the other hand, his comments

---

9. There is an English translation in *Writings from the Philokalia on Prayer of the Heart*, tr. E. Kadloubovsky & Gerald E. H. Palmer (London, 1951) 164–270.

10. *Nicodemos of the Holy Mountain: A Handbook of Spiritual Council*, tr. Peter A. Chamberas, intro. George S. Bebis (New York/Mahwah, 1989) 90.

on why human beings are macrocosms in microcosms contain much that is useful and certainly warrant proper *lectio*.[11]

But the fact of the matter remains that none of these practices is essential. If Christians wish to use them, they are there to be used, but when it comes down to it, what Orthodox spirituality really is, is the ordinary sacramental life of ordinary Christians. The road to deification can be no more and no less than going to church, receiving the sacraments and the grace that they channel, prayer, whether liturgical or personal, and following, as best we can, the injunctions of Jesus of Nazareth as they are revealed in the New Testament.

This last, of course, is no easy matter. The way of evangelical perfection is not restricted to Sundays, and when Jesus told us to love our enemies, he did not mean only on one day of the week. In fact, as we suggested at the beginning of this chapter, we might have preferred it if Jesus had kept his mouth shut on a number of issues. Nor is the matter made any easier by the problem of interpretation. We said in Chapter Six that Scripture must always be interpreted, but how is a member of the armed forces supposed to react to the principle of turning the other cheek (Lk 6:29)? Does it mean 'If an enemy torpedoes the port side of your aircraft carrier, turn to him the starboard side also'? And what about lending and expecting nothing in return (Lk 6:35)? Tell that to the chartered banks. And what about Luke 14:26: 'If anyone comes to me and does not hate their father and mother, wife and children, brothers and sisters, they cannot be my disciple'? That, surely, would appear to exclude most of the human race. There is strange stuff in the Gospels.

Some of this difficult material may reveal its secrets through *lectio divina*; some of it may not. But rather than pondering imponderables, we may find it simpler and probably wiser to follow the straightforward injunction in Luke 6:31: 'Do to others as you would have them do to you'. This is not an idea confined to Christianity, but it is a fairly safe yardstick for moral action. 'Others', we might add, are not just other human beings. It is not, of course, foolproof—we might not advocate it to a masochist, for example—but if we com-

---

11. *Ibid.*, 67.

bine it with its negative counterpart, 'Do not do to others what you would not have them do to you,'[12] it is as good a guide as any. None of this is possible without help. Indeed, to think that we can get through life and achieve salvation without help is both heretical and stupid. Happily, help is all around us, if we would only ask for it. The saints, for example, are not just good, dead people who are now lounging on deck-chairs beside the crystal sea enjoying eternal cigars and everlasting brandy. Their task is far more daunting, as is that of the angels, especially guardian angels (who must be eternally exhausted), to say nothing of the Mother of God and the very Trinity itself. Help, in fact, is nothing more and nothing less than grace, and grace, like help, is there if we seek it. All you have to do is knock, said Jesus of Nazareth, and the door will be opened. Grace was first given to each of us in baptism and chrismation, and is further offered in confession and absolution, but as we said at the beginning of this chapter, all the sacraments are, by definition, channels of grace. Yet not all the sacraments can be repeated, or, if they can, there are limits to the number of repetitions. One cannot be baptized twice, for example, and the number of times one may marry is restricted not only by canon law but also, presumably, by physical endurance. Fortunately, this is not the case with the Eucharist. The Eucharist is infinitely repeatable, and, in Orthodox belief, offers to struggling humanity a constant and unlimited source of grace, strength, assistance, and consolation. It will be the subject of our next chapter.

---

12. This is to be found in the Latin western text of Acts 15:29. It does not appear in the Greek.

13

THE BODY AND BLOOD OF CHRIST

THE ORTHODOX CHURCHES are at one with Roman Catholicism and most of Anglicanism in maintaining that at the Eucharist a real change occurs. After the priest has called down the Holy Spirit onto the bread and wine—the *epiclesis*—what remains on the altar is not bread and wine, but the true body and blood of Christ. It might not look like it and it might not taste like it, but that is what it is. In the Middle Ages, the Latin Church in the west was troubled by a number of eucharistic controversies deeply concerned with the question of the nature of the eucharistic change. If indeed the bread and wine are the body and blood of Christ, why don't they look like it? A number of early Fathers, eastern and western, had offered two answers, both of them eminently reasonable. The first was what Ambrose of Milan called *horror cruoris* or 'horror of blood'.[1] The vast majority of Christians would be revolted to find themselves chewing on a lump of raw human flesh—cannibalism is not considered good form—and a mouthful of blood first thing in the morning would be a repellent breakfast. Secondly, if the body and blood really looked like body and blood, where would be the need for faith? The very fact that they still look and taste exactly like bread and wine means that we must *believe* that they are, in reality, body and blood, and the Eucharist is therefore one of the greatest tests of faith.

Orthodoxy would agree, though the eucharistic controversies were entirely confined to the west. The Orthodox Churches simply

---

1. Ambrose of Milan, *De sacramentis*, IV.iv.20.

maintained, and still do maintain, that a real change does take place in the eucharistic elements and that that change is miraculous. That is all there is to it. Furthermore, the Orthodox Churches, in whatever language they use, simply talk about a 'change', and 'change' is not a theological or philosophical term. The Latin term transubstantiation, on the other hand, is decidedly theological, and we need to say something about it.

For the medieval west it was, in fact, a very useful term, and it offered a sound solution to the sort of question being asked in the 800s. The most important (and obvious) of these questions was whether the bread and wine on the altar were changed into the actual, physical, corporeal body and blood of Christ, and, if they were, why did they not show the actual, physical, and corporeal characteristics of human flesh and blood? It is all very well to speak of *horror cruoris* and the need for faith, but this merely sidesteps the essential basic question: is this the true flesh and blood of Christ, or is it not? The answer was provided by the term 'transubstantiation'.

The medieval theologians borrowed from the Greek philosopher Aristotle the distinction between substance and accidents. The substance of something is its inherent, essential, but intangible nature; the accidents are its outward qualities or characteristics. Using this distinction, medieval theologians maintained that when the miraculous change occurred, it was the *substance* of the bread and wine which changed into the body and blood of Christ, while the *accidents* remained the accidents of bread and wine. By substance they meant, in this case, the abstract incorporeal nature of 'fleshness' and 'bloodness', and were thus able to avoid the awkward problems of such things as bones and muscles. By accidents, as we have said, they meant those characteristics which were perceived by the senses, primarily the senses of touch, taste, and smell. The answer, then, to the question of whether the bread on the altar was really and truly the actual body of Christ was both Yes and No. Yes, it is the true body of the Saviour, but in its incorporeal or 'substantial' nature; No, it is not the actual physical body with its physical or 'accidental' characteristics. Christ is there present, we need have no doubt of that, but if we look for meat and muscles, we will not find them. The same, naturally, was true for the wine. It was indeed the true substance of the blood of Christ, but it would not taste or smell like blood—those were no more than 'accidents'. Transubstantiation, therefore—not 'trans-accidentification'—offered a neat and useful solution for the times, and the term, which first appeared in about 1140, came to be the official term used by the Roman Catholic Church to designate the eucharistic change.

The eastern Churches did not, in general, adopt it, primarily because it answered questions which, in the east, had not been asked. But in the seventeenth century some Greek and Russian theologians borrowed the term from the Roman Catholic west, and it was used officially by the Synod of Jerusalem in 1672. Quite how the bishops at Jerusalem understood the term is, however, not entirely clear, and, in any case, it was never popular. When Philaret Drozdov, Metropolitan of Moscow, wrote his *Catechism* in 1823, he said that all the word really implied was that there was a true and real change, and Philaret went on to quote Saint John of Damascus who had said that whatever happens happens through the power of the Holy Spirit. *How* it happens remains incomprehensible; *that* it happens is the teaching of the Church.[2] And that (if we may skip from John of Damascus to John Keats) 'is all / Ye know on earth, and all ye need to know.'[3]

It follows from this that the Eucharist is a sacrifice. Here again the Orthodox Churches are at one with Roman Catholicism. In the Eucharist Christ offers himself to us, and, through the priest, is offered up to the Father for us, on our behalf. It is a re-enactment of the great offering on Calvary, and what happened at Calvary happens again at every Eucharist. At the Eucharist, we ourselves are present at a re-enacted (but not repeated) Calvary, and in the Eucharist we receive once again the grace of forgiveness and the grace of redemption. God is not bound by time.

What, then, of the view of the Protestant Reformers and the Protestant tradition that Calvary was the one and only sacrifice? That nothing can be added or taken away from that sacrifice? And that at that sacrifice the salvation of the world and of the human

---

2. Philaret Drozdov, 'The Longer Catechism of the Orthodox, Catholic, Eastern Church', tr. R.W. Blackmore, in Philip Schaff, rev. David S. Schaff, *The Creeds of Christendom* (New York, 1931 [6th ed.]; repr. Grand Rapids, 1983) 497–498.

3. John Keats, *Ode on a Grecian Urn* (the last lines).

race was achieved once and for all? Neither Orthodoxy nor Roman Catholicism would or would wish to disagree. According to Saint Thomas Aquinas, the Mass was a sacrifice only insofar as it was an 'image' of the 'real sacrifice'.[4] Likewise, the Roman Catholic Council of Trent (1545–63) affirmed that the sacrifice of the Mass was indeed propitiatory, that it applied to and profited both the living and the dead, but that it did not in any way detract from the all-embracing sufficiency of the great sacrifice on Calvary.

What the Eucharist does is to transform a once-and-for-all event into an ever-present reality. It is the same grace, just as it is the same sacrifice. Nothing is added; nothing is taken away. At Calvary, grace was restored to a graceless world; at the Eucharist, the same grace flows into us and transforms us, if we are truly open to it, into temples of the living God.

Taking Communion, therefore, is a serious matter and the Orthodox Churches treat it seriously. Not to take it seriously would be the same as not taking the crucifixion seriously. But if we see in the crucifixion of Jesus of Nazareth just another example of yet another Jewish rebel being executed by the Romans for sedition (crucifixions were common in first-century Palestine), then we cannot honestly call ourselves Christian. Furthermore, since the bread and wine is no longer simply bread and wine, when we consume the eucharistic elements, we actually consume Christ himself. In the medieval west there was much discussion as to what this implied. If we consume the perfect and incorrupt body of Christ will it metabolize inside us and render us equally perfect and incorrupt? And will it have the same effect on good and bad alike?

The answer to the second question was No, it will not. Just as we need faith in order to see what appears to be bread and wine as being, in reality, flesh and blood, so we need the same faith if the flesh and blood we consume is to have any effect upon us. But what effect? According to Saint Gregory of Nyssa, when Christ blends himself with the bodies of his believers, the mortal is united with the immortal, and by virtue of this union human beings will, in the fullness of time, participate in Christ's immortality and in-

---

4. Thomas Aquinas, *Summa theologiae*, III.83.1.

corruption.⁵ We are mingled with Christ in soul, says Nicholas Cavasilas, united to him in body, and commingled with him in blood, and in this supreme incorporation, we become truly 'Christian'.⁶ We begin to live the life in Christ, and the life in Christ is Christ in our life. But this is not automatic. The Eucharist is not a pill. If we have a headache and take an aspirin, our headache will disappear whether we like it or not. The Eucharist does not work in the same way. It is true that those who partake of it may receive (in the words of the Divine Liturgy) 'purification of soul, remission of sins, the communion of the Holy Spirit, and the fullness of the Kingdom of Heaven', but only by willing, faithful, and faith-full cooperation—synergy—with the grace of God. But with faith, all these things are possible, and the deification we spoke about in Chapter Seven is inconceivable without regular Communion.

So how often should we communicate? If the Eucharist is so important, and, with faith, so effective, surely it is better to communicate as often as possible? Not every five minutes perhaps, but maybe every day? Saint Basil the Great certainly thought so. 'It is good and beneficial', he says, 'to communicate every day', and goes on to tell us that he himself communicated at least four times a week, and more often if there was the feast of any saint.⁷ Orthodox laity of today would be hard pressed to imitate Basil since a daily Eucharist (except in monasteries) is virtually unknown, but there is more to it than that.

During the fourth century, Christian congregations grew ever larger and the Divine Liturgy grew ever longer. By the second half of the century, the clergy were wearing rich and ornate vestments, they were using rich and ornate vessels on the altar, and the liturgy itself was rich, ornate, and splendidly dramatic. Much emphasis was placed on the miraculous and awe-inspiring nature of the eucharistic transformation—the altar became a place of 'terror and shuddering'⁸—and the officiating clergy were increasingly separated from the laity. Before the end of the century, the sanctuary was

5. Gregory of Nyssa, *Oratio catechetica magna*, 37.
6. *Nicholas Cabasilas: The Life in Christ*, tr. Carmino J. deCatanzaro (New York, 1974) 129–130.
7. Basil the Great, *Epistola* 93.
8. See Henry Chadwick, *The Early Church* (London, 1967; rpt. 1993) 267.

being screened off by curtains, and the first iconostasis appeared in the sixth century in Justinian's great church of the Holy Wisdom (Hagia Sophia) in Constantinople. The large numbers, the atmosphere of holy awe, and the separation of priest from populace all conspired to diminish the frequency of Communion. It is one thing to eat your lunch at your local cafe; it is quite another to dine at the Ritz, and not everyone feels at home at the Ritz. The same was true in the churches of the late fourth—and subsequent—centuries. If you're going to dine at the Ritz, you might want to take a shower, fix your hair, wear something formal, and starve for a day. So, too, for those who wished to take Communion from the late fourth century onwards. It was not something you did without proper preparation, and it was not something you did every week. You built up to it. You steeled yourself for it. And only when you felt really prepared did you venture to the altar, and, in fear and trembling, actually take into your mouth the very flesh and blood of your crucified and resurrected Lord.

The inevitable result, of course, was that frequency of Communion on the part of the laity diminished dramatically. Sometimes, too, the emphasis on proper preparation for such an awesome experience led those who needed it most to take it least. But we should not abstain from the holy table, says Nicholas Cavasilas, on the pretext that we are unworthy. On the contrary, it is the sick who need to go to the doctor, not those who think they're well.[9] If you're a sinner (and we all are), then the sacrament of confession is there to deal with the matter. The Eucharist was not instituted for the benefit of those who think they're perfect.

But what has all this to do with modern Orthodoxy? What have Basil and Nicholas to do with us? The answer, of course, is that for Orthodoxy, history is not just history: it can also be Tradition. The approach to the Eucharist which was characteristic of late fourth-century Byzantium is still, in general, characteristic of modern Orthodoxy. Many Orthodox Christians still communicate infrequently, though this is changing, and non-Chalcedonians tend to communicate more frequently than Chalcedonians. But the approach to the sacrament is still one of awe and wonder, and the

9. Cabasilas, *The Life in Christ*, 193.

changes which have taken place in the Roman Catholic eucharistic liturgy following the Second Vatican Council are not, at the moment, to be seen in Orthodoxy. Roman Catholicism has here looked back to the more familiar and intimate practices of the earliest Church, or at least the Church of the second century; Orthodoxy still preserves the glory of Alexandria and imperial Byzantium.

Part of the preparation for receiving Communion is fasting. This is also true of Roman Catholicism, but the changes that have taken place in Roman Catholicism in recent years have not taken place in Orthodoxy. Since 1964 Roman Catholics have been required to fast for only one hour before communicating; Orthodoxy demands more. Some Orthodox Churches maintain the traditional practice (which dates back to at least the fourth century) of fasting from the previous midnight. The Copts require at least nine hours. Certain other Orthodox Churches require six, but that (so far as I am aware) is the absolute minimum. Nothing at all may be eaten or drunk during this period.

In general, fasting plays a more important role in Orthodoxy than in any of the western Churches. With a few exceptions, all Wednesdays and Fridays are fast days (this is a tradition which dates back to the second half of the first century), and in addition to that, in the Chalcedonian Churches there are four other periods during the year when fasting is prescribed.[10] Of these, the most important and the longest is the Great Fast of Lent; but all in all, Greek and Russian Orthodox could find themselves fasting for just about half the year. And if this seems severe, it is much less severe than the situation in the non-Chalcedonian Churches. Coptic Orthodox Christians fast for more than two hundred and fifty days each year, and fasting, in both Chalcedonian and non-Chalcedonian Churches, demands, in theory, total abstention from all meat, fish, dairy products (including eggs), wine, and olive oil. But as we have had occasion to observe elsewhere, theory and practice are not the same thing.

There is no doubt that the pace and demands of life in the modern world have had a marked effect on the traditional rules of fasting, and there is wide variation in when and how it is practised. Nowadays, apart from the eucharistic fast, many Chalcedonian

---

10. For the details, see Ware, *The Orthodox Church*, 300.

Orthodox fast only during Holy Week, though less rigorous fasting at other times is not uncommon. There have, in fact, been calls for modifications to the rules of fasting to take account of the problems of modern society, but nothing official has yet been done or said. Indeed, at the Pan-Orthodox Synod which met in Geneva in 1982, the question of fasting was carefully avoided. Those responsible for drawing up the agenda had voted by a majority to exclude it.

Fasting is, in essence, penitential. It was rigorously practised in Judaism, and it was a standard part of earliest Christianity. Jesus of Nazareth certainly fasted. Fasting was intended to weaken temptation and strengthen spirituality, though on occasion (as a number of early writers make clear) it was no more than a hypocritical display of outward piety. Whether and to what extent it is useful is a matter for each individual, and modern Coptic Christians (for example) and modern Roman Catholic Christians look at it very differently. It would be absurd for us to say that one is right and one is wrong. But any healthy Orthodox who intends to observe all the fasts of the Church in all their rigour would be well advised to discuss the matter with his or her parish priest—or else enter a monastery. But let us return to the Eucharist.

We need not discuss here the actual eucharistic liturgies—that was done in Chapter Eight—but we will say something of the practical details of just how one communicates. Anglicans and Roman Catholics (since the Second Vatican Council) regularly communicate in both kinds. That is to say, they eat a morsel of bread and drink a sip of wine. Such was the practice of the early Church, and Communion in both kinds was the general practice of all Churches, eastern and western, until the twelfth century. Then, for reasons which are not here our concern, the Latin west adopted the practice of Communion in one kind—bread alone—and retained the practice until the 1960s. Even now, Communion in one kind is common in Roman Catholicism, especially if there is a large congregation. Members of the Anglican and Protestant traditions have always communicated in both kinds, and both the bread and wine are normally received separately.

There is, however, the possibility of what is technically known as *intinction*. We mentioned this in Chapter One. In intinction, the consecrated bread is dipped into the consecrated wine and then administered to the faithful, and one can find both Anglican and Roman Catholic churches where this is the regular practice, though it is by no means common. Some people prefer it because of fear of infection by the AIDS virus. In Chalcedonian Orthodox Churches, a form of intinction is the standard practice, though this is not always the case in the non-Chalcedonian Churches. How is it done?

In the Chalcedonian tradition, when the priest and deacon prepare the bread and wine in the room to the left of the sanctuary, the priest takes a little knife called the lance (it is shaped like a spear) and uses it to cut from the round Communion loaf a certain section. This portion is called the Lamb, and in due course it will become the Lamb of God. At the *epiclesis*, the Lamb is transformed by the power of the Holy Spirit into the body of Christ and the wine into his blood. But in Chalcedonian Orthodoxy, the consecrated Lamb is cut into small pieces and placed in the chalice with the wine, and when the faithful come up to communicate, the priest uses a spoon with a long handle (it is often gold-plated; sometimes actually of gold) to take from the chalice a morsel of the wine-soaked bread, and places this morsel in the communicant's mouth. Meanwhile, one or more of those assisting will hold a cloth under the communicant's chin, so that should there be an accident, the morsel of bread and wine will not fall onto the floor. Sometimes communicants are expected to hold the cloth themselves. This method of intinction explains why receiving first Communion is no problem for newly baptized and chrismated babies: they eat their baby food in the same way. After people have taken Communion, they normally kiss the foot of the chalice (which will be decorated with a little cross), and then make their way to a table where there will be a basket of bread and a little cup or little cups of wine. Why?

The wine is simply to wash down any morsels that may have been left in one's mouth; the question of the bread is a little more complicated. What we are dealing with here is called, in the Byzantine tradition, the *antidoron* (pronounced 'an-TEE-though-ron' with the accent on the second syllable). It is the *pain bénit*, the 'blessed bread', of French and French-Canadian Catholicism. It comprises what is left over from the Communion loaf after the priest has cut from it the Lamb, and it is blessed by the priest, but not consecrated.

The word *antidoron* means 'instead of the gift'—the 'gift' being the consecrated body of Christ—and although it was originally intended only for those who did not communicate, it is now distributed to everyone. You can eat it yourself, exchange it with or give it to your friends, or take it home to give to someone else, Orthodox or not.

Orthodoxy, like Roman Catholicism, restricts actual Communion to its own baptized and chrismated members. In the view of both Churches, intercommunion is not a path that leads to full communion, but a sign that it has been achieved; and although one can make a sound theological argument to the contrary, it is not the Tradition of the Church. Since, therefore, Orthodox and non-Orthodox Christians are not yet united in faith and Orders, intercommunion is not encouraged. But with the *antidoron*, we have a visible sign of the overall and ultimate unity of the Christian tradition, and to share the blessed bread with Roman Catholics, Anglicans, Episcopalians, and anybody else you wish is an important symbol of Christian love, and of hope for a more Christian future.

The practices of the non-Chalcedonian Churches are not greatly different, but in (for example) Coptic Orthodoxy, the consecrated bread and wine are not mixed together. The priest places a morsel of bread directly into the mouth of the communicant, and then uses the communion spoon to administer the wine. There is a rich theological symbolism in both intinction and non-intinction, but we will not elaborate on that here. This is not a text-book of theology. So how does a Coptic priest deal with the first Communion of a newly-baptised baby? He dips his finger in the wine, touches the bread with it, and then puts the tip of his finger into the baby's mouth.

Just as in the Roman Catholic tradition, Orthodoxy, too, reserves the sacrament. That is to say, somewhere in the sanctuary of an Orthodox church (normally on the altar) there will be a small ornamental casket—in the west it is called the tabernacle—in which is kept a small amount of the consecrated bread and wine. The practice is an ancient one and dates back to at least the second century. But when offering the reserved sacrament, the bread and wine are not mixed together as they are in the chalice: the priest just touches the consecrated bread with a drop of wine from the communion spoon. Unlike Roman Catholicism, however, there is no Orthodox equivalent of the ceremonies of Exposition or Benediction (save in some western-rite parishes of the Antiochian archdiocese in the United States), both of which were unknown until the fourteenth century. It is true that the consecrated eucharistic elements are used to bless the members of an Orthodox congregation, but only in the course of the Divine Liturgy. The purpose of reservation is primarily for the Communion of those who are sick (or in prison), but it is also necessary on those days in Lent and Holy Week when the Church celebrates the Liturgy of the Presanctified. In this liturgy (as we saw in Chapter Eight) there is no consecration, and Communion is given from the consecrated bread and wine reserved from the preceding Sunday.

The mention of the sick leads us conveniently and logically to the last of the sacraments, which is unction or anointing. All the Orthodox Churches—all Churches that use the rite, for that matter—trace it back to a passage in the letter of Saint James: 'Are any among you sick? They should call for the elders of the church and have them pray over them, anointing them with oil in the name of the Lord' (James 5:14). But whereas the Roman Catholic west, for many centuries, restricted the sacrament to those in danger of death (*in extremis* in Latin, from which comes the term 'extreme unction'), all the Orthodox Churches offer it to anyone who needs it. Indeed, it may also be used as a preventative. In theory, the celebration of the sacrament of unction requires the presence of seven priests, but, understandably, this rule is seldom applied. The sacrament is still effective with fewer priests (five or three), and if need be it can be celebrated by one alone. In addition to the actual anointing, the rite involves seven readings from the Epistles, seven from the Gospels, and a variety of hymns and prayers. Normally it takes place in church, but if a person is gravely ill, it can be done at home. And in some parishes (but by no means all), on the Wednesday of Holy Week (or, in Coptic Orthodoxy, on the last Friday before Holy Week), the entire congregation is anointed in church in preparation for receiving Holy Communion.

With this discussion of anointing we have completed our survey (and it is no more than a survey) of the seven sacraments, and it is now time to leave these theological questions and turn to a quite different matter. In all that we have said so far we have continually compared and contrasted Orthodoxy with other Christian traditions, especially Roman Catholicism, and we must now look at relations between the Orthodox Church and other Churches in a little more detail. What officially has been done in the matter of ecumenism and Church union, and where does Orthodoxy stand today with regard to Roman Catholicism, Anglicanism, and the wide-ranging diversity of Protestantism? That there are problems here is not in doubt, and they are not problems which can be glossed over. But an honest and non-partisan discussion of the situation is essential, and that is what we shall try to do in our next chapter.

14
ORTHODOXY AND THE WEST

IT IS NOT DIFFICULT to find within the Orthodox fold plenty of examples of those whose only reaction to ecumenism and the possibility of Church union is stubborn and sometimes hysterical opposition. On the other hand, it is not difficult to find similar reactions in other Churches as well. Orthodoxy is not alone in having its quota of bigots, and statements such as 'modern ecumenism is both a threat and an ecclesiological heresy', or modern ecumenism is 'a betrayal of the Holy Orthodox Church [and] a negation of its essence',[1] are not uncommon. High on a balcony overlooking the sea, the ultra-Orthodox monks of the Esphigmenou monastery on Mount Athos have placed a sign which reads, in Greek: 'Orthodoxy or Death'.[2] Indeed, I have a nasty suspicion that views such as these, if not quite so extreme, represent a majority viewpoint within the Orthodox world.

On the other hand, it cannot be denied that this is a logical viewpoint, given that Orthodoxy maintains (rightly or wrongly), that it, and it alone, has preserved intact the Tradition of the Church, and that if the 'deposit of faith' is to be found anywhere, it is to be found there. And, from one point of view, this is true. That is to say, it is true that Orthodoxy has seen fewer changes than any of the other major Churches, though the obvious rejoinder to this is that

---
1. These and similar statements are to be found on the website of the Orthodox Christian Information Center at http://www.orthodoxinfo.com/ecumenism.
2. See Speake, *Mount Athos*, p. 165, for a photograph. I do not know whether the sign is still there.

183

Orthodoxy has changed so little because it has simply turned a deaf ear to the promptings of the Holy Spirit. Be that as it may, Orthodoxy can and does claim a solid and unbroken continuity with the early Church, and it is easy to take this as a basis for declaring that Orthodoxy is the only true Church. If, therefore, you wish to be saved, become Orthodox. If Orthodoxy *is* the Church, then Orthodoxy need not and should not go forth, cap in hand, to the other Churches. On the contrary, let the other Churches come to the rock of salvation, the pillar of the faith, the foundation of the truth, and there find the pledge and guarantee of eternal life.

Such an extreme view is, as we have said, logical. Whether it is true is another matter entirely. But it is not the view of all Orthodox, and it is certainly not the view of most of the Orthodox patriarchs. There *is* a positive side to ecumenism, the World Council of Churches is not simply a mechanism for the propagation of Protestant doctrine, and, as Christian Orthodox as well as Orthodox Christians, one should at least make an attempt to love one's ecclesiastical neighbours and not merely condemn them—however sorrowfully—to eternal torment and everlasting pain.

But who are these neighbours and how should I relate to them? Sometimes, obviously, no relationship is possible. Given its foundation in Holy Tradition, the Orthodox Church clearly cannot look for any real rapport with a Church that does not believe that the one God is a Trinity, or which does not regard Christ as truly human and truly divine. There is really no point, therefore, in any dialogue between Orthodoxy and (for example) the Unitarian Universalist Association. Furthermore, Orthodoxy cannot look for any real rapport with a Church which is not, at basis, sacramental. In other words, there can be no re-union between Orthodoxy and the vast majority of the Protestant family of Churches, which emphasize preaching rather than sacraments, and with which there was never any union to begin with. This is not to say that members of these Churches should not be respected, admired, valued, and loved; it *is* to say that although some of them might be happy to have an Orthodox share in their celebration of the Lord's Supper, Orthodoxy cannot return the compliment. Members of these Churches are always welcome to attend the Divine Liturgy, but they may not receive Holy Communion.

Lutheranism, however, is not quite as Protestant as some other Protestant Churches, and some of Luther's own views were quite different from those of more radical Reformers such as Ulrich Zwingli or John Calvin. Some Lutheran Churches, for example, have bishops and recognize a form of apostolic succession. They also acknowledge the presence of Christ in the Eucharist, though they do not accept transubstantiation, and regard baptism and the Eucharist as sacraments. In recent years, therefore, there have been attempts at dialogue between Orthodox and Lutherans, but although we may admire the goodwill, we cannot say that there has been a great deal of success. The problem is that while Lutheranism and Orthodoxy can indeed embrace a number of common ideas, there are many other ideas on which they do not and, indeed, cannot agree. Justification by faith has only a superficial similarity to deification, for the central issue—whether 'works' can be effective in the search for salvation—is answered quite differently by the two groups. In theological terms, one maintains a doctrine of infused righteousness, the other of imputed righteousness, though this is not the place to enter into detail on the subject. Furthermore, Lutheran sacraments are not so much channels for grace, which is the Orthodox view, as symbols of grace already received, and there are only two of them. Ordination is not regarded as a sacrament, and when we come to the Lutheran doctrine of the priesthood of all believers, male and female, there can be little common ground between the two traditions. Nor can there be much overlap between Orthodox and Lutherans on the place of Mary and the saints, nor on the infallibility of the seven (fewer for the non-Chalcedonians) Ecumenical Councils. In short, although it is possible to select a few important items from the theological supermarket which both sides are prepared to share—sometimes, if we are to be honest, in a rather watered-down form—there remain many others which are unique to the two different groups, and the few items that have been selected have not been deemed sufficient for any true union.

If, then, we are thinking in terms of real union or re-union, we are clearly thinking in terms of Roman Catholics and, to some extent, Anglicans,[3] but here too there are problems. At present, the

---

3. The case of the Old Catholics will be considered later in this chapter.

Roman Catholic Church quite clearly demands recognition of the absolute jurisdictional primacy of Rome, whereas dealing with Anglican doctrine is like trying to grasp a heavy fog. It moves around, it slides about, it is eminently malleable, and—in accordance with the very reason for its creation—it can be all things to all men and usually (though not always) to all women. Anglicanism was devised to offer as broad a sweep of doctrine and practice as possible—it had to bridge post-Tridentine Roman Catholicism and the principles of the continental Reformation—and it achieved its task with commendable success. It boasts a fine spirituality (especially in the seventeenth century), a great deal of eminent and lucid scholarship, and, in the person of Michael Ramsey, who died in 1988, one of the great churchmen of the twentieth century. But it is hard to pin down. Within the broad fold of the Anglican tradition, it is not difficult to find Anglicans who are Orthodox in all but name, Anglicans who are Roman Catholic in all but name, and Anglicans who are fundamentalist evangelical Christians in all but name. So when we speak of uniting with Anglicanism, the first question we must ask is 'Which Anglicanism?, or even 'Which Anglican?'.

But despite this real problem, Orthodox-Anglican relations have been warm and profitable since the nineteenth century. The Anglican and Eastern Churches Association, whose purpose was to work and pray for the union of the Orthodox and Anglican traditions, was founded in 1864, primarily on the initiative of John Mason Neale, who added many eastern hymns to the western repertoire and who published *A History of the Holy Eastern Church* in five volumes between 1847 and 1873. It was a fine piece of scholarship for its day. A number of official and semi-official meetings between the two Churches then took place in the course of the twentieth century, and apart from certain setbacks involving the recognition of Anglican orders and (especially) disagreement over the ordination of women, a considerable amount of progress was made—at least on paper. In practice, however, little has been done. The parties meet, they discuss, they produce documents (some of them very fine), they agree on a number of points, they avoid others, they thank each other courteously for their respective contributions, and they take their leave.

There are those, therefore, who would say that the movement towards the reunion of Orthodoxy and Anglicanism is a purely documentary movement. This is not, in fact, entirely true, but it is not far wrong. Yet it is too easy to be pessimistic and dismissive. In the world of medicine, a great deal of basic scientific research is necessary before we move on to testing techniques on humans, and it may be years before we see the 'practical' consequences of a new line of thought. The same is true in ecumenism. At its meeting in October 1999, the International Commission of the Anglican Orthodox Theological Dialogue continued discussions on the nature of the Church which had begun in 1989. The delegates considered 'the nature and authority of the episcopal ministry and the question of conciliarity and primacy', and discovered an 'essential convergence'.[4] Subsequent meetings have examined the meaning of sacramental priesthood in the Church, its relation to the unique high priesthood of Christ, and other forms of ministry in the Church. This sort of progress is not to be despised, and we cannot hope for too much too soon. After all, the matters at stake are of first importance—if the delegates are not talking about salvation they shouldn't be there—and even if such dialogue serves, for the moment, only to help both Churches define or refine the content of their Tradition, that is no mean achievement.

On the other hand, all Christian Churches today are faced with a number of questions which are not only important theologically, but which are of immediate consequence to some, at least, of that large percentage of the general population who are not heterosexual males. Should women be ordained as priests or ministers? Should active gays or lesbians be ordained as priests or ministers? Should women be consecrated as bishops? And should priests or ministers conduct and bless same-sex marriages? The Orthodox answer to all four of these questions is, rightly or wrongly, a resounding No. There are, of course, Orthodox priests who are active homosexuals, but, in theory at least, they were not known to be that when they were ordained. In the Anglican communion, however, there are a

---

4. International Commission of the Anglican Orthodox Theological Dialogue, Communiqué, available on the Internet at http://www.anglicancommunion.org/ministry/ecumenical/dialogues/orthodox/index.cfm.

number of churches which, at the moment, are prepared to answer all four questions with a Yes, even if it is not a resounding Yes (it is sometimes hesitant in the extreme), and this can only drive a gulf between these churches and Orthodoxy. No Orthodox Church will unite with a non-Orthodox Church which ordains women, knowingly ordains actively gay males, consecrates women as bishops, or blesses same-sex marriages.

What, then, of Roman Catholicism? Here we have a Church which refuses to ordain women or (in theory) active gays, does not consecrate women as bishops, will not bless a same-sex marriage, and which clearly has much else in common with Orthodoxy. It is also a Church which, since the Second Vatican Council, has been open to cordial dialogue. In 1964, Pope Paul VI and Ecumenical Patriarch Athenagoras I met in Jerusalem, and in the following year the mutual anathemas of 1054 (which we discussed in Chapter Three) were solemnly revoked. This did not restore the two Churches to communion, but it was a necessary first step towards that possibility. Nor should the mutual revocation be looked on simply as a ritual or symbolic gesture. Both Orthodoxy and Roman Catholicism place great weight on ritual gestures.

Following this historic meeting of pope and patriarch (the last time they met had been five hundred years earlier at the Council of Florence), there were a number of other official meetings which resulted in useful consensus on the nature of the Church, apostolic succession, and the sacraments. Nevertheless, the fact remains that the real problem in Orthodox-Roman Catholic reunion is the problem of the papal claims, or, more precisely, the papal claim to supreme teaching authority. The old controversy over the *filioque*, which we discussed in Chapter Four, is not now of major consequence. Both Churches are in total agreement on the full divinity of the Holy Spirit, and both are in total agreement that the Church, guided by the same Spirit, is the vessel of grace. But what of the Roman primacy?

True, the term is rather old fashioned, as also are the terms 'primacy of honour' and 'primacy of jurisdiction' which we introduced in Chapter Three. But the essential question still remains: is the pope first among equals, or is he, in some sense, first above all? We are not talking here about political authority, those days are long past (nowadays the Papal States are only important to stamp collectors), but of teaching authority. As we saw in Chapter Three, this primacy is manifested in modern Roman Catholicism in three ways: (i) decisions made by Roman Catholic bishops (even unanimous decisions) are authoritative only if they are approved by the pope; (ii) the pope may speak on behalf of his bishops without actually consulting them (their tacit approval being assumed); and (iii) decisions of Ecumenical Councils are authoritative only if they, too, are approved by the pope.

The question at issue here is not that of papal infallibility, but something much wider. The doctrine of papal infallibility, in fact, is of less consequence in Orthodox-Roman Catholic relations than is often supposed. The doctrine of infallibility, which was proclaimed infallibly at the First Vatican Council in 1870, does not actually say that under certain circumstances the *pope* is infallible; it says that the teaching of the Church, as proclaimed under certain circumstances by the pope, is infallible, and that is a very different matter. We might add that it was not what Pius IX wanted ('*La tradizione son' io*', he said with magnificent arrogance: 'I am the Tradition!'), and it took some very deft footwork by Cardinal Guidi, Archbishop of Bologna, to change the title of the decree from 'On the Infallibility of the Roman Pontiff' (which was the original draft) to 'On the Infallible *Magisterium* [teaching authority] of the Roman Pontiff.' But in any case, apart from the papal statement proclaiming the doctrine, there is general, though not universal, agreement among Roman Catholic theologians that only one infallible statement has been proclaimed since 1870: the doctrine of the Immaculate Conception in 1954 (with which, it might be added, almost all Orthodox disagree).

On the matter of the infallibility of the Church's teaching, however, Orthodoxy would have no disagreement. The Church is infallible because the Church is taught by the Holy Spirit, and, according to Christ himself, 'when the Spirit of truth comes, he will guide you into all truth' (Jn 16:13). The fact that human beings have often made the most miserable hash of hearing what the Holy Spirit is actually saying is unfortunate, but it does not prove that Christ was a liar. As Sergius Bulgakov has said, 'the Church is infallible, not because it expresses the truth correctly from the point of view of practical expediency, but because it contains the truth.'[5] And for Orthodoxy, this infallibility is expressed primarily through councils, especially Ecumenical Councils, and not through any one individual. Nor would Orthodoxy agree that this one individual could overrule the majority of bishops, as may certainly happen in Roman Catholicism.

On the other hand, the question of whether a papal statement has or has not been uttered infallibly is, for the ordinary Roman Catholic layperson, irrelevant. What is technically called the 'ordinary *magisterium*' of the Church means that Roman Catholics are obliged to accept the teachings of the Church, and act in accordance with them, unless and until these teachings are changed by the Church *acting in and through the pope*. It is true that what is taught and what is actually done are sometimes far apart—the case of birth control is an obvious example—but the fact remains that papal statements are (in theory) to be regarded as authoritative by all Roman Catholics. Sometimes, as we have seen, a pope may forbid any further discussion of the matter, although (in practice) this prohibition is often ignored.

It is obvious that Orthodoxy must look on these ideas with grave disquiet. Ecumenical Patriarchs do not possess this type of authority—they may try to persuade, but they cannot overrule—and the greater powers possessed by Roman Catholic popes mean that their individual views, whether liberal or conservative, must necessarily have far-reaching influence. Pope John Paul II, for example, had a profound belief in the immense importance of his office. From the beginning of his pontificate he saw himself as an authoritative teacher, and had no hesitation in asserting his authority. He was also generally conservative in his views, and it is undeniable that, under his administration, the more conservative elements in the Roman Catholic Church, seriously shaken in the aftermath of the Second Vatican Council, were able to re-establish themselves.

As a Slav, however, John Paul II was more interested and more active than any of his predecessors in the Orthodox Churches, and in his hopeful encyclical *Ut Unum Sint*, promulgated in 1995, he asserted the fundamental unity of the 'sister Churches' of east and

---

5. Bulgakov, *The Orthodox Church*, 79.

west and left no doubt of his commitment to reconciliation. But in the same encyclical he also reasserted the primacy of Rome. It is the duty of the Successor of Peter, he wrote,

> to admonish, to caution and to declare at times that this or that opinion being circulated is irreconcilable with the unity of faith. When circumstances require it, he speaks in the name of all the Pastors in communion with him. He can also—under very specific conditions clearly laid down by the First Vatican Council—declare *ex cathedra* that a certain doctrine belongs to the deposit of faith.[6]

It is true that the document goes on to say that 'all this must always be done in communion', and it is also true that the doctrine of the Roman primacy is stated delicately and diplomatically, but there is no doubt that it is there. John Paul II did not regard himself simply as a bishop among bishops, as *primus inter pares*, and his understanding of the Roman primacy involved very much more than a simple primacy of honour.

Furthermore, in a document issued in June 2000 the term 'sister Churches' is clarified:

> In the proper sense, *sister Churches* are exclusively particular Churches (or groupings of particular Churches; for example, the Patriarchates or Metropolitan provinces) among themselves. It must always be clear, when the expression sister Churches is used in this proper sense, that the one, holy, Catholic and apostolic Universal Church is not sister but *mother* of all the particular Churches.[7]

Such a statement clearly has unfortunate implications for reunion. On the other hand, in the encyclical *Dominus Iesus*, issued on 6 August 2000, and which has proved so offensive to many non-Christians, the Orthodox communities are referred to as 'true

---

6. Paragraph 17 of the encyclical, available on the Internet at http://www.vatican.va/edocs/ENG0221/INDEX.HTM.
7. Congregation for the Doctrine of the Faith, Protocol 121/99-10995, available on the Internet at http://www.natcath.com/NCR_Online/documents/sisterchurches.htm, and elsewhere.

particular Churches',[8] and in the past, 'true' has been used to refer to the Roman Catholic Church alone.

At the moment, therefore, it seems that what Rome offers with one hand it takes back with the other (and vice-versa), and the preeminent view of the papacy held by John Paul II, rightly or wrongly (depending on your standpoint), cannot be seen as promoting Orthodox-Roman Catholic reunion. Under John XXIII the situation might have been different. What it will be under Benedict XVI is yet to be seen. But the salient fact remains: the papal claim to supreme teaching authority, however diplomatically stated, is a major problem—perhaps the major problem—for the Orthodox Churches in the quest for reunion. Orthodoxy remains adamant that the bishop of Rome is *primus inter pares*, first among equals. He does not and can not possess any additional charism above and beyond that possessed by the other bishops. It is true that Orthodoxy can and has reinterpreted *primus*—'first'—in more than one way, but in the quest for reunion, it is not so much what the patriarchs are prepared to offer which is important: it is what the papacy is prepared to accept.

There are, in fact, some Orthodox Churches already in communion with Rome. These are the Uniat (sometimes and less correctly spelled Uniate) Churches. They retain Orthodox rites and customs (including married clergy), but they acknowledge papal supremacy. All came into existence for a mixture of theological and political reasons, and the oldest of them is the Syrian Maronite Church, which entered into communion with Rome in 1182. The largest group is the Ukrainian Uniat Church which came into existence in 1595. They are sometimes referred to as Eastern Rite Catholics, and, in general, they have had an unhappy history. The other Orthodox Churches tend to regard them as traitors to the faith, and the Roman Catholic Church has sometimes had an uneasy relationship with them. After all, how can you defend a celibate Roman Catholic clergy if hundreds of your Eastern Rite Catholic clergy are married? In 1991, however, an official code of

---

8. Paragraph 94 of the encyclical, available on the Internet at http://www.vatican.va/roman_curia/congregations/cfaith/documents/rc_con_cfaith_doc_20000806_dominus-iesus_en.html.

canon law came into force for the Uniat Churches, and nowadays they certainly have a better relationship with Rome than they do with their Orthodox neighbours. There has been considerable tension (and sometimes considerable violence) between the two groups, not least in Ukraine, and many Orthodox still regard the Uniats with an unchristian mixture of contempt, disdain, distrust, and dislike.

What, then, of the Old Catholics? The Old Catholics consist of a small group of Churches in the Netherlands, Germany, Austria, Switzerland, Poland, and (as a result of immigration) the United States, and all of them have doctrines very similar to those of Orthodoxy. Theology and politics led to the formation of the Dutch group in the eighteenth century, and most of the others came into being in reaction to the First Vatican Council (1869–70). There were many who did not or could not agree with the views of Pius IX on the nature and extent of papal teaching authority, and shortly after the council was suspended in October 1870, they seceded from the Roman Catholic Church. As with Orthodoxy, the doctrines of the Old Catholics are based on the first seven Ecumenical Councils, and they accept other doctrines which came into being between 787 (the date of the Seventh Ecumenical Council) and the Great Schism of 1054. They are solidly sacramental, their clergy may marry, and their liturgy is in the vernacular, though it is not an Orthodox liturgy. They are, however, closer to Orthodoxy than any other western Church, and from the 1870s to the 1980s a number of conferences were held in which both Churches agreed on almost everything. Why, then, has there been no formal union?

Apart from the fact that these things take time—some would say too much time—there is a major problem in that since 1932 the Old Catholics have been in full communion with the Church of England. Intercommunion was also established a little later with the Episcopal Church in the United States and most other Anglican Churches. If, then, the Orthodox Church were to enter into full communion with the Old Catholics, what would that imply for Orthodox-Anglican reunion? Would the entire Anglican communion be drawn in on the coat-tails of the Old Catholics? Or would the Old Catholics have to de-communicate themselves from the Anglicans in order to re-communicate themselves with the

Orthodox? It is a tricky question, and a question, clearly, to which no one yet has come up with a satisfactory answer. One group of Old Catholics—the comprehensively named Anglican Catholic Byzantine Orthodox Church (ACBOC)—clearly had no problem in uniting with almost anyone, but the ACBOC was dissolved for legal reasons in 2003.

Despite their cautious approach to the question of ecumenism, most of the Orthodox jurisdictions are members of the World Council of Churches. The Council was formally constituted in 1948, and in 1961 defined itself as 'a fellowship of churches which confess the Lord Jesus as God and Saviour according to the scriptures and therefore seek to fulfil together their common calling to the glory of the one God, Father, Son, and Holy Spirit.'[9] It cannot be denied that there is a distinct Protestant disposition to the Council, and the Roman Catholic Church is not formally a member. Since 1961, however, it has involved itself with the work of the Council, first by sending observers, and then, even though not a member, by assisting in the drafting of certain of its documents. As we have said, the Orthodox Church is a member of the Council—one of its founding members, in fact—though not always a happy one. Some—and they are not few—would say that membership of an ecumenical organization compromises the claim of the Orthodox Church to be the one, true Church, and (like the Roman Catholics) they would prefer to attend only as observers. The Patriarchate of Moscow was particularly hesitant, and it was more than a decade before it applied to join the Council. Membership of the Council does not, in fact, compromise Orthodox claims, but it can look as if it does.

There have been times, too, when the Orthodox Churches have not been able, in all conscience, to put their signatures to certain documents, and have submitted minority reports. That this is no longer the practice is, for many Orthodox, a thing to be regretted. There is also the problem that the Council tends to be more concerned with socio-economic issues than with doctrinal questions, and while Orthodoxy willingly recognizes that such issues are important, legitimate, urgent, and Christian, it would also like to

---

9. World Council of Churches, Constitution, paragraph 1 (easily available on the Internet).

see theology and spirituality given if not equal, at least appropriate, consideration. It may be true that 'faith without works is dead, being alone' (James 2:17), but if we are justified by our works alone, then Saint Paul spent a great deal of time talking nonsense.

On the other hand, Orthodox membership of the Council profits both the Council and Orthodoxy. It cannot be denied that Orthodoxy has an arrogant tendency to keep itself to itself—if you're convinced you're the one, true Church, why bother talking to anyone else?—and this is not a good thing. There is a very great deal going on in modern Christian thinking, and although it varies immensely in quality—even in rationality—some of it demands careful consideration. The Ecumenical Patriarch Athenagoras I (1886–1972), a giant of a man physically, intellectually, and spiritually, clearly showed the way in this regard, and apart from keeping up with contemporary politics by reading *The Times* every morning, he was deeply interested in the trends and developments of modern theology. Contrary to the views of some ultra-orthodox Orthodox, the Holy Spirit does not confine its activities to Mount Athos.

It is also useful for the World Council of Churches to be in intimate communication, if not communion, with Orthodox and Roman Catholics. Without their contribution and, sometimes, opposition, the Council could easily become a pan-Protestant association concentrating on education, evangelism, justice, health issues, economic problems, poverty, refugees, and the consequences of war—all of which, we might add, are obviously of first importance. Sometimes the presence of the Orthodox members of the Council may be awkward and divisive, but Church councils (not least the seven Ecumenical Councils) have often been awkward and divisive. Indeed, they sometimes have to be awkward and divisive if they are to get at the truth. The scholastic method in the west may have led to problems, but it certainly showed that thesis and antithesis could lead to synthesis. A good argument can be a good thing, provided that both parties are at least partly prepared to try to see each other's viewpoint. If they are not so prepared, then we might as well give each of them a baseball bat, lock them up in a room for an hour, and see who comes out.

The related questions of ecumenism and Church union are not easy. It is one thing to have an enjoyable, interesting, long-lasting, and rewarding relationship with a person; it is quite another thing to marry them. Marriage is something that demands careful forethought, total commitment, and a great deal of hard work, and it is unwise—stupid is a better term—to enter upon it lightly. The same is true of the marriage of the Churches. Yet even now there is movement. Sometimes there is even progress, for movement and progress are not the same. But if those who read this book are looking for quick results, they will be disappointed.

We have been talking in this chapter about Orthodoxy and the west, more precisely about Orthodoxy and the western Churches, but what about Orthodoxy *in* the west? In these days, in the twenty-first century, those seeking spiritual fulfilment are not restricted to western traditions, and for those who are interested there is an enormous choice of spiritual paths available. Furthermore, for those who are seeking such fulfilment within the Christian tradition, they, too, have a much wider choice than was the case only a few years ago.

In 1960 the Anglican priest and preacher Austin Farrer delivered a sermon at Pusey House in Oxford in which he explained why he was and why he remained Anglican. There were, for him, two overriding considerations. The first was that he dared not dissociate himself from 'the apostolic ministry, and the continuous sacramental life of the Church extending unbroken from the first days until now'; the second was that he could not ally himself with Rome because of fundamental disagreements over the doctrine of papal infallibility and the Roman Catholic understanding of its *magisterium*.[10] So why not Orthodoxy? 'Because', says our author, 'I was not born a Greek or Slavic Christian.'[11] In 1960 that was true. Orthodoxy was ethnic Orthodoxy. In many places (alas!) it still is. But not in all. One does not, nowadays, need to be born into the tradition, and, for some of those seeking spiritual realization, Orthodoxy is just round the corner. Let us therefore say a word about Orthodoxy in the west, and even something about western Orthodoxy.

---

10. Austin Farrer, *The End of Man* (London, 1973-Grand Rapids, 1974) 50–51.
11. *Ibid.*, 51.

15

ORTHODOXY IN THE WEST

ORTHODOXY spread to the west in just the same way as Christianity spread to the west: actively and passively. Actively, it was brought by missionaries (primarily Russian Orthodox). Passively, it was brought by immigrants seeking a haven from persecution and/or a better life. If the immigrants were lucky, they found themselves in a place where there was an Orthodox church of their own jurisdiction. If they were unlucky, they either did without or allied themselves with another Orthodox tradition. In the early days of Orthodoxy in America, some Orthodox churches were microcosms of almost the entire Orthodox world.

It would be easy to fill this chapter with names, numbers, dates, and places. It would also be boring. In any case, those interested in such things may easily find the information elsewhere, especially on various websites. This chapter, therefore, is not intended to be a comprehensive survey of the Orthodox diaspora. Instead we will concentrate on the story of the Orthodox Church in North America and, to a lesser extent, in Europe. But even then our approach will be selective, and members of many smaller Orthodox and quasi-Orthodox communities may be disappointed to find that their names do not appear.

Greek Orthodoxy first spread to England in the seventeenth century, and among the Greeks who came to the country was the priest Nathaniel Canopius, who (according to tradition) was the first to introduce the English to the pleasures of coffee. The first Greek Orthodox church was established in 1677 in London on a site (appropriately) in present-day Greek Street, Soho, but there was strong opposition from the established Church of England, and in 1684 the church was taken from the Greeks and given to the French Protestants.

The Russians fared rather better. They established themselves in London early in the next century and catered to Greeks and Russians alike. Then, in 1837/8, the London Greeks were able to open their own church, and from then on there was a small, but constant Orthodox presence in England and Wales, especially in the cities of Manchester, London, Liverpool, and Cardiff. As for the non-Chalcedonian Churches, Armenian Orthodox communities have had a long history in London and Manchester; in 1995 the Antiochian Archdiocese received a notable influx of Anglicans who were unprepared to accept the ordination of women; and in 1994 the Coptic Orthodox Church underwent a curious renaissance when it took under its wing the British Orthodox Church. That, however, is a matter which must be left for discussion until later in this chapter since it cannot be understood without first saying something about Syrian Orthodoxy in the west; and Syrian Orthodoxy in the west cannot be understood without first turning our attention to Orthodoxy in the New World.

That story begins dramatically. Orthodoxy—Russian Orthodoxy—first came to the country in 1741 when a Russian expedition led by a Dane in the service of the Tsar, Vitus Jonassen Bering (the Bering Sea bears his name), landed at what is now Sitka on the southern coast of Alaska. Five days later, on 20 July 1742, the first Orthodox liturgy to be celebrated in North America occurred on the deck of Bering's ship. Bering's voyage was followed by a flood of unscrupulous Russian fur-traders, and Russian control over Alaska lasted until 1867. To serve these Russian Alaskans (and to convert the original inhabitants), a small mission was established in the last years of the eighteenth century. The mission also opened the first school for the indigenous peoples. Missionary work proceeded much more effectively in the next century as a result of the efforts of an extraordinary man, Ivan Veniaminov, who worked in Alaska for some thirty years.

Ivan Yevseyevich Veniaminov was born in 1797 in Siberia and began his career as a married parish priest, first in Irkutsk and then in Alaska. While in Alaska he became fluent in Aleut, devised an alphabet for the language, wrote the first grammar, and translated into Aleut the Gospels and the Orthodox Liturgy. After ten years in the Aleutians he moved to Sitka (then called Novo Arkhangelsk) and began missionary work among the Kolosh Indians. In 1840, when he was back in Saint Petersburg recruiting support for the Alaska mission, his wife died, and Veniaminov took monastic vows under the monastic name of Innocent (Innokenty in Russian). Soon afterwards he was consecrated bishop of the immense and newly-created diocese of Kamchatka, which embraced Kamchatka, Alaska, the region of Yakutsk, and the Kuril and Aleutian Islands. He established a seminary to train priests from the indigenous population and travelled the region for twenty-eight years, often in conditions of appalling hardship and great danger. In 1868 his time in Alaska came to an end when he was appointed Metropolitan of Moscow. As Metropolitan, he established the Orthodox Missionary Society which, until the 1917 Revolution, played an active role in the spreading of the Russian Orthodox tradition. Veniaminov himself died in his eighties in 1879 and was canonized as Saint Innocent Veniaminov on 6 October 1977.

Such were the dramatic beginnings of Orthodoxy in America, but the situation was soon to change. Waves of new immigrants flooded into the United States in the second half of the nineteenth century (more than twenty-three million arrived between 1865 and 1910), and many of them came from eastern Europe, bringing with them their own religious traditions. Many of these were Eastern Rite Catholics—i.e., Uniats—but when they reached America and found that the Roman Catholic Church of the time would not permit married priests, a large number of them allied themselves with Russian Orthodoxy. Indeed, Russian Orthodoxy became a sort of haven for the dispossessed, and in the early years of the twentieth century included under its capacious wing people of almost every variety of Orthodoxy, Chalcedonian and non-Chalcedonian alike. There were Albanians, Bulgarians, Greeks, Lebanese, Romanians, Serbs, Syrians, and Ukrainians, as well as Russians, and, with the encouragement and support of the Russian Orthodox archbishop, Tikhon, more and more English—the language of the immigrants' new homeland—was used in the liturgy. Tikhon (who would later become the first patriarch of the Russian

Church since 1700[1]) had foreseen the Americanization of his flock and acted accordingly. The Ecumenical Patriarchate never gave formal approval to this pan-Orthodox Russian Orthodoxy, but it was not unhappy to accept it, and until the Russian Revolution of 1917 the Russian Orthodox Church remained the only formally organized Orthodox presence in North America.

The consequences of the 1917 Revolution were disastrous. The administration of the Church collapsed, contact between America and Russia virtually ceased, and for about six years there was no effective leadership for the Orthodox in America. The Russian immigrants in America were often in disagreement with each other (especially on political issues), and the various national groups which had, from convenience and necessity, united under the Russian banner, began to seek their own ways and their own mother-churches. Furthermore, new immigrants continued to enter the country in an unceasing flow, and things as they were in pre-1917 Russia became no more than a memory of the Good Old Days. The Greeks set up their own archdiocese in 1922 (it is now the largest Orthodox group in North America), the other ethnic Churches followed suit, the Russians split (acrimoniously) into further independent and semi-independent jurisdictions, and the present situation in the United States, and, to a lesser extent, Canada, is complex and confused.

As we said a moment ago, the Greeks comprise the largest group, but Greek Orthodoxy still tends to be more ethnic than many other jurisdictions, and many Greek parishes still resist the increasing use of English in the Divine Liturgy which can be seen in almost all other American Orthodox churches. But the second largest group in the United States is the Orthodox Church in America (OCA), which is multi-national, sometimes almost pan-Orthodox, open to converts, and (in theory) English-speaking. How did it come into being and what is its importance?

The story goes back to 1920 when Tikhon, whom we met as a missionary above and who was by now Patriarch of Moscow, issued a decree designed to deal with problems consequent on the 1917

---

1. Basil Ivanovitch Belavin (1866–1925). He was canonized in 1989, and his feast day is 9 October.

Revolution. If Russian bishops found themselves unable to keep in normal and regular contact with the Patriarchate, they could establish temporary, independent jurisdictions of their own. Whether Tikhon intended this to apply outside as well as inside Russia remains unclear (he probably did not), but the bishops who had been exiled or who had fled the country were happy to interpret it as if it did.

The first thing they had to do was to convene a meeting to assess the situation, and a first meeting was held in 1920 at Constantinople (which was not renamed Istanbul for another ten years). More important was the meeting which took place the following year in what was then the city of Karlovtsy in what was then Yugoslavia. It is now Karlovci (or Sremski Karlovci) in Serbia. This meeting established a temporary administration for all exiled Russian Orthodox, and decreed that a synod of bishops would meet annually at Karlovtsy—the Karlovtsy Synod—to keep abreast of changing circumstances. From the start, relations between the Karlovtsy Synod and the Russian Church back home were sorely strained. The Moscow patriarchs obviously had to toe a delicate line with regard to Communism and the ruling regime. The bishops in exile, however, had the luxury of violently opposing Communism and, in 1921, unwisely called for the restoration of the Romanov dynasty. Inevitable tensions continued throughout the 1920s and '30s, and then, as a result of the turmoil of the Second World War, the synod moved its location from Karlovtsy to Munich, and in 1949 from Munich to New York. It is still there, where it is known as the Russian Orthodox Church Outside Russia (ROCOR) or the Russian Orthodox Church Abroad (ROCA). In May 2007, however, after a lengthy series of negotiations, an Act of Canonical Communion was signed by the Russian Orthodox Patriarch, Alexy II, and Metropolitan Laurus of ROCOR which reunited the Russian Orthodox Church Abroad with the Moscow Patriarchate. It must be added that not all members of ROCOR are happy with this reunification, and whether it will lead to division or even schism within ROCOR remains to be seen.

In the early 1920s, when the Karlovtsy Synod had first been established, almost all the Russian bishops in exile were eager to cooperate with it. This initial enthusiasm, however, did not last—

there were just too many divergent views—and in 1926 Metropolitan Platon, the Russian Metropolitan of New York, separated from the Karlovtsy Synod. Since he had already separated from the Moscow Patriarchate two years earlier, being unable, in good conscience, to pledge loyalty to the atheist Soviet government, what this meant was that from 1926 most of the Russian Orthodox in the United States were, to all intents and purposes, an independent group. In due course they adopted the title of the Russian Orthodox Greek Catholic Church of America. Not surprisingly, the newly formed Church was not officially recognized as being independent, nor would it be for more than forty years, but it continued to act as if it were independent while keeping one eye on the Karlovtsy Synod and the other on the Moscow Patriarchate to see how the wind was blowing. Overtures were made to Moscow in the 1940s to return to the fold, provided that the Patriarchate would recognize officially the Church's unofficial independence, but at the time this was found to be impossible. It would take many more years before the goal was achieved, but when it was, in 1970, the Church was granted not merely autonomous, but autocephalous status under a new name, the Orthodox Church in America (OCA). Not all the other Orthodox Churches were prepared to acknowledge its new status. Some still do not.[2] The Ecumenical Patriarchate of Constantinople certainly objected to the decision, rejected a similar request for autonomy from the Greek Orthodox archdiocese, and, at the time, short-sightedly reiterated its opposition to the use of English in the liturgy.

Since 1970 the Orthodox Church in America has been a rapidly growing and flourishing institution. There are more than five hundred parishes in the United States, more than ninety in Canada, and a handful—less than twenty all told—in Mexico, South America, and Australia. The precise number of believers is unclear, but it is estimated to be about a million. It has sought, with great success, to transcend what Ecumenical Patriarch Dimitrios I called the 'scandal' of Orthodox ethnicity, and in many parishes it has also succeeded in overcoming Chalcedonian/non-Chalcedonian divisions. I know of OCA churches where Greek, Russian, Syrian,

2. See Chapter Two, n. 8.

Coptic, and Ethiopian Orthodox worship God in English with every sign of true unity. Furthermore, the presence of converts (which, unlike certain other Churches, the OCA welcomes) means that new theological blood continually flows into the OCA genepool, and since many of these converts bring with them a solid theological background from other traditions, Orthodox theology can only benefit from the interchange.

The idea of a true American Orthodoxy which would transcend ethnic barriers was not new. Back in 1905 it had been a vision of Tikhon, the future Patriarch of Moscow, but although he tried to persuade the Moscow Patriarchate to establish an independent American Orthodoxy, the time was not yet ripe. Further moves, associated with a charismatic but controversial Orthodox archbishop of Brooklyn, Aftimios Ofiesh, were made in the 1920s, but they too were unsuccessful.

Aftimios was an interesting man. He was born in Lebanon in 1880, ordained as a celibate priest in the Syrian Orthodox Church, and, after becoming disillusioned with what he saw as Syrian ultraconservatism, he moved to New York in 1905. At that time, as we saw above, the Syrians (and virtually all other Orthodox) were under the jurisdiction of the Russian Orthodox Church, but tensions were growing between Syrians and Russians, and there was a strong Syrian separatist movement which wanted to secede from Russian Orthodoxy and re-align itself with the mother-church of Antioch. As it happens, the separatists won, and the Syrian Antiochian Orthodox Church in North America was established in 1916. Aftimios himself was staunchly pro-Russian, and, as part of the Russian counter-attack to the pro-Syrian movement, he was consecrated bishop of Brooklyn on 13 May 1917 in the Russian Orthodox cathedral of New York. He was a devoted and energetic pastor, but his episcopate was gravely troubled by the continuing bitter conflict between Russians and Syrians.

Despite his own pro-Russian position, Aftimios eagerly sought Orthodox unity. So, too, did some of the Russian bishops, and in 1927 Metropolitan Platon and certain of his colleagues issued a charter instructing Aftimios (now an archbishop) to establish an autonomous Holy Eastern Orthodox Catholic and Apostolic Church in North America which would be primarily English-speaking and which would transcend national and linguistic boundaries. But again the time was not yet ripe and the attempt failed, though there exists today a Church of this name which traces its lineage directly to Aftimios.[3] Aftimios himself then lost all credibility in Orthodox eyes by deciding to marry, and his archiepiscopate ended in 1933. He would spend the remaining years of his life in retirement, mainly in Kingston, Pennsylvania, and died aged eighty-six on 24 July 1966.

The Western Orthodox Church in America (which is wholly distinct from the Orthodox Church in America) also claims at least partial descent from archbishop Aftimios. But it also traces its lineage through a Brazilian Roman Catholic bishop, Carlos Duarte Costa, who separated from Rome in 1945 and founded the independent *Igreja Catolica Apostolica Brasileira* (Brazilian Apostolic Catholic Church). The details of this curious fusion are not here our concern, but it is a remarkable illustration of the fact that, in America, all things are possible.[4]

The Syrian Orthodox Church, in which Father Aftimios was first ordained, is now the third largest Orthodox Church in North America. As we saw above, the needs of the Syrian immigrants were initially met by the Russian Orthodox Church, but the pastoral care of the Syrian immigrants in New York and of scattered communities elsewhere fell on the shoulders of a Syrian bishop who had arrived in the United States in 1895. His name was Raphael Hawaweeny, and after almost a decade of hard and effective work in lower Manhattan and Brooklyn, he was consecrated bishop at Saint Nicholas's church in Brooklyn on 12 March 1904.

The new bishop, a missionary at heart, spent the next ten years criss-crossing the United States and Canada, but still found time to found a magazine for the Syrian Orthodox community and to publish a considerable amount of liturgical material in Arabic. He died young, only fifty-four, in 1915, and as we have already seen, the First World War and the Russian Revolution brought economic

---

3. The Holy Eastern Orthodox Catholic and Apostolic Church in North America, otherwise known as the American Orthodox Catholic Church, has (or had) a website at http://www.geocities.com/theocacna/index.html. There is much rancorous dispute as to exactly who has proper claim to the title.

4. Further information can be found at http://www.woca.org (woca = Western Orthodox Church in America).

and administrative chaos to Orthodoxy in North America. This was also the period of bitter conflict between those Syrians who wished to rejoin the Antiochian Patriarchate and those who wished to remain under Russian jurisdiction, but even those who wished to ally themselves with Antioch were by no means united in their views. It would take many years—decades, in fact—before the divisions were overcome; but from 1975, when unity was finally restored, the Antiochian Orthodox Christian Archdiocese of North America has been a vibrant and successful Church. The Syrians, we might add, agreed wholly with Archbishop Tikhon in his vision of an English-speaking American Orthodoxy, and the Syrian Church was one of the pioneers in the use of English in Orthodox liturgy.

In the number of its parochial communities, Syrian Orthodoxy is only about one fifth of the size of the Greek Orthodox Archdiocese and the Orthodox Church in America. The Coptic Orthodox Church is still smaller, though not by a great amount, but if the Church is not large, it is certainly alive. The Christian Coptic Orthodox Church of Egypt maintains a number of excellent websites which are as important for Coptic studies in general as they are for Coptic Orthodoxy, and the interested researcher can find a wealth of material on Coptic history, liturgy, music, chant, art, icons, textiles, saints, theology, and literature, as well as sermons and books by Pope Shenouda III. There are also lessons in the Coptic language, lectures in both Arabic and English, and a large variety of videos, tapes, and CDs. It is an extraordinary achievement.[5] The other Orthodox Churches—Serbian, Bulgarian, Romanian, Ukrainian, Armenian, Ethiopian, and the south Indian Malankara Orthodox Church—have still smaller representations, but most of them, too, have provided useful material on the Internet.

Let us now return to Europe. Orthodoxy, as we saw earlier, first came to England in the late 1600s, but for three centuries it remained primarily a Church run by immigrants for immigrants. In the nineteenth century, however, some curious developments took place which looked towards the formation of a British Orthodoxy, developments which centred around a French Roman Catholic

---

5. Those interested need only glance at the impressive menu for 'The Coptic Network' at http://www.coptic.net/CopticWeb.

priest who had separated from his Church and allied himself with Syrian Orthodoxy. His name was Jules Ferrette, and in 1866 he was consecrated as Bishop Julius, bishop of Iona and its Dependencies, by the Syrian bishop of Homs (Emesa) who, six years later, would be appointed Patriarch of Antioch. The new bishop was then sent off to the British Isles to establish an independent and indigenous Orthodox Church in western Europe—an undertaking, we might add, which was not well received by the other Churches in the country (including the Orthodox). To his credit, Bishop Julius persisted in his endeavours, and over a number of years (despite losing contact with the Syrian Patriarchate) built up a small group of faithful who comprised the Orthodox Church of the British Isles. Their number was never large, and for about a century they existed as no more than a scattered group of small local communities, independent of any Orthodox Church. In the 1990s, however, their numbers began to increase, and those who were administering the Church at this time realized the great advantage of associating themselves officially with one or other of the main Orthodox traditions. That tradition was to be Coptic Orthodoxy, and in 1994 the British united with the Copts as the British Orthodox Church within the Coptic Orthodox Patriarchate. Its Metropolitan is a full member of the Coptic Holy Synod.

Not all the members of the old Orthodox Church of the British Isles agreed with the move, and those who preferred not to unite with the Copts allied themselves with a French group, the Celtic Orthodox Church, which also traced its history back to Jules Ferrette. The Church exists today as the British Eparchy of the Celtic Orthodox Church. We should perhaps add that yet another group, known as the Celtic Orthodox *Christian* Church, is a different organization altogether.[6]

It cannot be denied, however, that the Celtic Orthodox Church and similar institutions (and there are a surprising number of them) are no more than intriguing curiosities of Orthodox history. The same cannot be said for the small but active Catholic-Orthodox

---

6. The British Orthodox Church, the Celtic Orthodox Church, the British Eparchy of the Celtic Orthodox Church, and the Celtic Orthodox Christian Church all have their own websites.

Church in France—the Église Catholique-Orthodoxe de France—which introduces us to the question of 'Western-rite Orthodoxy'. What are we talking about here? What we are talking about is Uniatism in reverse. Uniat churches use an Orthodox liturgy but are in communion with Rome; western-rite communities within Orthodoxy use a western (or semi-western) liturgy and are either independent or in communion with Antioch. There are not many of them. In the United States, save for some of the oddities we mentioned above, they are all under the jurisdiction of the Antiochian Orthodox Christian Archdiocese, and in 2007 there were twenty parishes. The western-rite tradition came into existence in 1958 in the hope that it might facilitate the conversion of non-Orthodox to Orthodox, but it had, at best, limited success. The parishes use two rites, one based on the 1570 Roman Catholic rite, the other on the Anglican *Book of Common Prayer*, though in both cases there are small but significant Orthodox amendments.

In France, western-rite Orthodoxy is confined to the Église Catholique-Orthodoxe de France which we mentioned above. It was founded just before the Second World War by Louis-Charles Winnaert, a Roman Catholic priest who had major disagreements with the Roman Catholic tradition, and who, in 1937 (the last year of his life), finally left the western Church to unite with the Moscow Patriarchate. By a special dispensation, he and his followers were permitted to continue using the western rite, though Father Winnaert's successor revised the liturgy to include a substantial number of Orthodox—specifically Byzantine—elements. What we really have here, therefore, is a semi-western-rite Orthodoxy. The Church has had an unhappy history. In 1953 it left the Moscow Patriarchate and existed independently for seven years before placing itself under the jurisdiction of the Russian Orthodox Church Outside Russia (ROCOR). This arrangement ceased in 1966, and the Church once again existed independently until it was received into the Romanian Orthodox Church in 1972. Unfortunately, there were problems from the start, and in 1994 the Romanian Patriarchate severed all its ties with the Catholic-Orthodox Church which now exists yet again—precariously—as an independent entity.

The idea of western-rite Orthodoxy undoubtedly poses problems—problems far more serious than a mere matter of ecclesiastical jurisdiction. The Divine Liturgy lies at the heart of the Orthodox Tradition—indeed, it *is* the heart of the Orthodox Tradition—and there are those who would say that it is no more possible to have an Orthodox western rite than it is possible to have a square circle. The jurisdictional aspect is essentially irrelevant. Just as the marriage of a man to a woman does not turn a male into a female (or vice-versa), so the fact that a western-rite parish might be under the jurisdiction of, say, Moscow, does not make it Orthodox.

On the other hand, Orthodoxy does not restrict itself to one liturgy alone—we saw in Chapter Eight that it uses five—and there is no doubt that, in their essential form, the Orthodox liturgies and the Roman Catholic and Anglican/Episcopalian liturgies are in harmony. They may not do quite the same things in quite the same way, but they certainly come out of the same pot. Is it reasonable, then, to maintain that only those Churches that use one of the five standard Orthodox liturgies can truly be called Orthodox? There is clearly an argument to be made both ways, but God forbid that Orthodox in North America should start treating western-rite Christians as other Orthodox, in recent years, have treated Uniats.

Paris (if we may return to France) was always the centre of Orthodox life in Europe. To a large extent, this was the result of Russians, especially upper-class Russians, fleeing the Russian Revolution in 1917. Good Americans, when they die, go to Paris, said Thomas Appleton; aristocratic Russian *émigrés* did not wait for death. Good and bad alike, they hastened to re-establish their Grand Ducal courts in the cultural capital of Europe.[7] They were, however, not the only ones to come, and Russian Orthodox philosophers and theologians (some of them priests) made major contributions not only to modern Orthodox theology, but to an ever greater public awareness of the Orthodox tradition. Prominent among them were men like Nicolas Berdyaev (1874–1948), Sergius Bulgakov (1871–1944), Georges Florovsky (1893–1979), Nicolas Zernov

---

7. You can visit 'Russian Paris' in English, French, and Russian on the Internet. Make a start with http://www.russianparis.com/eng/one_page.htm.

(1898–1980), Vladimir Lossky (1903–1958), and a number of others. Some of them were on the staff of the Parisian *Institut de Théologie Orthodoxe Saint-Serge*—the Theological Institute of Saint Sergius—founded in 1925, and almost all of them were staunch (though critical, in the best sense) supporters of the ecumenical movement.

Beyond this we cannot go. An exhaustive treatment of the Orthodox diaspora would include the history of Orthodoxy in Africa (African Orthodoxy, as distinct from Coptic Orthodoxy, arose after the First World War and was closely associated with the rejection of colonial rule), Australasia (where there are Greek, Russian, and Arab parishes, almost all post-dating the Second World War), the Far East (the history of Orthodoxy in China and Japan is a fascinating story), Eritrea, Estonia, Finland, Georgia, India, Latvia, Lithuania, Macedonia, Poland, and so on, and so on.[8] The tales are sometimes triumphant, sometimes tragic, but all worth the telling, and there is need for new and up-to-date studies. One thing is certain: Orthodoxy can no longer be considered simply as a religion of immigrants, and any discussion of the Christian religion in North America in particular must give it appropriate space.

So for those seeking spiritual fulfilment or a spiritual path, why not Orthodoxy? We must admit that there are reasons why not as well as reasons why, and we will try to summarize some of them in our final chapter.

---

8. Useful and up-to-date information may be found in *The Blackwell Dictionary of Eastern Christianity* under the names of the different countries.

16
ORTHODOXY: PRINCIPLES AND PROBLEMS

WE MAY SUMMARIZE what we have said in these pages by defining Orthodoxy as a biblical, theological, traditional, conciliar, sacramental, liturgical, communal, ecclesial, and hierarchical religious system. It is also trinitarian in that it worships the one in three of the Holy Trinity. It is incarnational in that it recognizes in Jesus of Nazareth God made human. It is pneumatocentric—'Spirit-centred'—in that it believes firmly in the help, inspiration, and guidance of God through the person of the Holy Spirit. It is Marian in that it venerates Mary as the *Theotokos* or God-bearer. And it also venerates angels and saints who are not mediators, but helpful and protective friends. It follows, therefore, that those who have major problems with any of these ideas cannot and should not be or become Orthodox. Nationality is not enough.

One cannot be Orthodox, for example, if one regards Christ simply as a good man. One cannot be Orthodox if one is not prepared to recognize that the Bible is an inspired book. One cannot be Orthodox if one regards the Eucharist as no more than a symbolic commemoration of the Last Supper in which no change whatever takes place in the elements of bread and wine. We could add many more matters to this list, but to make things clearer, let us look at the nine adjectives set out at the beginning of this chapter in a little more detail. Not much of what we say will be new, but it will do no harm to recapitulate.

Orthodoxy is biblical in that it is based on God's revelation in Scripture. On this point it is in agreement with the rest of Christianity. For Christians, rightly or wrongly, the Hebrew Bible is obviously the 'Old' Testament because it points the way to the New, and the New Testament is the fulfilment of the Old. Some parts of the Bible inevitably have greater impact than others, and there is no doubt that, for the everyday practice of Christianity, the Gospels are more important than, say, the two books of Chronicles. For biblical historians, the two books of Chronicles might be of greater interest than the Gospels.

In general, Orthodox Christians do not consider the Bible to be literally—word for word—factual. It is true that many fundamentalist Christians regard it as Muslims regard the Qur'ān, namely, as a book divinely dictated rather than divinely inspired, but that is not a view commonly held among Orthodox. That the Bible contains a great deal of truth is not in doubt, but truth and facts are not necessarily the same thing. Pilate would have had no need to ask Jesus of Nazareth 'What are facts?': the nature of facts is fairly clear. That Tokyo is the capital of Japan is a fact. He asked, instead, 'What is *Truth*? . . . and would not stay for an answer.'[1] We must remember, too, that inspiration responds to inspiration. If we read the books of the Bible merely as historical curiosities, they will satisfy only our historical curiosity. If we read them as *lectio divina* (which we discussed in Chapter Twelve), their impact will be very different.

The Bible is complemented by theology. Despite the endeavours of medieval western scholastics, theology remains an art rather than a science. The theologians of the Orthodox Church, from the early Fathers to inspired thinkers of the present day, have offered us signposts to the truth. Such sign-posts, as we suggested in Chapter Four, are no more than approximate—some certainly need correction—and their accuracy or otherwise varies in direct proportion to the inspiration of the Holy Spirit—or, more precisely, to the degree to which fallible human beings have been able to respond to that inspiration. But for Orthodoxy, the opinions of inspired theologians, and especially the opinions of inspired theologians meeting in Ecumenical Councils, are sure guides to the Christian life and Christian spirituality. As we said earlier, the Bible always needs to be inter-

---

1. Francis Bacon, *The Essayes or Counsels Civill and Morall* (first published 1625), Essay I 'Of Truth' (the first sentence).

preted, and it is the view of Orthodoxy that the interpretation of the Church is a safer guide than that of idiosyncratic individuals. This idea naturally leads us to Tradition, 'the living memory of the Church'.[2] Holy Tradition lies at the very centre of Orthodoxy. Sometimes it has been actively defined by theologians and councils. Sometimes it has developed passively as the Church itself has developed. Often it has been actively defined after it has passively developed. But however it has come about, Orthodox Tradition remains the guide to Orthodox life.

This, as we know, can be both good and bad. In theory, Tradition is an ever-evolving process responding to the ever-present inspiration of the Holy Spirit. In practice, it can too often become a species of ultra-conservatism, a sort of theological ossification, an ecclesiastical museum piece. But a Tradition which is not a *living* Tradition is a useless Tradition. True Orthodoxy, says Bishop Kallistos Ware,

> can never rest satisfied with a barren 'theology of repetition', which, parrot-like, repeats accepted formulae without striving to understand what lies behind them. Loyalty to Tradition, properly understood, is not something mechanical, a passive and automatic process of transmitting the accepted wisdom of an era in the distant past. An Orthodox thinker must see Tradition *from within*, he must enter into its inner spirit, he must re-experience the meaning of Tradition in a manner that is exploratory, courageous, and full of imaginative creativity.[3]

Of all the sources of Tradition, some of the most important are the seven Ecumenical Councils from Nicaea I in 325 to Nicaea II in 787. They are certainly not the only sources of Tradition, but they are of immense consequence. The Orthodox Church may therefore be said to be a conciliar Church, although, as we have seen, not all the Orthodox Churches accept the authority of all the councils. The idea of conciliarity is a reflection of the related idea that all duly consecrated bishops possess the same charism, that one bishop cannot be any more episcopal than any other. Many Orthodox,

2. Bulgakov, *The Orthodox Church*, 19.
3. Ware, *The Orthodox Church*, 198.

therefore, are certainly prepared (happy would be too strong a word) to acknowledge the bishop of Rome—the pope—as first among equals, to accede to him a primacy of honour, but they cannot, in all conscience, accede to him a primacy of jurisdiction. The teaching authority of the Church lies not with any one individual, but with the entire bench of bishops—the post-apostolic college—and the clearest way of determining what might be called the 'sense of the Church' is by means of a council operating by, in, and through the inspiration of the Holy Spirit. Without that inspiration, a council is no more than a secular board meeting. To respond to the Spirit's inspiration demands a high degree of selflessness, openness, honesty, and devotion on the part of those assembled. They must also be prepared to listen. That this is not always the case is only to be expected, for God's exasperated denunciation of Israel as a stiff-necked people was not confined to Israel alone.

A graceless council is therefore a useless council, for the Church can exist only in the grace of the Holy Spirit, just as the grace of the Holy Spirit exists in the Church, though not only in the Church. Orthodoxy, therefore, shares with Roman Catholicism and much of Anglicanism an essentially sacramental nature. As we said above, Orthodox do not regard the Eucharist merely as a symbolic reenactment of the Last Supper, they do not regard marriage only as legal wedlock, they do not regard baptism simply as a convenient way of having someone else bathe the baby, and so on. Faith, grace, and the sacraments are inextricably intertwined, and one cannot be Orthodox (or Roman Catholic or Anglican for that matter) without believing that certain visible, physical actions, under certain specific conditions, may be channels for divine grace.

Orthodoxy freely admits that something peculiar happened in the process of evolution which has rendered us more inclined to be selfish than selfless. The technical term is Original Sin. But Orthodoxy does not agree with the Augustinian tradition that original sin renders us wholly incapable of doing any good at all. It is true that without God's grace we cannot do enough good to achieve salvation, but salvation is freely offered and, in synergic cooperation with that grace, we may freely accept it. Grace is all around us, though in Orthodox eyes it is to be found especially (though not uniquely) in the Church; and within the Church it is to be found especially (though not uniquely) in the sacraments. To non-Christians the same grace is offered just as effectively in different ways and through different channels, but that is not our concern in these pages.

The most important of the sacraments is undoubtedly the Eucharist, and the Eucharist cannot be separated from the Divine Liturgy. In the course of the Liturgy, the bread and wine become the body and blood of Christ, and in the Liturgy the mystical Body of Christ (the believing faithful) and the eucharistic Body of Christ are united. Each of us becomes a Christ-bearer, which is not only a great grace, but also a great responsibility. Orthodox life is therefore liturgical or eucharistic life (the two amount to the same thing), and it is difficult (though not impossible) to be Orthodox in the absence of a local church.

Participation in the life of a local church is also a reflection of the communal nature of the Orthodox tradition. The Orthodox way is not generally the way of the hermit, though Orthodox hermits are far from unknown. We are, whether we like it or not, integral parts of the human race, and Orthodoxy would agree with a twelfth-century Catholic archbishop of Canterbury who made it perfectly clear that you cannot love God unless you also love your neighbour:

> Since God has no need of any benefits himself, he has put in his place, as it were, our neighbours who do need these things so that they might receive from us the outstanding benefits due to Him. None of us, therefore, should flatter ourselves in thinking that we love God if we do not love our neighbour. . . . How else can we offer benefits to God save by offering them to those in whom God does have a need, though he in himself needs nothing? It is God who, in his members, asks and receives, who is loved or despised.[4]

Being, in general, egocentric human beings, we may not much like this idea, but it is a central feature of the Christian tradition.

---

4. Baldwin of Forde, *Sermo* 15.65; *Corpus Christianorum Continuatio Mediaevalis* 99 (1991), 245. English translation by David N. Bell in *Baldwin of Ford: Spiritual Tractates*, Cistercian Fathers Series 41 (Kalamazoo, 1986) 2:180.

Charity does indeed begin at home, but it can also begin within the congregation of one's local faith-community, Orthodox or otherwise.

It follows, therefore, that Orthodoxy is an ecclesial system: it is centred on the Church and its liturgy. Every baptized Christian is, by definition, a member of the Body of Christ, and the Body of Christ is the Church. We progress towards deification as members of the Church, and the members of the Church include both the living and the dead, the saints and the angels, and the Mother of God herself. The Orthodox tradition is not an individualistic tradition, though there is certainly room for individualism, and the slow course of our redemption takes place within the ecclesial community.

The ecclesial community, however, is neither democratic nor egalitarian. Orthodoxy, like many other varieties of Christianity, is strictly hierarchical. The responsibilities to govern the Church, administer the sacraments, and preach the Gospel were handed down from the apostles to their successors, and from an early date—certainly as early as the second century—the successors of the apostles were considered to be the bishops of the Church. If local parish priests also administer the sacraments and preach the Gospel, they do so by license from their bishops. They do not possess these privileges by right.

This is not to say that the laity do not play a role in the life of the Orthodox Church. They do, though it cannot be denied that the role they play is limited. In the Byzantine tradition, when a priest is ordained, he is ordained in the presence of the laity, and at a certain point in the ceremony the assembled laypeople acclaim the ordination by shouting 'He is worthy'. On the other hand, if the assembled laity does not approve of the new priest and has shouted that he is *not* worthy (and this has very occasionally happened), their disapproval has had no real effect. The ordination has proceeded anyway, though from the point of view of ecclesiastical law this is illicit. But it cannot be denied that the *whole* Church, not just the ordained clergy, is the people of God—the Second Vatican Council was right to emphasize the fact—and, in theory, the ultimate test of both doctrine and tradition is that they be accepted by the whole people of God. But the exact manner in which both clergy *and* laity are, as Saint Peter said, 'a holy priesthood'

(1 Pet 2: 5) has not been defined in Orthodoxy. The Second Vatican Council dealt with this question more openly, though it cannot be denied that the ideals of that Council are not always to be seen in the daily operation of the Roman Catholic Church.

So much, then, for the central features of the Orthodox tradition. All of them can be found among other branches of Christianity, though the emphases differ, and it is the way in which they are manifested in practice that will or will not attract a person to Orthodoxy. There are those who love liturgy, but who prefer a modern version with modern music accompanied by guitars: Orthodoxy is not for them. There are those who believe that Peter's idea of a 'holy priesthood' removes all distinctions between ordained clergy and unordained laity: Orthodoxy is not for them. There are those who love the idea of Tradition, but see the decisions of the Ecumenical Councils as being of interest only to historians of Christian theology: Orthodoxy is not for them. There are those who have an admiration for icons, but consider kissing them to be rank idolatry: Orthodoxy is not for them. Such examples can easily be multiplied.

There are also other problems, and one of the worst, as we have seen, is ethnicity. This is less of a problem now than it was a few decades ago, and although in North America it is slowly being overcome, a problem it remains, and a major problem at that. In the past, ethnicity played a vital and decisive role in preserving the identity of the various immigrant groups, but (if we may quote the great Chinese philosopher Mencius) that was Then, this is Now.

The impact of ethnicity may be seen in two main ways. From an individual point of view, certain of the Orthodox jurisdictions do not always welcome converts who do not speak the native language of most of the parishioners. From a political and administrative point of view, the various Orthodox Churches are not always on the best of terms—Ukraine and the Balkans remain a major problem—and even within specific ethnic groups (especially the Russians) there are wide divergences of opinion and loyalty. In North America and the English-speaking world, English-speaking children and grandchildren and great-grandchildren of non-English-speaking immigrants are naturally having a profound influence on the local situation, but the warmth with which potential converts are welcomed still varies considerably. Some ethnic parishes still prefer a closed shop, despite the fact that this is neither Orthodox nor Christian. But Orthodox are not alone in this.

On the other hand, ethnicity can also have a dangerous attraction. There is an undoubted exoticism about worshipping God in Old Slavonic in a Russian Orthodox church surrounded by candles and icons with magnificent music in a superbly choreographed liturgy. But those who come to Orthodoxy solely for its exoticism come for the wrong reason. If Orthodoxy is to be effective, either on a personal or communal level, it will not be because it is exotic, but because it participates in Truth.

A second problem, as we have already said, lies with the all-important concept of Tradition. Tradition can all too easily degenerate into ultra-conservatism, but even if it does not, and even where creative change takes place, it tends to take place very slowly—too slowly for many people. Those, therefore, who wish to see the ordination of women to the priesthood (not just to the diaconate) may not find themselves at home within the Orthodox tradition. Those who wish to see the sacramental blessing of gay and lesbian relationships or a more liberal attitude to divorce will likewise find more sympathetic ears elsewhere.

On the other hand, there is much more room for individual opinions within Orthodoxy than many people may think. Orthodoxy has never attempted to legislate the Christian life to the same degree that Roman Catholicism has (though even there, what is actually taught and what is actually done seem to be growing ever further apart), and, as we said in Chapter Four, the decisions of the Church are better seen as sign-posts pointing the way rather than walls imprisoning the conscience. In some matters, of course, one is legally bound by ecclesiastical law, but even there there can be considerable latitude. Legally, for example, an Orthodox who marries in a non-Orthodox church is barred from receiving the sacraments until he or she remarries in an Orthodox church. We mentioned this in Chapter Ten. In practice, the rule is sometimes relaxed. Much depends on priest, parish, and jurisdiction.

This is not to suggest that an Orthodox Christian can deny the Trinity, doubt the Incarnation, and spit on the saints while remaining wholly Orthodox. It *is* to say that he or she may have doubts about the need for sacramental confession, or disagree with the

Church's stand on the ordination of women, or see no problem with instrumental accompaniment to the Divine Liturgy, or wholeheartedly reject the Pauline acceptance of the institution of slavery, and still remain solidly within the Church. Orthodoxy seeks to persuade rather than enforce, and, unlike Roman Catholicism, it does not try to silence its more creative theologians. Sometimes specific teachings may be condemned, but that is very different from commanding the teacher to be silent. In 1935, for example, the Holy Synod of the Russian Church condemned certain ideas of Sergius Bulgakov (he was accused—unjustly, as it happens—of making Divine Wisdom a fourth person of the Trinity[5]), but Bulgakov continued to teach freely until his death in 1944.

Orthodox Tradition, therefore, is more elastic than it may appear, and Orthodoxy in no way seeks to stifle the intelligence, creativity, or conscience of the individual believer.

There is one area, however, in which Orthodoxy does not seem to offer what many people today are actively seeking: mystical experience. In recent years we have seen a great resurgence of interest in spirituality and mysticism—there is a huge amount of material in all forms of media—and there can be no doubt that many people are eager to experience Altered States of Consciousness. To examine the nature of these states is not our business in this book, but whatever they may be, Orthodoxy does not pander to them. It is true that the old hesychast tradition was a formidable and effective mystical system, but it is not now widely used, and nowadays the practice of the Jesus Prayer is spiritual rather than mystical. It may certainly lead to mystical experience—the Spirit blows where it wills—but it is not necessarily designed to do so.

Furthermore, the sensual and sensuous nature of some western mysticism is not to be found within the Orthodox tradition. We do not find, for example, contemplative techniques centred on the wounds of Christ, we do not find the quasi-sexual unitive experiences undergone by a number of later medieval visionaries, we do not find meditative exercises intended to recreate in the imagination

---

5. Bulgakov's ideas were shared by a number of other Russian theologians and are generally referred to as 'Sophiology': see *The Blackwell Dictionary of Eastern Christianity*, 455.

the agonies of the suffering Saviour. What we *do* find is a spirituality centred on the Divine Light, a spirituality centred on the Jesus Prayer, a spirituality which is essentially ecclesial, and a spirituality which tends to be image-less rather than image-full.

Orthodoxy is less concerned with an egocentric seeking for spiritual highs than with the experience of grace, and the concept (and practice) of what Nicholas Cavasilas called the 'life in Christ' is more important than any Altered State of Consciousness. In any case, Altered States of Consciousness are not difficult to achieve—they can easily be induced by drugs or alcohol, for example—and if you want to experience a permanent Altered State of Consciousness, all you need do is hold your breath for ten minutes. What these states are, however, and what they reveal is quite another matter, but that, as we said above, is another subject for another book.

Sometimes, what looks like mysticism is not. In his *Way of Salvation*, for example, the nineteenth-century *starets* and spiritual teacher Theophan the Recluse (1815-94) states that the purpose of the Christian life is union with God. But what does he mean by this? He does not mean the Plotinian flight of the alone to the Alone, the submerging of the soul in God, but the grace-full indwelling of God in the human heart.[6] For Theophan, the business of a Christian is not so much to experience union with God in a mystical sense as to live in union with God in a sacramental sense. Should the latter lead to the former, all well and good, but that is God's decision, not ours.

This is not to say, of course, that descriptions of mystical experiences are not be found within the Orthodox tradition. They are. Saint Symeon the New Theologian (949-1022), for example, tells us that one evening, while he was praying an early form of the Jesus Prayer—'God have mercy on me, a sinner' (Lk 18:13)—his room was suddenly filled with divine light. He lost all consciousness of his surroundings and saw nothing but light. He seemed, in fact, to have become one with the light, to have been transformed into light, and to have left this world altogether. He was overcome with

---

6. See Bolshakoff, *Russian Mystics*, 203. A better title for Bolshakoff's book would be 'Russian Spiritual Teachers'.

tears, yet the experience also filled him with inexpressible joy.[7] Symeon, however, was what we might call a 'natural' mystic—there have been others—who regularly experienced some sort of mystical union, and could not really understand why others did not do so as well. As far as he was concerned, such experiences were a normal occurrence for anyone living a truly Christian life, and if we do not ourselves experience it, it is because of the number of our transgressions, our neglect of the commandments, and our insufficient love for God.[8]

Symeon's monks, we might add, were by no means convinced of this, and nor need we be. Symeon was clearly an exception, and mystical experiences of this nature are *not* standard fare for ordinary, everyday Christians, Orthodox or otherwise. Orthodoxy, while acknowledging Symeon's charism, and bowing appropriately to the hesychasts, generally prefers to tread the path outlined by Nicholas Cavasilas, Theophan the Recluse, and many, many others. The goal of Christianity is deification, and as we said in Chapter Twelve, we can progress a long way towards our goal by going to church, receiving the sacraments, praying, and doing, to the best of our ability, what Jesus of Nazareth told us to do in the pages of the New Testament.

Those, therefore, who seek in Orthodoxy a *mystical* tradition may not find quite what they seek. Those who seek a *spiritual* tradition will not be disappointed.

Orthodoxy, then, cannot be all things to all people. Why should it be? Despite the fulminations of fanatics, there are many ways to God, and the Holy Spirit was not baptized an Orthodox Christian. But for those who seek a Christian path, the Orthodox Church has, perhaps, more to offer and fewer problems than many might suspect. Some of what it offers and some of the problems I have attempted to outline in these pages.

Conversion, of course, is never wholly explicable. There must obviously be some logical basis—you cannot, for example, be converted to Judaism or Christianity or Islam if you do not believe in

---

7. Symeon's autobiographical account, written in the third person, appears in his *Catechesis* 22.88–100; *Sources chrétiennes* 104 (1964) 372.
8. See Bell, *Many Mansions*, 164–167.

one God—but the question of why one tradition should appeal more than another can be extraordinarily difficult to answer. Sometimes, certainly, the answer is easy: I am X or Y or Z because that is how I was brought up, and what was good enough for my parents is good enough for me. In this case, one is simply socialized into a particular system, and that is all there is to it. But for those who wish to look further or deeper, or who find too many problems and disagreements with their own tradition, there are plenty of others to choose from. But to change takes both courage and work.

That it takes courage cannot be doubted. It is no small matter to relinquish the security and familiarity of one's religious home and venture out into unknown territory. But that is where the work comes in. Only a fool would convert to a tradition of which he or she knows nothing, and, in any case, if one is thinking of converting to, say, Presbyterianism, one owes it to Presbyterianism to find out as much as one can of what it teaches and what it demands. It is true that both head and heart must be involved in the decision, but embracing a particular tradition simply because it is convenient or feels good is no good reason to embrace it. It may certainly be a start, for inspiration moves in mysterious ways, but the emotional attraction must be supplemented by down-to-earth questions. What does Xism or Yity have to say about God, gods, angels, birth control, abortion, divorce, wealth, heaven, reincarnation, alcohol, working on certain days of the week, prophets, prophecy, vegetarianism, polygamy, homosexuality, saints, spirituality, diet, trance states, celibacy, sex, ecology, gardening, watching TV, cats, dogs, computer games, and anything else you can think of? Part of the business of this book has been to answer some of those questions from an Orthodox point of view. Whether it has succeeded is a matter for the judgement of the individual reader.

Index

Abbots, authority of, 141
Abortion, Orthodox attitudes towards, 127–128
Abraham (patriarch)
icon of the Hospitality of Abraham, 70, ill. 4
Absolution, 119–122
indicative v. precatory formula, 120
necessity (or otherwise) of sacramental absolution, 119
see also Confession
Acacian Schism (482–519), 42
Administration and organization of Orthodox Churches, chapter 3 passim
Affusion, 114
Africa, Orthodoxy in, 209
Aftimios Ofiesh, Archbishop of Brooklyn (d. 1966), 203–204
Alaska, Orthodoxy in, 198–199
Aleut language, 198–199
Alexandria, patriarch and patriarchate of, 29, 36, 107, 177
Alexy II (Russian Orthodox Patriarch), 6, 201
Altar (Holy Table), 16, 101
Altar girls, and Orthodox Tradition, 15

Ambrose of Milan (d. 397), 171
America, Orthodoxy in, chapter 15 passim
Ananael (archangel), 160
Anastasius of Sinai (d. c. 700), 48–49, 59
Angela of Foligno (d. 1309), 145
Angels, 12, 17, 159–160, 161, 169, 211, 216, 222
guardian angels, 17, 48, 49, 51, 59, 70, 87, 160, 169
the Way of the Angels, 136, chapter 11 passim
see also Ananael, Barachiel, Gabriel, Michael, Raphael, Sakakael, Salathiel, Sarathael, Surael, Uriel
Anglican and Eastern Churches Association, 186
Anglican Catholic Byzantine Orthodox Church, 194
Annulment of marriages, 132–133
Annunciation, the, 65 (n. 6)
Anointing, at baptism and chrismation, 115–116
Antidoron ('in place of the gift'), 179–180
Antioch, city and patriarchate, 14, 36, 205, 206

223

Antiochian Orthodox Christian Archdiocese of North America, 205, 207
Antiochian Orthodox Church, 3, 30, 198
Antony of Egypt/Antony the Great (d. 356), 92, 93, 139–140, 151
Apokatastasis: see Satan
Apostolic Catholic Assyrian Church of the East, 3–4, 7, 9, 30, 31, 33, 63
Apostolic Succession, 37, 185
Apostolic Tradition, 73
Aquinas, Thomas: *see* Thomas Aquinas
Archimandrite (title), 136
Archpriest (title), 136
Aristotle (d. 322 BCE), 172
Arius (d. 336) and Arianism, 1, 20–22, 55, 77
Armenian Orthodox Church, 4, 30–31, 32, 37, 42, 198, 205
administration of, 30–31
Asceticon (by Basil the Great), 141–142
Assumption of the Mother of God, 3
doctrine of the, 66–67
feast of the, 66, 102
Assyrian Church: *see* Apostolic Catholic Assyrian Church of the East
Athanasius of Alexandria/ Athanasius the Great (d. 373), 22–23, 63, 77, 89, 102, 139–140
Athenagoras I, Ecumenical Patriarch (d. 1972), 44, 188, 195
Athos, Mount: *see* Mount Athos
Atonement, doctrine of the, 88, 89

Augustine of Hippo (d. 430), 56, 57, 85–87, 93, 96, 112
Augustinian Canons, 144
Australia, Orthodoxy in, 202, 209
Authority, problem of, chapter 3 *passim*
Autocephalous Churches, 32, 36, 52, 115, 135
list of, 32
Autonomous Churches, 32, 52
list of, 32 (n. 9)
Avatārs in Hinduism, 20

Bacon, Francis (d. 1626), 212 (n. 1)
Baldwin of Forde (d. 1190), 215
Baptism and chrismation/ confirmation, 113–118, 214
anointing at baptism and chrismation, 115–116
baptism by affusion, 114
baptism by total immersion, 114
baptism in the name of Jesus Christ or the Lord Jesus, 125 (n. 1)
conditional baptism and chrismation, 117–118
exorcisms in baptism, 114
infant baptism, 118
meaning of 'confirmation,' 115–116
names given at baptism, 114–115
'second baptism': *see* Penance
separation of baptism from confirmation in the West, 116
significance of baptism, 113–114
who can perform baptism, 114

Index

Barachiel (archangel), 160
Baradaeus, Jacob, bishop of Edessa (d. 578), 30
Barlaam the Calabrian/Barlaam of Seminara (d. 1348), 94–96
Bartholomew I, Ecumenical Patriarch, 62
Basil of Caesarea/Basil the Great (d. *c.* 379), 51, 77, 78, 118, 141–142, 144, 175
  see also Liturgy of Saint Basil
Basilica, 99
Beards and bearded priests, 15–16, 52, 108
Bears, 152, 153
Beatific Vision, 91
Beautiful Gate, 101
Benedict XVI, Pope, 44, 192
Benedictines, 144
Benediction, rite of, 181
Benedictus, 17
Benz, Ernst (d. 1978), 72
Berdyaev, Nicolas (d. 1948), 208
Berengar of Tours (d. 1088), 112
Bering, Vitus Jonassen (d. 1741), 198
Berlioz, Hector (d. 1869), 105
Bernard of Clairvaux (d. 1153), 65
Betrothal, ceremony of, 130
Bioethics, 6, 53
Birth control, 39, 53, 128, 190
Bishops
  always now unmarried, 134
  as successors to the Apostles, 37, 216
  authority of, 37–40, 213–214, 216
  Lutheran, 185
  married bishops in the early Church, 134
Bogomils, 1

Book of Common Prayer, The, 207
Bortnyansky, Dmitry Stepanovich (d. 1825), 16, 104
Brazilian Apostolic Catholic Church: *see Igreja Catolica Apostolica Brasileira*
Bread, leavened and unleavened: *see* Eucharist
British Eparchy of the Celtic Orthodox Church, 206
British Orthodox Church, 206
Buddhism, 11, 93, 164–165
Bulgakov, Sergius (d. 1944), 91, 189–190, 208, 219
Bulgarian Orthodox Church, 6, 36, 205
Bull, papal, 43 (n. 3)

Cabasilas, Nicholas: *see* Nicholas Cabasilas
Calendars
  Julian and Gregorian, 82–84
  Old and New, 82–84
Calvin, John (d. 1564), 86, 185
Canada, Orthodoxy in, 200, 202, 204
Candles, use of in Orthodoxy, 12, 102
Canons Regular, 144
Canopius, Nathaniel: *see* Coffee drinking in England
Cappadocian Fathers: *see* Basil of Caesarea, Gregory of Nazianzus, Gregory of Nyssa
Carey, George, former Archbishop of Canterbury, 127
Carroll, Lewis (Charles L. Dodgson) (d. 1898), 51 (n. 5)
Casti Connubii (papal encyclical; 1930), 39
Catherine, Saint, monastery of (Mount Sinai), 59

Catherine of Genoa (d. 1510), 145
Catherine of Siena (d. 1380), 145
Catholic Orthodox Church of France: see Église Catholique-Orthodoxe de France
Catholicates (of the Armenian Orthodox Church), 30–31
Catholicos (title), 30–31
Cave monasticism, 146
Caves, monastery of the (Kiev), 146 (n. 7)
Celibacy, clerical, 42, 75, 133–134, 192, 199
Celtic Orthodox Christian Church, 206
Celtic Orthodox Church, 206
Cenobitic monasticism, 140–141, chapter 11 *passim*
Cerularius, Michael: see Michael Cerularius
Chalcedon, Council of (451 [Fourth Ecumenical Council]), 4, 7, 27–28, 29, 30, 32, 33, 47, 54
Chalcedonian and non-Chalcedonian Churches, chapter 2 *passim* (especially 28, 29, 30, 32, 33)
Chalcedonian Definition of the Faith, 27, 28, 32
Chancel-screen, 13
Chantal, Jeanne-Françoise Frémyot de (d. 1641), 145
Cherubic hymn, 16
Choir-screen, 13
Chrism, 115, 116
Chrismation: see Baptism
Christ: see Jesus Christ
Christodoulos, Archbishop of Athens and All Greece (d. 2008), 44

Church
  as a microcosm of the world, 158
  as a School for Sinners, 158
  as a training ground for love, 158–159
  as infallible, 189–190
  as the Mystical Body of Christ, 161, 216
  as the People of God, 216
  as the Vessel of Grace, 157, 160
  'sister churches' defined, 191
Church buildings, Orthodox
  architecture, 11–12, 99–100
  dedications, 12
  furnishings, 12–13, 100–103
  lack of seating or pews, 12, 103
Cistercians, 143
Clement of Rome (Pope Clement I) (*fl. c.* 96), 7–8, 40
Clysma, Mount, 139
Coffee drinking in England, 197
Communion, 174–181
  and deification, 175
  effects of taking communion, 174–175
  frequency of communion, 175–177
  in one kind and in both kinds, 178
  intercommunion, 180
  methods of administering communion, 17, 178–179, 180
  of the sick or those in prison, 181
  seriousness of taking communion, 174
  see also Eucharist
Communion of the Saints, Orthodox understanding of the, 51, 161

Communion spoon, 179
Confession, 119–122
  frequency of, 122
  necessity (or otherwise) of sacramental absolution, 121, 218
  not necessarily made to a priest, 119–120
  rite for confession, 122
Confessionals, 122
Confirmation: see Baptism
Constantine I (emperor) (d. 337), 19–20, 21, 35
Constantinople, 14, 16, 26, 29, 36, 42
  as 'Second Rome,' 36
  Sack of Constantinople (1204), 44
  see also Ecumenical Patriarch and Patriarchate
Constantinople, Councils of
  381 (Second Ecumenical Council), 24, 33 (n. 10), 36, 47, 55, 57
  543 (Synod of Constantinople), 92
  553 (Fifth Ecumenical Council), 47, 64–65
  680-681 (Sixth Ecumenical Council), 47
  869–870 (Fourth Council of Constantinople), 52
Contraception: see Birth control
Conversion to Orthodoxy, 116–117, 221–222
Coptic Orthodox Church, 3, 4, 5, 29, 31, 37, 107, 116, 121, 122, 131–132, 160, 163–164, 177, 180, 181, 205, 206, 209
Corinth, 40, 135
Councils and Synods: see Chalcedon (451), Constantinople (381, 543, 553, 680–681, 869–870), Ephesus (431), Florence (1438–1439), Geneva (1982), Jassy (1642), Jerusalem (1672), Karlovtsy (1921), Lyons (1274), Nicaea (325, 787), Toledo (589), Trent (1545–1563), Vatican Councils, First (1869–1870) and Second (1962–1965)
Costa, Carlos Duarte, patriarch of the *Igreja Catolica Apostolica Brasileira* (d. 1961), 204
Creeds, 17, 73, 111
  Nicene Creed, 23, 54, 77
  'Nicene-Constantinopolitan' Creed, 54–55
Crete, icon painting in, 63
Cross, Orthodox, 12, 100 (with illustration)
Crossing oneself
  as a ritual gesture, 96, 102
  in Orthodoxy, 81, 96
  its significance in the Schism of the Old Believers (q.v.), 81–82
Crowning, its place in the marriage ceremony, 130
Crucifixion, the, 88, 95, 174
  death by, 100
Crusades
  impact of the Fourth Crusade (1202–1204), 43–44
Cyril VI (Coptic Orthodox Patriarch) (d. 1971), 132, 148
Cyril of Alexandria (d. 444), 25, 27, 57

Damasus I, Pope (d. 384), 40
David the Dendrite (d. 540), icon of, 71

Deaconesses, 135–136
  ordination of, 135
  vestments of, 135
Deacons, 135
Deification, 18, 23, 67, chapter 7 *passim*, 89–91, 96, 159, 161, 167–168, 175, 185, 221
  and angels, 159
  and communion, 175
  and demons, 159
  and ecology, 90
  and justification by faith, 185
  and participation in the Divine Attributes/Energies, 89–90, 95
  and reincarnation, 93
  and the corporeal assumption of Mary, 67
  and the sanctification of matter, 66-67
  as a communal/ecclesial process, 90, 216
  as an eternally continuing process, 90–91
  as the goal of Christianity, 221
  as the heart of Orthodox spirituality, 161
  of the universe, 159
Demons, 159
Desert Mothers, 78, 144
Desert spirituality, 144
Dimitrios I, Ecumenical Patriarch (d. 1991), 202
Diocletian (Gaius Aurelius Valerius Diocletianus) (emperor) (d. 313), 69
Dionysius the Pseudo-Areopagite (*fl. c.* 500), 77, 163
Diophysites: *see* Dyophysites
Diptychs, affair of the, 42
Discus/*diskos*, 106
Divorce, 131–133, 218
  grounds for, 131
  remarriage after, 132
Docetism, 64
Dominicans, 144
Dominus Iesus (papal encyclical; 2000), 57, 191–192
Dormition, Feast of the: *see* Assumption of the Mother of God
Drozdov, Philaret, Metropolitan of Moscow (d. 1867), 173
Dyophysites, 28, 33, 47

Eastern Orthodox (term), 4–5, 7, chapter 2 *passim*
Eastern Rite Catholics, 192, 199
Ecology, Orthodoxy and, 61–62, 157
Ecumenical Patriarch and Patriarchate, 4, 6, 39, 40, 42, 115, 150, 190, 200, 202
  first use of the title, 40
Ecumenism, and Orthodoxy, chapter 14 *passim*
  see also Union and Reunion
Eden, Garden of, 85, 87, 125
Église Catholique-Orthodoxe de France, 206–207
Egyptian Orthodox Church: *see* Coptic Orthodox Church
Elijah (prophet), 66
  icon of, 71, ill. 6
Eliot, George (Mary Ann Evans) (d. 1880), 145
Elisha (prophet), 71
Elizabeth of the Trinity (d. 1906), 145
Emergency Contraceptive Pills (ECPs), 53, 129
Engagement: *see* Betrothal
England, Orthodoxy in, 197–198, 205–206

Index 229

Enoch (patriarch), 66
Entrances
 Great Entrance, 16, 105–106
 Little Entrance, 15, 16, 105
Ephesus, Council of (431 [Third Ecumenical Council]), 26, 47, 63, 87
Epiclesis/epiklesis, 106, 171, 179
Eritrean Orthodox Church, 4–5
Esphigmenou monastery (Mount Athos), 148, 183
Estonia, Orthodox Church in, 6
Etchmiadzin, 30
Ethiopian Orthodox Church, 2, 4, 29, 31, 37, 107, 205
Ethnicity, problems of, in Orthodoxy, 196, 200, 202–203, 217–218
Eucharist, 105–106, 160, 167, 169, chapter 13 *passim*, 185, 211, 214–215
 as a sacrifice, 173–174
 as a test of faith, 171
 eucharistic change (transubstantiation), 171–173, 175–176
 eucharistic fast, 177–178
 horror cruoris ('horror of blood'), 171, 172
 reservation of, 180–181
 use of leavened and unleavened bread, 42, 43, 57
 see also Communion, Liturgy
Exorcisms in baptism, 114
Exposition, rite of, 181
Extreme unction, 181
Ezekiel (prophet), 159

Fall, the
 consequences of, 85–87, 91
 see also Sin and its consequences

Farrer, Austin (d. 1968), 196
Fasting, 177–178
 days of fasting, 177
Fathers of the Church, 76–79, 88, 159, 212
Ferrette, Jules, bishop of Iona and its Dependencies, (d. 1904) 206
Filioque, Controversy over the 54–58, 188
 see also Holy Spirit
Flesh, Christian attitudes towards the, 93–96
Florence, Council of (1438–1439), 44, 111, 188
Florovsky, Georges (d. 1979), 208
Founders' monasteries, 146–147
Fount of Wisdom, The (by John of Damascus), 77
France, Orthodoxy in, 208–209
'Russian Paris', 208 (n. 7)
Franciscans, 143
Free will, 85–88, 96
 see also Synergy

Gabriel (archangel), 160
 icon of, 101
Geneva, Pan-Orthodox Synod held in (1982), 178
Georgian Orthodox Church, 31, 36
Gnosticism, 92
Godparents, 114, 115, 131
Golden Legend, The (by James of Voragine; d. 1298), 69
Grace 13, 18, 38, 51, 65, 86–88, 89, 96–97, 111–112, 115, 118, 120, 121–122, 130, 132, 157, 160, 167, 168, 169, 175, 185, 214–215, 220
 and Christ, 87
 and non-Christians, 215

and sacramentals, 112–113
and the Eucharist, 173–174
and the Immaculate
    Conception, 65
and the sacraments, 111–112,
    113
infused and imputed grace, 185
the Church as the Vessel of
    Grace, 157, 160, 188
Great Entrance: *see* Entrances
Great Schism (1054), 41–45, 188,
    193
Gregorian Calendar, 82–84
Gregory I/Gregory the Great,
    Pope (d. 604), 40
Gregory XIII, Pope (d. 1585), 82
Gregory of Nazianzus/Gregory
    the Theologian (d. 389/90),
    77, 118
Gregory of Nyssa (d. *c*. 395), 77,
    78, 92, 118, 174
Gregory Palamas, the 'Light of
    Orthodoxy' (d. 1359), 78,
    95–96
Gretchaninov, Alexander
    Tikhonovich (d. 1956), 104
Guidi, Filippo Maria, Cardinal-
    Bishop of Bologna (d. 1871),
    189

Habit, monastic, 149
Hagia Sophia, church of, 43, 176
Hawaweeny, Raphael, bishop of
    Brooklyn (d. 1915), 204–205
Headgear, clerical, 108
Heaven, 91, 92
Hell, 91, 92, 93, 120, 121
Hesychasm and the Hesychast
    Controversy, 94–96, 145, 155,
    162–165
Hesychast techniques, 163–165
Hieromonks, 143–144, 149, 150

Hildegard of Bingen (d. 1179), 145
Hinduism, 11, 20, 93
History of the Holy Eastern Church,
    A (by John Mason Neale), 186
Holy Door, 101
Holy Eastern Orthodox Catholic
    and Apostolic Church in
    North America/
    American Orthodox Catholic
    Church, 203–204
Holy Mountain, the: *see* Mount
    Athos
Holy Spirit, 27, 42, chapter 4
    passim, 211
and Holy Tradition, 74
and infallibility, 189
as guiding the Church, 54, 56,
    58, 189
as inspiring Church Councils
    54, 165, 190, 213–214
doctrine of the, 23–24, 77
in baptism and chrismation,
    114, 116
in the Eucharist, 106
procession of the, 42, 55–57
see also Filioque, Controversy
    over the
Holy Table: *see* Altar
Holy Trinity, monastery of the
    (Russia), 152
Homilies: *see* Sermons
Homosexuality, Orthodox
    attitudes towards, 126–128
Hōnen (d. 1212), 165
Humanae Vitae (papal encyclical;
    1968), 39
Humbert, Cardinal-Bishop of
    Silva Candida (d. 1061), 43
Hymns, Orthodox, 14
    Cherubic Hymn, 16
    Hymn to the Mother of God,
        17

Iconoclastic Controversy
 (726–843), 49, 59, 60–62, 145,
 165
Iconostasis, 12–13, 101–102, 176
Icons 12–13, chs. 4–5 *passim*
 and redemption, 72
 and relics, 51
 and the Communion of the
  Saints, 51, 59
 and Tradition, 76
 as theological statements,
  60–62, 72
 history of, 48–49, 67, 152
 human beings as icons, 72
 in an illiterate society, 60
 in Orthodox churches, 101
 meditation on, 165–166
 nature of, 12, 48, 59
 praying with icons, 166 (n. 6)
 subjects of, 48, 59, 60, 70–71
 the Bible as an icon of the
  Word of God, 166
 veneration of, 12, 50–51, 59,
  102, 217
 wonder-working icons, 59–60
 see also Abraham, David the
  Dendrite, Elijah, Gabriel,
  Iconoclastic Controversy,
  Jesus Christ, Mary,
  Mother of God, Michael,
  *Panagia Nikopoia, Pantocrator/
  Pantokrator, Theotokos
  Glycophilousa, Theotokos
  Hodegetria*
Idiorrhythmic communities,
 149–150
Ignatius of Antioch (d. c. 107), 77
Ignatius of Xanthopoulos (*fl.* late
 14th cent.), 167
Igreja Catolica Apostolica Brasileira
 (Brazilian Apostolic Catholic
 Church), 204

Image of God, 87–88, 128, 162
Immaculate Conception,
 doctrine of the, 65–66, 189
Incarnation, 211, 218
 and icons, 60–61
 as a consequence of human
  sin, 88
 doctrine of the, 20, 24–29, 31,
  52, 60–62, 64, 66–67, 77, 95
 in Hinduism, 20
Incense, use of, 16
India, 30
Indulgences, 120
Infallibility
 of Ecumenical Councils, 190
 of popes, 189
 of the Church, 189–190
Innocent I, Pope (d. 417), 40
*Institut de Théologie Orthodoxe
 Saint-Serge* (Theological
 Institute of Saint Sergius,
 Paris), 209
International Commission of
 the Anglican/Orthodox
 Theological Dialogue
 (1999), 187
Intinction, 17, 178–179, 180
Iraq, Christianity in, 4
Irenaeus of Lyons (d. c. 200), 23, 77
Irkutsk (Alaska), 198
Isaiah (prophet), 89
 Dance of Isaiah, 130
Ivan the Terrible/Ivan IV
 Vasilyevich, Tsar of Russia
 (d. 1584), 60
Iviron monastery (Mount Athos),
 150
Iznik: *see* Nicaea

Jacobites: *see* Syrian Orthodox
 Church
Jainism, 93

James, Saint, 181
   see also Liturgy of Saint James
Jassy, Synod of (1642), 53
Jehovah's Witnesses, 20
Jerusalem, 36, 55
   Synod of Jerusalem (1672), 53, 173
Jesus Christ, 37, 70, 168, 178, and *passim*
   as Saving Victim and Triumphant Victor, 88–89
   as the Sun of Righteousness, 99
   brothers and sisters of, 64
   icons of, 13, 60–63, 101
   see also Incarnation
Jesus Prayer, 152, 154, 162–165, 166, 219–220
   its context, 167
   its effects, 154
John, Saint, 94, 158, 167
John XXIII, Pope (d. 1963), 76, 192
John Chrysostom, patriarch of Constantinople (d. 407), 77, 81, 112
   see also Liturgy of Saint John Chrysostom
John of Damascus (d. *c*. 750), 50, 77, 173
John of the Ladder/John Climacus (d. *c*. 649), 77
John Paul II, Pope (d. 2005), 39, 44, 57, 75, 190–192
John the Baptist/John the Forerunner, Saint, 71, 101
John IV the Faster, Ecumenical Patriarch (d. 595), 40
Joint Commission of the Theological Dialogue between the Orthodox Church and the Oriental Orthodox Churches, 7
   First Agreed Statement (1989), 7
   Second Agreed Statement (1990), 33, 52–53
Joseph, Saint (husband of Mary), 64
Judgement, 91
   individual judgement after death, 91
   Last Judgement, 91
Julian Calendar, 82–84
Julian of Norwich (d. after 1416), 79, 145
Julius Caesar, Gaius (d. 44 BCE), 82
Junia (female apostle), 74
Justification by faith, 185
Justin Martyr (d. *c*. 165), 77
Justinian I/Justinian the Great (emperor) (d. 565), 176

Kadiköy: *see* Chalcedon
Kallistos II Xanthopoulos, Ecumenical Patriarch (d. 1397), 167
Kamelavchion/kalymmavchion, 108
Karlovtsy Synod (1921), 201–202
Keats, John (d. 1821), 173
Keroularios: *see* Cerularius
Kiev, 146
Knights Hospitaller, Order of the, 143
Knights of Malta, 143
Kontoglou, Fotis (iconographer) (d. 1965), 71, ill. 6
Kowalska, Mary Faustina (d. 1938), 145

Ladder of Divine Ascent, The (by John of the Ladder), 77
Laity, place of, 216–217

Lamb, the (the portion of the communion loaf to be consecrated), 179
Lance (spear-shaped knife), 179
Laurus, Metropolitan of ROCOR (d. 2008), 201
Lavra, 146
Last Judgement: *see* Judgement
Learning: *see* Scholarship
Lectio divina ('sacred reading'), 166–167, 168, 212
Lent, fasting in, 177
Leo I/Leo the Great, Pope (d. 461), 40, 41
Leo IX, Pope (d. 1054), 42–43, 57
Leo III the Isaurian (emperor) (d. 741), 49, 50
Leonine Doctrine of the Roman Primacy, 41
Letters to a Beginner on Giving One's Life to God (by Thaisia of Leushino), 145
Leushino, monastery of (Russia), 145
Licinius, Valerius Licinianus (emperor) (d. 325), 19
Light
  and mystical experience, 220–221
  and the transfiguration of Saint Seraphim, 153
  created and uncreated, 94–95, 163, 220
  of the Transfiguration, 163
  symbolism of, 13
Limbo, 91
Litanies, Orthodox, 14–17
  Great Litany, 14–15
  Litany before the Lord's Prayer, 15
  Litany for the Catechumens, 15

Litany for the Departed, 15
Litany of Fervent Supplication, 15
Litany of Supplication, 15, 17
Little Entrance: *see* Entrances
Liturgy, Orthodox, 64, 144, 175, 181, 200, 208, 215
  and Western-rite Orthodoxy, 208
  chanted and sung, not said, 13–14, 104
  in English, 200, 203–204, 205, 217–218
  length of, 15, 102–104, 175
Liturgy of Saint Basil, 107
Liturgy of Saint James, 107
Liturgy of Saint John Chrysostom, 107
Liturgy of Saint Mark, 107
Liturgy of the Presanctified Gifts, 107, 181
Logacheva, Anastasia/Athanasia, abbess of the monastery of Saint Nicholas the Wonder-worker (Siberia) (d. 1875), 153
Lombard, Peter: *see* Peter Lombard
Lord's Prayer, 111
Lossky, Vladimir (d. 1958), 209
Luke, Saint, 67
Luther, Martin (d. 1546), 185
Lutheranism, 185
Lyons, Council of (1274), 44

Mabillon, Jean (Maurist; d. 1707), 144
Macarius III (Coptic Orthodox Patriarch), 132
Macarius Notaras of Corinth (d. 1805), 78, 79–80, 167
Macrina the Younger (d. 380), 78, 144–145

Magisterium, ordinary, 190
Malankara Orthodox Church, 29–30, 205
Mamre, 70, ill. 4
Mani (d. 276) and Manichaeanism, 93
Marcion (second-century heretic), 62
Margaret of Antioch, Saint, 68
Marie/Mary of the Incarnation (d. 1618), 145
Marina, Saint: *see* Margaret of Antioch
Mark, Saint, 29
Mark of Ephesus (d. 1444), 78
Marriage, chapter 10 *passim*, 214, 218
    marriage ceremony, 129–130
    of an Orthodox Christian in a non-Orthodox church, 126
    of close relatives, 131
    of Orthodox and non-Orthodox Christians, 125–126
    same-sex marriages, 126–127, 187, 188, 218
    unmarried mothers, 129
    wedding rings, 130
    see also Annulment, Divorce
Martène, Edmond (Maurist; d. 1739), 144
Mary (Jesus's sister), 64 (n. 4)
Mary, Mother of God
    and Theophanes of Nicaea, 65
    icons of, 13, 48, 67, 70, 101, ill. 2
    perpetual virginity of, 63–65, 67
    titles of, 25–27, 63, 64
    worthy of *hyperdouleia* or 'more than veneration,' 63, 65, 67
    see also Assumption of the Mother of God; Immaculate Conception
Mary of Egypt (5th cent.?), 3, 68
Mass of the Presanctified, 107
Matins, 104
Matta el-Meskeen: *see* Matthew the Poor
Matthew, Saint, 139
Matthew the Poor (Matta el-Meskeen) (d. 2006), 148
Maximus the Confessor (d. 662), 77, 92
McGuckin, Eileen (iconographer), 71, ill. 4, ill. 5
Meetings of the Heads of the Oriental Orthodox Churches in the Middle East
    Fourth Meeting (2001), 7
    Seventh Meeting (2004), 8
Mencius (Mêng Tze) (d. 288 BCE), 217
Metropolitan (title), 38
Mexico, Orthodoxy in, 202
Michael (archangel), 160
    icon of, 71, 101, ill. 5
Michael Cerularius, Ecumenical Patriarch (d. 1058), 42–43, 57
Milan, 19
    Edict of Milan (313), 16–17
Ministry of the Word, 105
Mitres, 16
Monasticism: *see* Monks and monasticism
Mongols, 30, 31, 151
Monks and monasticism, 134, 136–137, chapter 11 *passim*,
    cave monasticism, 146
    Egyptian monasticism, 139–141
    idiorrythmic monasticism, 149–150
    monastic habit, 149

on Mount Athos, 147–148, 150, 152
Russian and Slavic monasticism, 146–147
skete monasticism, 146–147, 150–151
Monophysites, 4, 28, 33, 47
Moral Rules (by Basil the Great), 141–142
Moscow, 70, 102, 151
patriarchate, 6, 8, 32, 173, 194, 201–202, 207
Moses (patriarch), 62, 94
Mothers of the Church, 78–79
Mount Athos, monasticism on, 147–148, 150, 152, 195
Moussa (Coptic bishop), 163–164
Music, in Orthodox churches, 13–14, 16, 104–105, 217, 218
Mysticism and mystical experience, 219–221
see also Hesychasm, Spirituality, Orthodox

Neale, John Mason (d. 1866), 186
Nestorian Church: *see* Apostolic Catholic Assyrian Church of the East
Neametz/Niamets, monastery of (Romania), 152
Nestorius, patriarch of Constantinople (d. after 451), and Nestorianism, 25–28
Newman, John Henry, Cardinal (d. 1890), 158–159
Nicaea, Councils of
325 (First Ecumenical Council), 22, 25, 33 (n. 10), 35–36, 47, 55, 69, 213
787 (Seventh Ecumenical Council), 47, 49–50, 51, 52, 53, 54, 193, 213

see also Creeds, Nicene Creed
Nicene Creed: *see* Creeds
Nicholas Cabasilas (d. after 1387), 80–81, 109, 175, 176, 220, 221
Nicholas of Myra/Nicholas the Wonderworker (4th cent.), 68, 69–70, ill. 3
his relics at Bari, 69–70
monastery of, in Siberia, 153
Nicodemus of the Holy Mountain (d. 1809), 78, 79–80, 167–168
Nuns, Orthodox, 15, 140, 143, 144–145, 148–149, 167

OCA: *see* Orthodox Church in America
Old Believers, Schism of the 1, 81–82
Old Catholics, 193–194
Omophorion ('bishop's stole' or pallium), 70
Opus Dei ('God's Work'): *see* Liturgy
Orders, Holy
and marriage, 134
Major and Minor Orders, 133
see also Bishops, Deacons, Readers, Subdeacons
Orders, monastic, 143
Ordinatio Sacerdotalis (papal encyclical; 1994), 75
Ordination
and approval by the laity, 216
of homosexuals, 127, 187, 188
of monks, 143–144
of women: *see* Women, ordination of
Organization and administration of Orthodox Churches,

chapter 3 *passim*
Oriental Orthodox (term), 4–5, 7, chapter 2 *passim*
Original Guilt, 85–86
Original Sin: *see* Sin
Orthodox Church in America (OCA), 4, 8, 32, 83, 108, 117
  history of, 200–203
Orthodox Church of the British Isles, 206
Orthodox Missionary Society, 199
Orthodoxy
  meaning of the word, 19
  essential principles of, chapter 16 *passim*
  problems of, chapter 16 *passim*

Pachomius (d. 346), 68, 140–141, 144
Pain bénit ('blessed bread'), 179
Pan-Orthodox Synod
  calls for, 6
  Geneva (1982), 178
Panagia Nikopoia ('The All-Holy, Bringer of Victory'), icon of the Virgin, 48
Pantocrator/Pantokrator ('All-Sovereign' or 'Ruler of All'), icon of Christ, 62–63, 68, ill. 1
Pantokrator, monastery of the (Mount Athos), 150
Papal States, 189
Paris: *see* France
Paten: *see* Discus/*diskos*
Patmucan, 2
Paul, Saint, 7, 22, 36, 49, 74, 88, 89, 115, 135, 154, 219
Paul VI, Pope (d. 1978), 39, 44, 188
'Pauline Privilege' for divorce, 133

Payne, Mother Bernard, abbess of Stapehill (England) (d. 1968), 161, 166
Pelagius (d. *c.* 420?) and Pelagianism, 85–87, 91
Penance, 118–122
  as 'second baptism,' 119
  history of, 118–119
  see also Absolution, Confession
Pentarchy, 36
Pentecost, 76
Persecution, 30, 31
Peter, Saint, 7, 36, 41, 75, 191, 216
Peter Lombard (d. 1160), 111
Peter I the Great, Tsar of Russia (d. 1725), 152
Pews, lack of in Orthodox churches, 12, 103
Philokalia (by Nicodemus of the Holy Mountain and Macarius Notaras of Corinth), 79-80, 81, 144, 152–153, 154, 167–168
Pilgrim's Tale, The, 154–155, 166–167
Phoebe (deaconess of Cenchreae), 135
Photian Schism (863–867), 42
Photius I/Photius the Great, Ecumenical Patriarch (d. *c.* 895), 77
Physis ('nature'), ambiguity of the word, 27–28
Pius IX, Pope (d. 1878), 65, 189, 193
Pius XI, Pope (d. 1939), 39
Pius XII, Pope (d. 1958), 66
Platon, Metropolitan of New York (d. 1934), 202, 203
Platonism, 89, 93, 96, 159
Plotinus (d. 270), 220

Pope
  as successor to Saint Peter, 191
  authority of popes, 39–41,
    53–54, 188–192
  title of, 29
  see also Benedict XVI,
    Clement of Rome,
    Damasus I, Gregory I,
    Gregory XIII, Innocent I,
    John XXIII, John Paul II,
    Leo I, Leo IX, Paul VI,
    Pius IX, Pius XI, Pius XII,
    Urban II
  see also Bishops, Leonine
    Doctrine of the Roman
    Primacy, Primacy
Possessors and Non-Possessors,
  147
Prayer, 167
  prayers for the dead, 92
  private prayer, 161
  unceasing prayer, 80, 154, 164
  see also Jesus Prayer, Lord's
    Prayer
Predestination, 86
Priesthood of All Believers,
  doctrine of the, 185, 217
Primacy
  of honour, 40, 188–189, 214
  of jurisdiction, 40, 53, 188–189,
    214
  of Rome, 40–42, 77–78, 186,
    214
  see also Bishops, Leonine
    Doctrine of the Roman
    Primacy
Procession of the Holy Spirit, 78
  Double Procession, 56–57
  Single Procession, 56
  see also Filioque, Controversy
    over the
Pure Land Buddhism, 164–165

Purgatory, 91–92, 120

Qabbalism, 93
Qamis, 2
Qurʾān, 212

Rachmaninov, Sergei Vassilievich
  (d. 1943), 104
Ramsey, Arthur Michael, former
  Archbishop of Canterbury
  (d. 1988), 186
Raphael (archangel), 159, 160
Readers, 133
Redemption, chapter 7 *passim*,
  173
  icons and redemption, 72
  universality of, 61, 95
  see also Satan, redemption of
Reincarnation, 2, 93, 222
Relics, 51
Resurrection, 66, 91
  baptismal resurrection,
    113–114
  of Christ, 88–89, 95
  of the body, 66, 91, 93
Rings, wedding, 130
ROCA: see Russian Orthodox
  Church Abroad
ROCOR: see Russian Orthodox
  Church Outside Russia
Romanian Orthodox Church,
  36, 205, 207
Rome, 14, 29, 36, 42, 55, 196
  primacy of: see Primacy of
    Rome
Rood-screen, 13
Royal Door, 101
Rublev, Andrei (iconographer)
  (d. 1430), 70–71, 102
Russian Orthodox Church
  Abroad (ROCA), 201

Russian Orthodox Church Outside Russia (ROCOR), 201, 207
Russian Orthodox Greek Catholic Church of America, 202
Russian Revolution (1917), consequences of, 200, 204–205, 208

Sacrament and sacraments, chapters 9-10 *passim*, chapter 13 *passim*, 214–215
  conditional performance of, 117–118
  defined, 112
  evangelical or dominical, 112
  meaning of the word, 111
  number of, 111–112
  reservation of, 180–181
  see also Baptism, Chrismation, Eucharist, Marriage, Penance, Orders, Unction
Sacramentals, 112–113
Saint John Ambulance Brigade, 143
Saint Petersburg, 100, 102
Saints, 3, 8, 12, 17, 48, 50–51, 59, 60, 63, 67–70, 71, 76, 90, 101, 102, 158, 161, 169, 185, 205, 211, 216, 218, 222
  doubtful and non-existent saints, 68
  feast days, 59, 115, 175
  icons of, 68–69
  saints' names and baptismal names, 105
  the Church of the Saints, 158
  the Communion of the Saints, 51, 59, 96, 161
  universal and local saints, 68
Sakakael (archangel), 160
Salathiel (archangel), 160
Salome (Jesus's sister), 64 (n. 4)
Salvation Army, 111
Sanctus, 17
Santa Claus: *see* Nicholas of Myra
Sarathael (archangel), 160
Satan, 89
  redemption of (*apokatastasis*), 92
  renunciation of Satan in baptism, 114
Scholarship
  monks and scholarship, 144
Scripture, 105, 127, 168, 211–213
  and *lectio divina*, 166–167, 168
  and Tradition, 73–74, 76
  the Bible as an icon of the Word of God, 166
  Sola scriptura, 73–74
Sententiae divinitatis ('Sentences on Divinity'), 111, 112
Seraphim of Sarov (d. 1833), 153, 163
Serbian Orthodox Church, 36, 205
Sergius (Sergei) of Radonezh (d. 1392), 151–152
Sermons, Orthodox, 15, 105
Servant of the Servants of God (papal title), 40
Sex and sexual intercourse, chapter 10 *passim*
  outside marriage, 127
  transmission of Original Sin through sexual intercourse, 93
  within marriage, 125, 128
Shenouda III (Coptic Orthodox Patriarch), 5, 132, 148, 205
Shvedov Konstantin Nicolaevich (d. 1954), 104
Sin and its consequences, 85–87
  and the sacrament of penance,

118–123
mortal and venial sin, 118, 120, 121
Original Sin, 85–87, 93, 214–215
Seven Deadly Sins, the, 157
transmission of Original Sin through sexual intercourse, 93
'Sister Churches', defined, 191
Sitka (Alaska; formerly Novo Arkhangelsk or New Archangel), 198, 199
Skete monasticism, 146–147, 150–151
Slavery, 219
Slavs, conversion of the, 36, 42
Sophiology, 219 (n. 5)
South America, Orthodoxy in, 202
Speake, Graham, 148 (n. 8), 150
Spirituality, Orthodox, chapter 12 *passim*, 219–220
as ordinary sacramental life, 168
Starets (plural *startsy*; 'Spiritual Guide'), 119, 151–155
Sticharion, 2, 135
Subdeacons, 133
Subordinationism, 20–22, 58
Sudan, 29
Sufism, 164
Surael (archangel), 160
Sybilline Oracles, 160
Symeon the New Theologian (d. 1022), 78, 80, 220–221
Synaxis, 105, 106
Synergy, 63, 87, 175, 214–215
see also Grace
Synodical Period (1700–1917), in Russian Orthodoxy, 152
Syrian Antiochian Orthodox Church in North America, 203
Syrian Catholics, 30
Syrian Maronite Church, 192
Syrian Orthodox Church, 4, 29–30, 37, 203, 204–205, 206
Syrians, monastery of the (Wadi Natroun, Egypt), 148
Syro-Malabar Church, 29–30
Syro-Malankara Church, 29–30, 205

Tabennisi, near Thebes (Egypt), 140
Tabernacle, 180
Tchaikovsky, Piotr Ilyich (d. 1893), 104
Tendai Buddhism, 97
Teresa of Ávila (d. 1582), 78, 79, 145
Tertullian (d. *c.* 225), 31
Thaisia, abbess of Leushino (d. 1915), 145
Theodore of Studios (d. 826), 142
Theodosius II (emperor) (d. 450), 26
Theophan the Recluse (d. 1894), 220, 221
Theophanes of Nicaea (d. 1381), 65
Theotokos ('God-bearer'), title of Mary, 25–27, 63, 65, 211
Theotokos Glycophilousa ('The Loving God-bearer'), icon of the Virgin, 48
Theotokos Hodegetria ('The God-bearer Showing the Way'), icon of the Virgin, 48, 67, ill. 2
Thérèse of Lisieux (d. 1897), 145
Thessaloniki (Greece), 71, 95
Thomas, Gospel of, 62
Thomas Aquinas (d. 1274), 65, 111, 174

Tikhon (Basil Ivanovich Belavin), Russian Orthodox Patriarch (d. 1925), 199–201, 203, 205
Tobias, 159
Toledo, Third Council of (589), 55–56
Tonsure
  at baptism, 114
Tradition, nature and importance of, 5, 7–8, 24, chapter 6 *passim*, 176, 180, 183, 213–214, 217
  and ecumenism, 183–184
  and the number of the sacraments, 112
  Apostolic Tradition, 73
  as authoritative, 75
  as dynamic, 78, 81
  as protection, 76
  as stagnation, 75–76
  as the living memory of the Church, 213
  as the witness of the Holy Spirit, 76
  its use and abuse, 73, 74, 213, 218
  Scripture v. Tradition, 73–74
  sources of, 76–78
  Tradition and traditions, chapter 6 *passim*
Transepts, 99
Transfiguration, the, 163
Transubstantiation, 172–175
  meaning of the term, 172–173
  use of the term in Orthodoxy, 173
Trent, Council of (1545–1563), 111, 174
Trinity, doctrine of the, 20–24, 31, 35, 52, 56, 77, 211, 218
  in Hinduism, 20
  Old Testament Trinity, ill. 4

Triumph of Orthodoxy, Feast of the, 50
Turks, 31, 32, 44

Ukraine
  monasticism in, 146
  Orthodox Church in, 6, 193, 217
Ukrainian Orthodox Church in America, 205
Ukrainian Uniat Church, 192
Unction, sacrament of, 181
  form of the rite, 181
  when performed, 181
Uniat Churches, 192–193, 199, 207
Union and reunion with non-Orthodox Churches, chapter 14 *passim*
  its limits, 184
  with Anglicanism, 185–188, 193–194
  with Lutheranism, 185
  with Roman Catholicism, 185–192
  with the Old Catholics, 193–194
Unitarianism, 20, 184
United States of America (USA)
  Antiochian Orthodox Christian Archdiocese in the USA, 30
  Greek Orthodox Archdiocese in the USA, 6
  Orthodoxy in the USA, chapter 15 *passim*
Urban II, Pope (d. 1099), 70
Uriel (archangel), 160
USA: *see* United States of America
Ut Unum Sint (papal encyclical; 1995), 190–191

Vatican Councils
  First (1869–1870), 189, 191, 193
  Second (1962–1965), 52, 74, 76, 177, 178, 188, 190, 216–217
Vatopedi monastery (Mount Athos), 150
Velichkovsky, Paisius (Paissy) (d. 1794), 152–153
Veniaminov, Ivan Yevseyevich/ Innokenty (Innocent) Veniaminov (d. 1879), 198–199
Vespers, 104
Vestments, Orthodox, 16, 109, 175
  history of, 108–109
  of bishops, 16, 70
  of deaconesses, 135
  of priests, 16, 109
  see also Habit
Vita Antonii ('The Life of Antony', attributed to Athanasius), 139–140

Wadi Natroun (Egypt), monasteries of the, 148
Ware, Bishop Kallistos (Bishop Kallistos of Diokleia), 1, 3, 213

Way of a Pilgrim, The: see Pilgrim's Tale, The
Websites, Orthodox, 8–9
Western Orthodox Church in America, 204
Western-rite Orthodoxy, 207–208
William of Saint-Thierry (d. 1148/49), 89
Winnaert, Louis-Charles (d. 1937), 207
Women
  as *startsy*, 153
  in eastern and western spirituality, 78–79
  included among the Apostles, 74
  ordination of, 8, 15, 74–75, 186, 187, 188, 198, 218, 219
  their contribution to spirituality and monasticism, 144–145
  see also Deaconesses, Nuns
World Council of Churches, 184, 194–195

Zernov, Nicolas (d. 1980), 208–209
Zwingli, Ulrich (d. 1531), 185